Praise for *Guerrilla Grunt*

This is a superb account of what actually happened in the planning, buildup, training, and prosecution of the Vietnam War. I personally lived, breathed, and observed what Colonel Fischer writes about. He was—and still is—a visionary who strongly advocates what so many forget: that we should learn from our rich war histories. This book is a brilliant recording of the colloquial and sycophantic processes we as a nation go through in preparing for and executing our wars. He and I agree: "Fight to win!"

— **Grady T. Birdsong,** Marine Corps Vietnam veteran (two tours Northern I Corps), author, retired telecom, data, and fiber optics business development professional, veterans' advocate and volunteer

Guerrilla Grunt is an incisive account of one Marine officer's pioneering efforts to develop the 2nd Marine Division Counter-guerrilla Warfare Center (CGWC), and the only authentic Vietnam combat training center in America, at Camp Lejeune, North Carolina, in 1965. It is the story of Colonel Robert L. Fischer's foresight and determination to endure when confronted by ingrained, institutional leaders who were unable to change how we fight our wars at a critical time in our history.

The history of how the CGWC came to be also parallels the evolution of our involvement in the Vietnam War. It offers important lessons not just for historians and today's military professionals, but for those who yearn to understand with greater clarity the reasons why we entered that conflict when we were so lacking in our knowledge and ability to fight it.

Guerrilla Grunt is both an impressive analysis of the complexities of shifting from conventional war to fighting a counterinsurgency (COIN) and a compelling personal memoir of how Colonel Fischer was able to overcome the resistance of those who failed to recognize that current doctrine left us unprepared to face a guerrilla enemy we barely knew.

Guerilla Grunt is an exceptional book that will appeal to a wide range of readers.

— **Dan Guenther,** former captain, U.S. Marine Corps; Vietnam veteran; and author of *China Wind, Dodge City Blues,* and *Glossy Black Cockatoos,* the 2010 Colorado Authors' League Award selection for Genre Fiction

Praise for *Guerrilla Grunt* (continued)

Guerrilla Grunt personifies the true essence of "adapt and overcome." Colonel Fischer's personal account, which chronicles the pivotal change in the 1960s Marine Corps to comprehend a nontraditional enemy and conflict that was difficult for our American culture to understand, is vital to today's leaders, educators, and military. The reader walks—and even jumps out of planes—right along with Colonel Fischer on his mission to transform conventional thinking to defeat a multifaceted enemy.

This nation should be grateful to Colonel Fischer, who fought on more than one front: the war in Vietnam and the struggle to alter established training doctrine and methods. Thank you, Colonel Fischer, for your sacrifice, extraordinary perseverance, and effort and willingness to educate us all. *Guerrilla Grunt* is a must-read in today's times.

— **Carron Barrella,** U.S. Marine Corps veteran and author of *More Than 36 Days* (the story of four Marines who survived Iwo Jima)

GUERRILLA GRUNT

How One Enterprising Marine Helped Change the Way
Marines Fight Their Wars

Robert L. Fischer, Colonel (Ret.), USMC

Guerrilla Grunt

Robert L. Fischer, Colonel (Ret.), USMC

Library of Congress Control Number: 2013902197

Printed in the United States of America

ISBN: 978-162137-221-9 (softcover), 978-162137-222-6 (ebook)

This book is written from the author's perspective, to convey his recollections and experiences, and is not representative of the official view of the United States Marine Corps or the Department of Defense.

Table of Contents

Acknowledgments

Almost 50 years after I first proposed and then established the 2nd Marine Division Counter-guerrilla Warfare Center (CGWC) at Camp Lejeune, North Carolina, that trained 20,000 Marines for the Vietnam War, a few Marine Corps pals, also veterans of that war, convinced me to tell my story. Its early focus on guerrilla warfare has so many lessons that apply today. I am glad I listened to them.

I want to point out that I was not the first Marine to study and experience the emerging guerrilla wars. Lt. Colonel Bill Corson, (professor and dean), Bing West, Colonel Mike Wyly, and Colonel Bruce Meyer were among the first. In 1964 and 1965, pre-war Marine Corps advisors to my own Vietnamese Marine Corps, such as Colonel (then Major) Pete Eller and Lt. Colonel Bill Leftwich, were the first of our new breed of Marine guerrilla grunts who fought large main-force Viet Cong and People's Army of Vietnam (PAVN) regiments in the *first* major battles of that war when the first enemy regiments and division size units appeared. And Marine helicopter units, the Shu-Flys, were also in the *first* pre-war battles when they hauled South Vietnamese forces into their *first* air-mobile battles and alerted us that U.S. Marines had better learn how to fight a different and difficult enemy.

If the CGWC made any contribution to the training and readiness for this war, it must be credited to our visionary Marine Corps generals like Wallace Greene (Commandant of the Marine Corps), Victor Krulak, Ormand Simpson, and Lew Walt. They knew that we had to orient our training towards Vietnam and a guerrilla enemy, but not to the sole exclusion of our amphibious warfare role and doctrine. Yet many opposed doing even that. *Guerrilla Grunt* is my personal account of overcoming that resistance, even after the Vietnam War began and our grunts were fighting an enemy we barely knew or even recognized.

Major credit for the success of the CGWC must go to my combat-experienced training cadre, whose knowledge made it the most successful, realistic counter-guerrilla training course in America. The commandant, many foreign visitors, combat authors and writers, and even a large number of the returning Vietnam veterans confirmed that we had done it right. Gunny Bob Atkinson created a village that was so realistic that trainees who later made the 1967 Deckhouse V amphibious landing in Vietnam confirmed that it was exactly like the CGWC had taught them. Gunny Jordan's ambush course and the Gurkha Drill (right out of the Malaya Jungle School) were also a reflection of his own ambush experience in Vietnam. Thanks to Corporal Harrington, the booby-trap trail was so realistic that Vietnam combat writer Malcolm Browne documented it in his 1966 *True* magazine article entitled, "The Devil Weapons of the Viet Cong." Many other writers would visit the training center and write similarly glowing accounts of the CGWC and my guerrilla team, which spoke little English but instilled the special lessons of guerrilla fighting in all that were fortunate to attend the school.

There were few who believed in my radical venture in its earliest days, but they ran interference for me and believed in me. My thanks must first go to Lt. Colonel Ken Clifford, a Fordham University professor and Marine Corps historian, who was on his two-week reserve training tour at Camp Lejeune when he heard me talking up my ideas in the officers' club bar. He obviously was so impressed with my proposal that he personally took it to General Simpson, greasing the skids at a time when I was very unpopular on that base. My 500-man guerrilla grunt force had just decimated a 2500-man Marine brigade in a large counter-guerrilla exercise at Camp Pickett, Virginia. In 1965, it was also Major Tom Glidden, a Marine Corps friend from my days as a lieutenant to my retirement ceremony as a colonel, who became my mentor and a true believer in me.

Finally, but hardly least, my wife Gwenny and my four lovely girls, who endured and still managed to enjoy up to 25 house moves as their Marine dad transferred from base to base. My gratitude was immeasurable—and it still is today.

Our Marine wives are the real heroes in our military careers. They hold down the fort and bear *all* of the family responsibility and the burdens when we Marine dads ship out, again and again. It took a very special woman to support her Marine the way she did, for 35 years. Gwenny also had a change agent to deal with. In every military assignment and challenge I took on, she was there for me. Sadly for the girls and me, she died in 1990 and now rests in Arlington Cemetery. She loved "her Corps" and her Marine.

I also want to thank the following people and institutions that helped me research, write, and publish *Guerrilla Grunt*:

Karen, my wife, best friend, and loving companion, for your continuing support and patience when I needed you most in my lengthy writing days.

Alexi Paulina, editor and advisor to this heavy-handed grunt. Your expertise and gentle style are truly unique.

My Vietnamese Marine advisor friends, living and dead: Bill, Larry, Don, Bob, Tom, Herk, and 300 who served.

Colonel Milt (Bull) Hull who started me on this path—early when my career began in the 4th Marines, and later he would command the same regiment in Vietnam.

Marine Corps commanders who helped and hindered me. Your positives were appreciated, but your negatives drove me on.

Major Gerry Devlin, U.S. Army (Ret.), whose friendship and humor helped me survive the U.S. Army Infantry Career Course—and is also the finest soldier I ever met.

Grady Birdsong, Marine Corps Vietnam veteran, advisor, and author of *A Fortunate Passage*. He is a military advocate and reliable "right arm" in promoting the Rocky Mountain Hyperbaric Institute and treatment clinic in Louisville, CO.

Dan Guenther, Marine Corps Vietnam veteran and inspiration for my own book—hopefully as good as his novels, *China Wind* and *Dodge City Blues*. Both provide exceptional insights into that tough war we shared.

Vietnam veterans Bob Averill, Wes Love, Larry Quinn, Tim Hall, C.R. Cusack, Al Cupps, Mike Frazer, Dean Glorso, Peter Schlesiona, Ed Barnholt, and their families.

My cover artist, Nick Zelinger, whose artistry and skill has created and captured the essence of a guerrilla grunt.

Paula Sarlls, Woman Marine and former president of the Woman Marine Association, a dedicated, loyal friend.

Cooper's Troopers, a lunch-bunch group of Marine and Navy veterans of every Marine battle in World War II and Korea. They tolerate us Vietnam, Iraq-Afghanistan vets.

Carron Barrella, Woman Marine veteran, friend, and author of *More Than 36 Days and Counting: Four Ordinary Men Face Extraordinary Circumstances* (about four veterans of Iwo Jima and also Cooper's Troopers).

Colonel Jim Wilson, protégé, student, furniture mover, and "Uncle Willie" to my girls in all their growing years. He was always there for them and for me.

Colonel Ken Turner, assistant G-3 officer, 2nd Marine Division at Camp Lejeune, who took the hits and warded off the threats, but ensured the survival of the CGWC.

Major General Ormand R. Simpson, CG, 2nd Marine Division, who saw the need for specialized training, then fully supported it and rewarded us for our efforts.

Colonel Bob Lucy, battalion commander, leader, and Marine visionary who thankfully understood this grunt.

Every Marine who stepped up and put it on the line in those difficult days and long years in the early 1960s.

To the wives of my Marine friends, who suffered the worst loss and never shared the better days with them.

To my stepsons Darrin and Kevin, whose support and acceptance of a Marine stepfather is appreciated if often not understood.

To my five wonderful grandchildren, Nickie, Richard, Laura, Madeline, and Vivian—may you all remember granddad's past and learn from it many things.

Introduction

In today's world of insurgents and terrorists, we tend to forget there were similar precedents that took place many centuries ago. Sun Tsu, the famous Chinese general, gave us the first original handbook that defined this irregular and different form of warfare that he successfully practiced 2500 years ago. In the early 1800s, a major cause of Napoleon's defeat was the irregular war he fought on the Iberian Peninsula. Guerrillas—50,000 of them—helped inflict 250,000 casualties. This huge loss contributed to his defeat in Europe. It also is common knowledge that in World War II, Russian, Chinese, and French guerrillas wore down much larger forces. In the Balkans, local guerrillas harassed and impeded superior German armies that had invaded their territories. Few military scholars took note of such successes in those limited wars by forces and tactics labeled *guerrilla, irregular, unconventional,* or *asymmetric.* Finally, in 2006, we labeled it *insurgency.*

Many excellent books document the guerrilla tactics and techniques employed by our enemies. It is not surprising that Mao Tse-tung, Ho Chi Minh, and Vo Nguyen Giap wrote their own accounts. We assume that our military schools also were teaching these available "lessons," and that our military units were trained in this kind of warfare. It is shocking to discover that, from the earliest observation and actual experience in the early 1960s, the United States (U.S.) military services ignored these lessons. We continued to maintain institutional ignorance after World War II, into Vietnam, and even into our recent experiences in Iraq and Afghanistan. Finally, thanks to a few open-minded military professionals who actually fought these wars, the lessons are now given some attention! Rigid, conventional brain-lock, in both civilian and military "leadership," was replaced by the ideas of imaginative, "out of the box" thinkers to eliminate the ingrained, institutional ignorance that was practiced and defended by pompous Pentagon paragons and their malleable military. Such "leaders" ensured the unsuccessful outcome in Vietnam.

In the early 1960s, Fidel Castro and Che Guevara employed guerrilla warfare to defeat the corrupt Cuban president, Fulgencio

Batista. They had studied the writings of Mao Tse-tung, Ho Chi Minh, and Vo Nguyen Giap, who had successfully employed this unconventional, irregular form of warfare to defeat a superior enemy. And they were not alone. Those outgunned, outmanned revolutionaries and future insurgents were reading and listening. Few in U.S. military leadership even turned a page to gain an understanding. What was truly dumbfounding for twentieth-century military leaders (who won massive battles in World Wars I and II by deploying their large armies against the large armies of their enemies) was the subtle simplicity of guerrilla warfare and later, the Iraq insurgency. It did not make logical sense that an inferior, poorly equipped guerrilla force could not only weaken and wear down a much larger military unit, but that with time, patience, and perfect execution of this protracted form of warfare, it could defeat the armies of very powerful nations. It was a lesson that simply would not be learned! Philosopher George Santayana provided the best maxim to apply to this contradiction:

"Those who forget the past are doomed to relive it."

But the issue is much more than forgetting our past and our fighting guerrilla warfare, or the asymmetrical, irregular, and unconventional warfare we have experienced since Chesty Puller and the U.S. Marine Corps guerrilla fighters engaged the native bandits and insurgents in Haiti, and Nicaragua. The U.S. Army also engaged the Huk Balahap in the Philippines. This guerrilla suppression happened early in the twentieth century, when the Marines wrote their *Small Wars Manual* to document how rebellious bandits could be countered. Yet the real lessons were still not learned. This information was not considered appropriate for our military schools or the obsolete type of warfare we continued to train for. Guerrillas, and the insurgents themselves, were dismissed as aberrations and totally ignored. The knowledge did not merit a footnote in the syllabus of military schools, which quickly returned to their study of "the last war" and what had been employed in it. Soldiers and Marines learned to march and take orders in boot camp. Then they trained to charge up hill after hill, units massed for the attack.

2

We trained for World War II by employing the tactics and techniques of World War I. Next, we trained for the Korean War by applying what was done in World War II, and so on. It was no big surprise that after the end of the Korean War, in the 1950s and 1960s, the U.S. continued to train military units in the same old way while Mao, Ho Chi Minh, and Giap fought their guerrilla wars in Asia. They employed a totally different form of warfare—one that we would ignore, right up until the day we entered their domain and quickly learned that very little of our conventional military training applied. "Two-up, one back, and hot chow in the rear" was passé. Its day had long gone. No more were our enemies dug into the hills and beaches, just waiting for us to charge and assault their positions. Instead, a frustrating, protracted form of warfare engulfed us. We did not have the training, temperament, or tactics to cope with it. That we would fight four different types of warfare in a single conflict (village-level guerrilla war to the high-tech air war) was unthinkable. But our enemy did, and we had to learn how to shift the gears of that different war, the hard way. We not only forgot the past, we didn't even consider it!

It would take more than 40 years before a few intelligent, disgruntled military leaders would finally convince a pathetic Pentagon and badly advised President that there was a much better way to counter an insurgency. Two brilliant field commanders, Army General David Petraeus and Marine General James Mattis, wrote the joint Army and Marine Corps Field Manual. General Mattis is a modern-day Chesty Puller, always up front where the bullets are flying. He sized up his enemy and the population with visionary, out-of-the-box solutions. It led to our current counterinsurgency (COIN) program. A *true grunt*, he learned from the past and recognized that both the enemy and the Iraq population had to be handled much like Bill Corson did with his unconventional Combined Action Program in Vietnam in 1965. Tom Ricks sums up the Mattis approach in his book, *Fiasco,* with "Mattisisms" such as:

"No Better Friend, No Worse Enemy."

"I come in peace; I didn't bring artillery. I'm pleading with you, with tears in my eyes. If you f--- with me, I'll kill you."

3

To Afghans who slap their women: "It's fun to kill you."

General Jim saw the light early in the Iraq War, when he took the initiative to implement a 21st century version of COIN warfare. It added a valuable dimension to the lessons he had learned from Vietnam. Today, David Kilcullen, senior counterinsurgency advisor to General Petraeus, dramatically changed the way we viewed our current wars when he analyzed the big global "war on terrorism" and how it is related to many small wars across the globe. He also warns that the U.S. has done a poor job of applying different tactics to these different situations and has been unable to "shift the gears of war." We still fail to make a real distinction between local and global struggles, thus complicating our challenge even more. Local insurgents may have very different goals from Al Qaeda. Kilcullen's book, *The Accidental Guerrilla,* changes the way we see war. We can learn to develop strategies that deal with global threats but still *avoid* local conflicts and, if possible, win them both. His successful "surge" strategy in Iraq proved this, but we must also learn that *neutral can be a powerful gear*. It took almost 40 years to progress from the U.S. Army Special Warfare School's *Counterinsurgency Planning Guide* – ST-31-176 (1963) to the joint *Army and Marine Corps Field Manual* – FM-3-24 (2007). This *alpha to omega* evolution from controlling and securing a simple village in Vietnam to a full-scale urban and national counterinsurgency program is now acknowledged as a sound strategy.

In Vietnam, our earliest counterinsurgency operations featured securing hostile areas, merging our U.S. troops with local forces and police, and then implementing population and resources control. In Iraq this was absolutely critical to maintain and secure essential infrastructures when General Shinseki warned, "We must have sufficient troop depth to accomplish this as well as to fight the war." Important areas include urban populated areas, local police and military units, shops and schools, utilities like water and power, and the road networks. Mao's "fish in the sea" would be without their protective sea if the local intelligence and our joint civil and military forces exposed the insurgents. The idea was not revolutionary. In World War II and Korea, we had to control the population centers

4

before we moved on. Often we relied on local indigenous forces. Even Japanese soldiers were employed in Indochina, just months after surrendering. Why didn't we use Iraqi soldiers for this purpose during this conflict? In many respects, it could have become a modern version of the Combined Action Program (CAP) that General Victor Krulak, General Lew Walt, and Lt. Colonel Bill Corson implemented as early as 1965.

But in 2006, three full years after the U.S. entered Iraq to topple Saddam Hussein and his thug army, this counter-insurgent strategy still wasn't understood or even accepted by the Pentagon. They were vehemently opposed to any hint of a guerrilla war, much less an insurgency emerging right before their eyes. Having based their current war strategy on twenty-first century military technologies and overwhelming "shock and awe" military power, the Pentagon leaders succumbed to their institutional propensity to "fight the last war" again—right to its bitter end. Hadn't they just successfully fought one on almost the same kind of battlefield in Desert Storm? But then, all that was lacking in that brief "war" was the insurgency! So, the "big boom, big bucks, and big budget" technology toys were aggressively employed, even when it was obvious they were ineffective in 2003 when the Iraqi insurgents emerged with their unconventional, asymmetrical guerrilla tactics. The U.S. military didn't change its approach in Vietnam in the 1960s, and it seemed that history was still repeating itself. Because Rumsfeld refused to listen to his few competent generals, the Iraq war also went very badly. Yet a few persistent generals began to change things by 2006, when the first comprehensive studies in counterinsurgency appeared in U.S. military schools.

Thanks to General Petraeus and General Mattis, who co-authored and jointly published their *Counterinsurgency Field Manual-FM-3-24*, we now can study and employ a *full-scale* counterinsurgency strategy and tactics. With it, the Iraq war was saved from Vietnam's fate. It was not too late to salvage and stabilize Iraq, when we finally understood it was another "people's war," and that it required a very different strategy. Thankfully, two visionary generals provided it, just in time. We also must be cautious not to put all our eggs into just one basket. A full-scale conventional war costs many *lives*. A long, drawn-out, protracted counterinsurgency strategy can take many *years*. But it would also save many lives. Americans favor neither, as our current military history is proving. We should have learned that it is no longer an either/or conflict, war or insurgency. It may well be a combination of conventional or counterinsurgency as the "surge" demonstrated. But one major lesson must be applied: our entrance and exit strategies must be based upon sound local intelligence and the correct application of diplomatic, political, economic, and even a military solution. This can ensure a successful outcome in both resourcing and winning a major war, suppressing a local rebellion, or resorting to a full-blown counterinsurgency that can be troop-heavy in controlling populations and their infrastructures. Today, our young troop leaders must be trained to shift these gears of war. They are now educated, and they even operate in insurgent areas.

When I first became aware of the emerging guerrilla wars in Southeast Asia, 50 years ago, we lacked the recognition, knowledge, and capacity to conduct the counter-guerrilla and counterinsurgency tactics and technologies we implement today. In addition, we now have the experience of Iraq and Afghanistan. But politically and diplomatically, we still may ignore and reject the existing threats posed by insurgents in other parts of the world. Today a major insurgent threat exists in Africa, from Yemen, Somalia, and all of North Africa where weak and struggling nations lack leadership to cope with Al Qaeda–led revolutionaries and rebel factions. Much like Southeast Asia in the early 1960s, another large insurgent region is emerging. Will we fail to recognize the next Mao, Ho, and Giap?

Will we once again forget the past and be doomed to relive it?

In 1963 I experienced this kind of pivotal time in our military training and war-fighting strategy. Back then we did not know our enemy in Southeast Asia, and even believed we were trained and equipped for any kind of war. The closed-minded institutionalism of our political and military leaders also failed to give us a defined entry and exit strategy for that complex war—nor did they realize how poorly prepared we were to fight guerrillas. I was one of a very few Marines who did not forget what he actually saw and

6

experienced in Southeast Asia in the early 1960s. *Guerrilla Grunt* is my personal account of trying to wake up a Marine Corps that had forgotten its past—a past that included fighting guerrillas.

Chapter 1: Those Who Forgot the Past

In 1963 I returned to the U.S. when my command of the Marines aboard the 7th Fleet flagship ended. Thanks to our Admiral, C.D. Griffin, Commander, 7th Fleet, we visited 22 different ports in my two years aboard. In the early 1960s, with communism expanding into many Asian countries, he visited a number of hot-spots like the Philippines, Vietnam, Cambodia, Thailand, Malaya, and Indonesia. I was fortunate to have a front-row seat where I was able to study the former, current, and emerging insurgencies—especially in Malaya, where I did have the opportunity to meet and interview their senior military and civilian leaders who were just completing their own 12-year "emergency" (as they called it).

At the same time, I read the major guerrilla writers like Mao Tse-tung, Lin Piao, Ho Chi Minh, and Vo Nguyen Giap and also was able to learn exactly how this unique form of irregular warfare was being implemented in Southeast Asia. It also became obvious that the great majority of the U.S. military leaders paid little attention to this threat. Instead, we focused on the Soviet Union and the nuclear battlefield in Europe. We firmly believed that huge conventional armies with atomic weapons would clash there, probably very soon. We also had survived a real atomic threat in the recent Cuban Missile Crisis. We just could not and would not accept that another form of warfare would ever emerge.

From my earliest days in the Corps, I heard my instructors and commanders lecture us with this maxim: *know your enemy*. We certainly studied the Germans and the Japanese, and to some extent, China and the Soviet Union. But our Vietnamese enemy was almost virtually ignored. We knew little about their historic, 2000-year struggle to ward off four major invasions by the Chinese who occupied most of northern Vietnam (*Dai Viet*) for 1200 years. Yet their customs, culture, and resiliency remained as it would during our years in Vietnam. They describe this as the flexible bamboo reed that sways with the wind, but *always* returns to its original condition.

Few of us knew that in the 13th century, Vietnamese General Tran Hung Dao led his Dai Viet *guerrilla* armies to repel and defeat *two* of Kublai Khan's Mongol invasions. Khan already had conquered most of Eurasia and even China. General Dao's crushing defeat of Khan's 500,000-man invasion force is cited among the greatest military victories in world history. It is ironic that his primary weapon was the insidious *punji* stake we would encounter many years later. They inflicted most of the Mongol land army casualties. But it was even more creative when he used thousands of steel-tipped bamboo poles that were inserted deep into the muddy basin of the Bach Dang River, where Dao's much smaller naval fleet lured 800 of Khan's troop-laden ships into the shallow waters of the river's mouth. The rapidly sinking tide lowered the hapless ships onto the swarm of stakes and sank more than 500 of them. This forced Khan's defeated armies to withdraw from Vietnam. General Dao's People's Army became the model for General Giap's People's Army some 700 years later. The same resiliency, combat skill, and resourcefulness would also gain the grudging admiration of our best grunts when they too fought the modern version of Tran Hung Dao's guerrilla army and weapons. Giap employed almost the same organization of the populace as Dao had, except he fought a modern French military force with his People's Army of Vietnam's tactics and techniques. He also won.

I had to continue my Marine Corps career, so I requested to attend the U.S. Army Airborne School at Fort Benning, Georgia, just to jump out of airplanes. Not only was my request approved, I was also ordered to attend the Career Infantry School with eight other Marine officers. It was the same school that Lewis Burwell "Chesty" Puller had attended right after World War I, and he had two tours fighting bandits and guerrillas in Haiti and Nicaragua. He was the most decorated U.S. Marine in history, and he retired as a lieutenant general. His cousin George Patton (the legendary U.S. Army general) attended the same school in the same building. Ours would be the last class to use it. Jump school (airborne) and Fort Benning's part of Ranger School would be add-ons to the primary course.

It was a choice tour for a captain, and I looked forward to hearing about the emerging guerrilla wars in Asia. To my surprise, not a single scheduled course addressed it in the school syllabus. On my first day of class, I shared a desk with a mustang Army officer who had scattered big piles of papers and books across the whole desktop. Gerry Devlin, a highly qualified senior parachutist and recent veteran of the Berlin blockade in Germany, obviously was a special breed of doggie. When I asked if he planned to attend the course, he replied, "Bob, I never let my studies get in the way of my education." And he didn't! In fact, during nine months of sharing that desk, Gerry managed to write a real Army bestseller, *Paratrooper*. I marveled at his tenacity and ability to focus on his research and writing while never getting caught off-guard—and I nudged and alerted him a lot that year.

One day when we were getting our mail, Gerry asked if I knew who the mail room officer was. The officer was a young Cuban who had recently joined the Army. I replied that I didn't have a clue. "That's Pepe Perez," Gerry revealed. "He led the Bay of Pigs invasion two years ago." Pepe had been jailed by Castro in Cuba. One year later, the U.S. managed to buy him (and the other lucky survivors of Pepe's regiment) their freedom with massive quantities of farm equipment and other unmentioned goodies the U.S. had ponied up. Pepe and I spoke often (in Spanish) for months. He also gave Gerry and me a taped interview that lasted more than two hours and covered all the details of the entire failed operation. It soon became obvious that he had little regard for his Central Intelligence Agency (CIA) "managers" and for President Kennedy, who had made a last-minute decision to abandon Pepe and his entire landing force on the beach (hence his hasty capture and imprisonment in a Cuban prison). We promised that we would never publish what Pepe had told us. He was writing his own book about the failed invasion, titled, *Turn Right to Havana*.

Pepe and I also spent a lot of time discussing my interest in guerrilla warfare in Asia. He revealed that Castro and Che Guevara were already in the process of exporting the same insurgent strategy into other countries in Latin America. They had learned from Mao Tse-tung's and General Giap's guerrilla writings. Guevara would be the point for it. The U.S. had turned a blind eye to that probability as well. Pepe had joined the U.S. Army in hopes that he and his Cuban

11

fighters might counter those very insurgencies in Latin countries. It would not happen until many years later, when Pepe had already left the Army and, out of complete frustration, shot himself. Two other tragedies also would occur. President Diem of South Vietnam would be assassinated to remove him from office—with U.S. assistance. And U.S. President John F. Kennedy would be shot in November 1963. Many foreign students openly wept in class at that tragic news.

I cannot say that the course material was very interesting. Most of it could have been written 10 years earlier, and probably was. Ten-foot-tall Russians, thousands of Soviet bloc battle tanks, and the ominous battlefield nuclear missiles dominated our instruction. As lowly, mid-rank captains, we drew large, sweeping arrows across Europe, the obvious nuclear battlefield if a war should start. The international geopolitical scene was anchored in the many dimensions of the Cold War. But China under Mao Tse-tung, a relative newcomer in the overall Communist picture, had already helped destabilize Asia with its support for North Korea in their war and the rest of Asia, especially Southeast Asia. That area was vulnerable to Communist expansion, and the U.S. was prepared to support and intervene if necessary against any serious threat to our South East Asia Treaty Organization (SEATO) partners. We had a treaty and allies to defend.

Politically we were alert and involved, but militarily we were still studying yesterday's way to fight—especially at Fort Benning, where the curriculum was boring and obsolete. In a few years I would find this same mental block and ignorance in the senior Army generals who tried to lead us in Vietnam. They too knew, and had experienced, only the methods used in World War II, and that's what they brought to Vietnam. They rejected any study of unconventional warfare that the British were experiencing.

Gerry, however, took the best course of action and rarely let the lectures interfere with his endeavors unless he was called upon, then it was my job to nudge him. So, we maneuvered *pentomic* (separated into five battle groups) divisions and heavy armor all over the map. We also had a Nuclear Weapons Employment course that lasted four weeks. My poor eyesight was further compromised by my plotting hard-to-read and multi-line *nomograms* (charts representing numerical relationships) and CEPs (atom-bomb radii, identified by the acronym for the French *Centre d' Expérimentations Nucléaires du Pacifique*) all over France. I also recalled Lenin's ploy that kept an enemy engaged in one threat area while his primary goal was to weaken and undermine him in another. It would work in Vietnam.

In just a few months I had come a long way from my brief, remote Asian education and experience. The nine Marine Corps officer students were given the improbable role of being "enemy" aggressor commanders, as dozens of Army tanks and personnel carriers chased our tiny tank units across the hills of Fort Benning. It was awesome to see a distant hill disgorge a massive tank force bearing down on a few hapless jarheads and our mini-force. Many years earlier, Chesty Puller had achieved a remarkable aggressor feat when he was given the same job we were given: aggressor. That feat was still remembered and discussed when I was at the school. In Chesty's days, the horse-mounted cavalry was in vogue, and horsemanship was their prime skill. Tanks would come later, when George Patton proved their worth. Chesty, who had already fought Haitian bandits and wore a Navy Cross medal, had also employed horses and mules in combat. Wily and imaginative as ever, Chesty's aggressor team stole into the "enemy" camp long after midnight and quietly removed all the horses. The next day, angry columns of haggard, dusty cavalrymen, minus their horses, limped the 20 miles back to Fort Benning, totally outwitted.

Finally, near the end of the course, with some news about Vietnam filtering back via the Army Special Forces teams (although not one appeared to instruct at Fort Benning), the school decided that we should have an hour devoted to fighting guerrillas. With a course exercise likely taken from some Boer War scenario, we were tasked with guarding 30 or 40 miles of a railroad. Whoopee! We had a limited number of soldiers to do the job, and endless patrols were out of the question. So, I constructed about 50 guard towers, every half mile or so, posted tower sentries, and had a rapid-reaction force standing by in case a guerrilla attack occurred along the line. I received a top grade for my imaginative solution, but knew that the scenario had little relevancy to Vietnam or the kind of guerrilla war we might fight there.

Across the base, the 11th Air Assault Division had begun to experiment with helicopter-borne troops and mustered the first battalion of the now-famous Army Air Cavalry. In fact, Lt. Colonel Hal Moore (later the commander at the famous Ia Drang battle and author of the book, *We Were Soldiers Once...and Young*) had formed and trained his battalion—for a heli-borne war. He had actually taken the time to read and digest the French lessons. Also on the base, an enterprising Army captain named McCarthy had managed to construct a Vietnam village to give live demonstrations for Fort Benning students who watched it from bleachers and saw how such a village was searched and destroyed. I spent some time with him, only to learn what a difficult time he had getting the project started. He too paid the price of resistance. But once it had proven its worth, *his* village demonstration was no longer his, but had inherited a number of senior "fathers" and sponsors when the Commanding General (CG) had declared it a winner. All the credit-takers came out of the woodwork. Little did I know that I would experience the same resistance and then, just as quickly, would get their "sponsorship."

Finally, the rugged airborne course started, right after we graduated from the Career Infantry Course in June 1964. It was blistering hot when we began the first week. We chugalugged gallons of water and were hosed down every hour as we went through the strenuous drills and exercises wearing our heavy parachute gear (less the chute) *at all times*. It weighed 40 pounds when dry, but was about 60 pounds when soaked, which was difficult to endure in that heat. Eight of the nine Marines volunteered for the course. Fortunately, all of us Infantry School students had been under the Ranger School instructors and had completed the Fort Benning portion of that course during the previous nine months. I thought we were in very good shape, and I knew one of our Marine grunts who was really ready: Captain Barnie Brause. While I puffed around the three-mile track, months before our jump school began, Barnie zoomed around the track effortlessly, smoking his damn Dutch Master cigar—all the way.

In steamy mid-June, some of the reservists who had just arrived from cooler climes barfed and dropped from the smothering heat and fiendish drills. With just one day left in my second week, and looking forward to the "easy" jump week, I managed to blow it—my left knee, that is. On my first of two 250-foot tower jumps, I dropped straight down with no choice of doing a parachute landing fall. I tore the cartilage off my twisted knee and exited the training site in the back of an ambulance. With just hours left to complete the course, the hard part was to give it up.

In less than an hour I was on crutches, hurting like hell physically but even more so emotionally. My wife, Gwenny, saw me hobble up the front walk and shook her head, saying, "I guess that ends it for you." I sure thought so, since I could not walk at all without those crutches. An hour later, Barnie Brouse, who had just come from the field, asked me if I wanted to finish. "Heck, Bob, you have only one hard day to go to finish." Barnie was our class character, and I knew he was being daffy when he made that comment. "I'm not kidding, Fish. I know an Army doctor who will give you something for the pain and help you finish the course."

To this day, I am not quite sure why I limped into Barnie's car, but within five minutes we were at the home of one of Barnie's many "contacts." The Army captain, a medical officer, asked me if I really wanted to finish the course that badly. I said I did. He gave me little white pills—pure codeine, enough for 10 days. His comment as I was leaving his home implied that Marines had to be just plain loony or the dumbest bastards he'd ever seen. The next morning, with a braced knee, I completed the three-mile run, made half a dozen 34-foot tower jumps, ran all over the training field, and even made my second 250-foot tower jump—without injury or pain this time. I had completed the really tough part.

The following week all we had to do was jump from a plane— five times. That, I could do. And I really didn't need the airplane that Monday. I was so high on four days of the codeine pills that I almost didn't need the parachute! On my first jump, I managed to do everything wrong that a jumper can do. I came down right in the middle of the gravel road, the only road on the whole Friar Field. I came in backward—my heels hit first, then my butt, and I slammed the back of my head onto the hard road. It tore the lining out of my helmet and left it dangling half-cocked on my head. I was in a daze and could hardly stand up when the instructor bellowed in my face, "Get up and run around that chute—sir!" I did, as fast as I could.

Standing just off the drop zone was my author buddy Gerry, with a big, smirking grin on his pink Irish face. "Now, that was about the worst parachute jump I have ever seen! I may have to put that one in my book. I hope you do better tomorrow, or you'll be dead if you do that again." Back at the post that afternoon, we were euphoric as we shared our "jump tales" like the old salts we had become. Several jumpers shared terrifying but hilarious experiences. An Army doctor who had been assigned to an airborne unit in Germany finally accepted the fateful challenge of his buddies to qualify. He had been scared witless from the start and regaled us with exactly how he would die on the drop zone. It nearly happened on his very first jump. We had been taught almost all the emergency procedures we should take if a mishap occurred. In the doctor's case, one did. Sure as blazes, he managed to land on another jumper's chute, while his chute collapsed on top of him. The solution called for him to run right off the chute—into space, a hairy thought at best. Wading in that parachute up to his knees, the doctor quickly pondered taking the ride down and just staying there—but he remembered that you do wind up dead that way. So, he shut his eyes and "ran like hell" right into space, which filled his own chute with air once more. I could only imagine the terror this must have evoked! A young black kid also managed to get a fouled chute on his first jump. He hit the ground so hard that he was bleeding from his mouth and nose; he was totally dazed and almost dead. Fortunately, a quick-thinking airborne instructor had the solution: "Get up and run around that chute!" He did, and then staggered off the field with it.

I managed to make the next four jumps and began to realize that I was not going to do this as an occupation. Sure to blazes, I landed in a blackberry patch and had to cut and claw my way out. On my third jump, I narrowly missed the irrigation piping in a nearby field. Fortunately, I lived and completed all five jumps. I admit that one of the most impressive graduation ceremonies I've ever attended was in the old rigging sheds of Fort Benning. There, thousands of World War II (and later) paratroopers received their cherished jump wings. We were among the last to train in them.

Didn't need an airplane—already spaced out!

I was really proud of my wings, so was Gerry Devlin, my writing pal, who that summer received his orders to Vietnam as a Vietnamese Ranger Battalion advisor. I later read that he fought his unit out of a deadly ambush after receiving mortar shrapnel in his stomach and intestines, which almost killed him. For his extreme heroism Gerry Devlin received the Distinguished Service Cross, just one medal below the Medal of Honor. What else would I have expected from this remarkable soldier? Unfortunately, his stomach wounds were so severe that Gerry received a medical discharge at the rank of major. Years later, I saw him regularly on the History Channel as an expert on parachute operations. That was no surprise—he wrote the book while sitting next to me!

In July 1964, after buying a new Pontiac station wagon, I received my orders to Camp Lejeune, North Carolina. But first, my family and I went to see Grandma and Grandpa in my hometown of Dubuque, Iowa. In addition to the interesting school year and my desire to jump out of planes, my wife Gwenny and I now had our fourth daughter, Kathy, who was born on February 4, 1964, at the Martin Army Hospital, Fort Benning. Amazingly, Gwenny was in and out of the hospital in less than two days, and our last baby joined us. My mom had come to Benning to assist Gwenny, as well as to carry and spoil that precious little girl all day long. But when she went home, Kathy demanded the same treatment all night long, and she got it until we found out that her formula was wrong for her. Once the formula was corrected, she too became a good sleeper. Nevertheless, everyone managed to spoil her all over again during our two weeks at home.

I really enjoyed returning to my roots to see one of the most beautiful places on earth, my hometown that was situated on the tall Mississippi River bluffs. There, Grandpa managed to charm the girls as well. Each day would start off with Kim, Kerrie, and Kristy parked at the kitchen table as my dad whipped up one more delight, which the little girls devoured before heading out to play in his huge backyard, where he had built a stand-in playhouse under one of the cherry trees. Then, Grandma would have the girls help her pick berries, beans, corn, and tomatoes from the lush garden that she and my dad planted every year. We sure hated to leave, but we had another life. Little did I know then what was in store for me next, which would hardly be termed "conventional." The pivotal point in our country's military history lay just ahead, and I was one of the few who were ready for that major change—and its impact on our conventional, traditional Corps.

Chapter 2: "Swamp" Lejeune, North Carolina

In August 1964, I reported to the 2nd Marine Division at Camp Lejeune, North Carolina, or, as we fondly remembered it, *Swamp* Lejeune. Many years before World War II, several Marine Corps generals began to search for a location for a new Marine base where "marine" landings could be made. The beaches at Lejeune have exceptional, gently rolling surf on long, sloping, sandy beaches. "Perfect," they reckoned, assessing the huge swamp that had plenty of mosquitoes, snakes, and hot, sandy, humid, and miserable weather. "This is the place!'' Why? Because the sandy beaches were perfect for amphibious landings and the assaults against bunkers. Amphibious warfare, the Marine Corps' specialty, was developed on the beaches of the Caribbean and later at Camp Lejeune and Little Creek, Virginia. At that time it was expertly employed against the Japanese in World War II in the Pacific island landings that stopped their imperial expansion all the way to Australia and Hawaii. General McArthur and our 1st Marine Division also employed it, and encircled dumbfounded North Koreans.

Camp Lejeune also had many things we liked, such as its training areas, barracks, and remote location. In the evolution of modern warfare, marine amphibious landings rank as one of the most successful tactical techniques ever devised to engage a difficult, entrenched enemy ashore. Imagine landing thousands of Marines under withering fire, as was done in World War II. With horrendous naval gunfire and integrated air support, the Marines took every island, beachhead, and objective in that war. The U.S. Marines have never been repulsed, even though we faced superior Japanese odds in the first major landing in World War II on Guadalcanal. There, Marine Corps General Vandergrift, a future commandant, was abandoned by the Navy as a huge Japanese naval force bore down on his division and he was left to fight with the meager resources they had managed to get ashore. General Holland McTyeire "Howlin' Mad" Smith and the other Marines who would fight island battles in that war did not forget that experience. Such endeavors became routine for Marines.

From the time I entered the Marine Corps, I studied this type of warfare, practiced it, developed it, and then restudied it to have a new understanding of the latest doctrinal changes that were made. When I signed aboard at Camp Lejeune, I fully expected to deploy on another of those amphibious ventures in the Caribbean. It was what we did best, and why not? We developed it, tested it, and proved that it works. At Fort Benning, it was obvious that the Army had great difficulty coordinating its land warfare with the Air Force's air support. They groped for a way to support troops *when* they needed to. The Army envied the way the Marines put it all together with the Navy's amphibious shipping, naval gunfire, landing craft, and our own amphibious tractors (Amtracs). At the time, *only* the U.S. Marine Corps had totally integrated all of its ground weaponry and aircraft. This projection capability let us send ashore the Battalion Landing Teams (BLT), our Marine Expeditionary Forces (MEF), our very large Marine Amphibious Forces (division size), and other Marine task-organized units that were required for any small emergency.

The enemy situation and terrain determined if we landed by sea or focused more on the heli-lift. Even in the very mobile desert war of Desert Storm, it was the threat and successful feint of an amphibious landing off the beaches of Kuwait that forced Saddam to shift a large number of his ground units. It seems that the threat of 17,000 Marines landing there had petrified him and occupied 120,000 of Saddam's "elite" Republican Guard units. Instead, the main Marine Corps assault force charged into Kuwait airport, right out of the desert. Marines were the only land-mobile armored force that didn't stop, slow down, or let any of Iraq's forces deter our assault. General H. Norman Schwarzkopf hailed this quick victory. Even "Stormin' Norman" could readily see that "his" Marines could "fight in any clime and place, from dawn 'til setting sun." Ironically, his seagoing grunts had mastered desert warfare.

Thanks to innovative Marines like Lt. General Victor Krulak, my pint-sized, brilliant leader and former boss at Marine Corps Recruit Depot, San Diego, the Marine Corps often was on the point when it came to tactical innovation and training for any mission. As a young captain, he was the key developer of our Marine amphibious tractors at Culebra Island in the Caribbean. As he progressed up the ranks, I continued to read about this very unique Marine officer at the forefront of any new initiative, including the guerrilla warfare to come—which would be soon. Krulak's genius was irritable to some. From the earliest days of our Corps, we knew only one way to fight: straight into the heart of the enemy, where logic says they can be quickly destroyed.

Congress also supported our development of this very unique doctrine. With the addition of our own successful employment of vertical assault, as an airborne complement to our ship-to-shore movement, we reached totally new levels of tactical innovation. I was proud to be part of the first Marine Corps organization (4th Marine Regiment–Hawaii) to employ heli-borne Marines as a tactical extension of our amphibious role—and, very successfully! We Marines pride ourselves on our unique ship-to-shore control system that employs helicopter, vertical takeoff craft, and high-speed hovercraft that zoom over the waves toward the shores.

I had been assigned to the 3rd Battalion, 8th Marines (3/8), and hoped I would have another chance to command grunts again in a totally different environment from Hawaii. At Camp Lejeune, we were the force in readiness for any emergency that arose in the whole Caribbean area. Prior to 1965 and our entry into Vietnam, it included some tense situations in Cuba, Panama, Haiti, and the Dominican Republic. Marine battalions deployed for four-month tours of duty with Marine Amphibious Units (MAUs) that included amphibious ships and our new helicopter carriers. It was no longer "pretend time" like I had experienced in Hawaii. Real combat emergencies existed, and the Marines at Camp Lejeune seemed to be in the thick of it. Naturally, I expected that my first assignment would be with a MAU as a company commander and that I would spend months afloat. Europe and the Caribbean were *the* priorities at that time.

When I reported in, the executive officer (XO) briefed me quickly and then assigned me to India Company, a rifle company. I was elated to command my fourth company. The major had also been to the Army Infantry School at Fort Benning, as had Major

Tom Glidden, the S-3 (Operations and Training) officer. Neither had elected to attend either the Airborne or Ranger training that were add-ons to the Infantry School; I felt they had missed a real opportunity that few Marines would ever get to experience. It was virtually impossible to get this unique training assignment unless you were a member of our Force Reconnaissance Companies.

Tom and I had served in the 4th Marine Regiment, and years later I would join him again at Fleet Marine Force, Pacific (FMFPAC), where he was chief of staff during my last Marine Corps tour. He remained a lifelong friend. I would also briefly meet the new battalion commander, a tall, gangly man who reminded me of Ichabod Crane. He was obviously relishing a rare moment in his life as a Marine Corps commander of the 3rd Battalion, 8th Marine Regiment, 2nd Marine Division. He gave me the routine platitudes of, "Welcome aboard. I'm glad to have you, and I know you will do a good job." I was happy to be assigned to another rifle company and have an opportunity to command Marines again. The rest wasn't too important to me. Instead of going to sea, I was told to prepare my new company for an extensive, large-scale counter-guerrilla exercise in October at Camp Pickett, Virginia. It was called "Grassroots '64." The Cold War in Europe would have to wait.

As a guerrilla-oriented Marine, I thought I was hearing things when my commander told me to first get my family settled—which meant finding a home in the nearby city of Jacksonville and waiting a year to move onto the base. We found a neat little three-bedroom house, near the schools and other Marine families in the same situation. Our household effects arrived on schedule. With our family nicely settled in, my wife Gwenny, with her usual efficiency and outgoing friendliness, got to know half the neighborhood within a few days. Most of our neighbors also were Marines, and our wives carried the burden of schooling and raising the families. This impressive ability of the wives allowed us to go overseas for months and not worry about their welfare. A military wife deserves great admiration; few women could tackle their tough job. I always admired the "can-do" approach that my beautiful, titian-haired Australian wife took when she was faced with a difficult situation—

she just stepped up! Marine wives endured such situations, rarely complaining. They instinctively knew the pressures their husbands also endured. What marvelous women they are! And what a marvelous gal I had.

I was so fortunate to have found Gwenny, and on a blind date at that. We had four beautiful little girls that Gwenny doted on. They were already becoming young ladies, the Aussie way, how Gwenny herself grew up. Until then, only Kim and Kerrie, my two oldest, began to sense that their dad was leaving again. They had seen it in spades in Japan, where I managed to be home less than one week a month. The youngest two had not experienced an absent dad, but soon would learn that he had some kind of work that made him go away and they wouldn't see him for a long time. Many years later, I would look back and reflect on those sad, family times and feel a sense of guilt. But my wonderful wife put it in perspective: "You are a Marine. It's your job!"

I returned to my new priority, guerrilla warfare. I knew that the East-coast Marines knew little about that remote "Asian" subject; Marines at Camp Lejeune worried about Castro and the Russians in Europe. But the Korean War had already taught us who our real Asian enemies were: Russia and China. America had just completed another proxy war in Korea, and a real threat in Europe kept us preoccupied. A 1960 *Life* magazine cover showed a world map with the red sprawl of Communism emanating from Russia and China, with its large red arrows sweeping across the globe toward its many targets. Southeast Asia was in that path, and we were preparing for many falling dominos in the whole region. Even heavily populated Indonesia was a fertile spawning ground for insurgencies, with President Sukarno cozying up to Ho Chi Minh, Giap, and Mao Tse-tung. They recognized that the French colonial empire had ceased to exist and that Asians would control the future destiny of Asians. Sukarno even offered Ho Chi Minh and General Giap one million Indonesian men to assist them in securing Malaysia and the other vulnerable countries in Southeast Asia. He obviously believed that Communism would spread throughout all parts of his Asian world. Sukarno wanted his share and supported the "domino" theory.

It was an ominous time for America and its allies in that part of the world, and I had a front-row seat to observe and study this threat from 1961 to 1963. America was at a pivotal point in its history but did not know it yet. And so was my own Marine Corps. With our major priorities in Europe and in Latin America, it seemed that our existing amphibious training was all we required. Lt. Colonel. Bill Corson, who was "stationed" in Hong Kong, and Major Hugh Bumpas, a Marine Corps foreign-area specialist in Taiwan, gave me my first real education into the emerging Communist insurgent threats we now faced. Both Bill and Hugh were CIA agents, but we would not find out for years.

It took an Australian writer, Denis Warner, to produce the best insight into Vietnam's Communist leaders in his book, *The Last Confucian*. He told, in explicit detail, how Ho Chi Minh organized five Communist insurgencies in Southeast Asia and how he systematically massacred, terrorized, and removed all opposition to his Communist cause. The seemingly benevolent nationalist (often termed the "Abraham Lincoln of Vietnam") was a cold, calculating murderer, as was his right-hand henchman, General Giap. Both of them and their communist cadres carried out the execution of many thousands of influential anti-Communists all over Vietnam when they dared to voice their opposition. Giap had just defeated the French at Dien Bien Phu, by employing a totally different form of warfare. It ended their colonial rule. General Giap was also ready to take on America if we dared venture into their domain. Sadly, we failed to learn any lesson from that defeat.

It was well known that one million North Vietnamese, mostly the oppressed Catholic and Buddhist populations, chose to leave North Vietnam to seek safety and freedom during monitored partitioning of North and South Vietnam in 1954. But the calculating Ho had already established his Communist cadres in the south, where the fledgling Diem government struggled to survive. Diem urgently appealed for American help. His U.S. visit appeared on television and in all of our major publications. President Dwight D. Eisenhower even hosted President Diem's visit, yet gave his cause a very low priority at that time.

In 1964 when I first reported to Camp Lejeune, Marine Corps advisors were already serving with the Vietnamese Marine Corps. In December 1964 my Naval Academy classmate and pal, Pete Eller (who introduced me to my wife, Gwenny), was already fighting main-force Viet Cong regiments. I saw his picture in the Washington Post with his nose heavily bandaged, so I knew he had taken a serious hit. Pete's 4th Vietnamese Marine Battalion had just fought the largest pre-war battle, three months before U.S Marines first landed in Vietnam. It was a time of great turmoil after President Diem was assassinated. General Nguyen Chi Thang, Political Commissar of South Vietnam's B-2 region and the Central Office for South Vietnam (COSVN), had his main force regiments attack many of Diem's weak strategic hamlets and expand his control outside the major population centers. On December 28, 1964, they attacked and occupied the village of Binh Gia, northeast of Saigon. Two companies of the 30th Ranger battalion responded to a report of heavy enemy activity in the village and was driven off. On December 30, the rest of the 30th battalion, with the 33rd Ranger battalion supporting, was ordered into the battle, and two air-mobile helicopters were shot down. The determined Rangers secured a foothold and held out during the night, but were overrun by the stronger Viet Cong regiments. It was obvious that a sizeable enemy force was now controlling the village.

On December 29, Pete's 4th VNMC battalion was ordered into battle. They quickly occupied the village and evacuated the Ranger casualties from their earlier battle. Later that day, an armed helicopter attacked a sizable Viet Cong force 1500 meters southeast of the village and was shot down and burned. III Corps ordered a company-sized patrol out the next morning "to determine the situation" at the helicopter site. Pete accompanied the patrol, but sensed that it was very risky because the patrol had no artillery support (although it did have its own crew-served weapons and supporting armed helicopters). Then, before the helicopter crew could be recovered, the company came under heavy attack from different directions. Pete called air strikes near the perimeter as casualties began to mount. He was knocked down by an enemy sniper. Amazingly, that bullet hit the rim of his helmet and shattered, with portions of it almost severing his nose and causing other facial wounds. The company withdrew back to Binh Gia under covering fire, taking its wounded but having to leave the bodies of 12 Marines and those of the helicopter's 4 crew members. Pete was evacuated to the Saigon Naval Hospital for facial surgery. Later that day, the rest of the battalion was ordered back into the rubber plantation where the helicopter had previously crashed. Elements of two reinforced Viet Cong regiments of the recently formed 9th Division were led by battle-hardened North Vietnamese officers. They quickly attacked and overwhelmed the outnumbered battalion with an estimated eight-to-one advantage in soldiers, 81mm mortars, field artillery, recoilless rifles, and heavy machine guns. For his actions at Binh Gia, Pete Eller received the Silver Star commendation medal.

In July 1965, Bill Leftwich displayed exceptional heroism and combat skill as senior advisor to Task Force Alpha. Local intelligence had disclosed that a regimental sized main-force Viet Cong unit had set up an ambush just outside Bong Son where Bill's task force would move through, en route to relieve the besieged Special Forces camp at Duc Co. More evenly matched than Pete's 4th Battalion at Binh Gia, Bill was able to muster air and artillery and then change their route and tactical position to outflank the 32nd Viet Cong Regiment and soundly defeat it. That decimated regiment took almost one year to recover and appear on the battlefield again. Then Task Force Alpha moved on to relieve the Special Forces camp. The impressive Bong Son battle took place just five months before the Air Cavalry met main-force PAVN regiments at the Ia Drang. It was another fixed-position battle decision of General Thang, who firmly believed his PAVN and main-force Viet Cong regiments could stand and fight Vietnamese or U.S. forces and render such large casualties and attrition that it would demoralize U.S. fighters and families back in the United States. Bill's task force suffered light casualties and impressed General Westmoreland so much that he called Bill "the best advisor" in Vietnam. American newsmen rushed to accompany Bill on future operations, and Task Force Alpha would continue its battlefield success against other main-force units. But like Pete's experience at Binh Gia, Bill also suffered a facial wound and would carry a nasty scar across his face for the rest of his life. In each case, had those snipers been only millimeters off, both *covans* would have met the same tragic fate.

Prior to March 1965, Marine Corps battalions also were assigned to Special Landing Forces (SLFs) that mustered in the Philippines and floated offshore to provide our historic amphibious capability if so ordered. But that combat scenario would find it ill-suited and untrained. Earlier Vietnam visits to the area by Commandants David Shoup and Wallace Greene had indicated there was high-level Marine Corps interest in that different kind of war, but General Shoup, while supporting a low-intensity commitment that featured Special Forces and advisors, would later vehemently oppose the commitment of Marines. Yet on Okinawa we were starting to train in counter-guerrilla warfare. The focus was primarily on jungle and mosquito survival in the overgrown Northern Training Area. Few U.S. Marines had experienced actual guerrilla warfare— not since Chesty Puller and some of our "Old Corps" Marines had fought the bandits in Haiti and Nicaragua in the 1930s.

In 1954 a few on-the-job observers, such as Lt. Colonel Victor Croizat, went to Vietnam to monitor the partitioning of the Vietnams. Victor was the first to organize the Vietnamese Marine Corps. They had been French commandos aboard their river fighting-boats in the Viet Minh War. French writer Bernard Fall called them the best fighting force in that war. Almost all of the South Vietnamese military forces were patterned after U.S. organizations—learning tactics right out of World War II that were totally unsuited for countering insurgents. But prior to the U.S. entering the war, the Vietnamese Marines obtained actual experience in fighting guerrillas when they cleaned out "bandits" that were hiding out and striking Saigon and nearby cities from the Rung Sat Special Zone. This zone was an immense, 450-square-mile swamp between Saigon and the South China Sea. From May to July 1967, my own 6th VNMC battalion also would hunt and kill Viet Cong in that same lousy swamp.

The most effective counter-guerrilla fighters were the British who, with their Gurkhas and Australian units, finally won their 12-year terrorist "emergency" in Malaya. But their adversaries, the

Communist terrorists (CTs), numbered less than 30,000 in a totally different scenario and unique geographical location. Malaya was a very long peninsula bordered only by the waters that the British Navy completely controlled, while Vietnam had many hundreds of miles of difficult jungle terrain that bordered on nearby Laos and Cambodia. In the early 1960s, we hardly considered such complexities and also underestimated the enemy we would one day fight. However, during my visit to Malaya, I was able to observe and study the war they were still fighting. More importantly, the British had written their own books. Luckily, I procured *Anti-Guerrilla Operations in Southeast Asia* and *Anti-Terrorist Operations in Malaya*. Little did I realize at that time what a major role they soon would play in my own guerrilla "operations" back in the U.S.

In 1963, just as I returned to the States, guerrilla warfare training actually made it into the training syllabus at Camp Pendleton, California. Before I left my flagship tour, I found an opportunity to attend this fledgling course. Unfortunately, the Marines who conducted that course hadn't been near Malaya or Vietnam. Their training was motivated by Marines just returning from Asian tours, who talked it up in the "slop-chutes" over a few too many beers. Somehow, the guerrilla subject gained command acceptance. A "school" was set up. It would have been much more effective if it had remained in the slop-chutes! What I experienced during a week of "counter-guerrilla training" was so far off the mark that any Marine who was "trained" there would have experienced one of the most useless training weeks in his career.

After a few vague and largely disoriented classroom lectures about the "bad guys" (there was nothing taught resembling actual guerrilla tactics and techniques), we trainees took to the barren bills of the Cleveland National Forest, just east of the base. There, we had to chase a half-dozen "guerrillas" over the hills and dales for several futile days—with no contact, no ambushes, and no counter-guerrilla tactics for those long, useless days. We kept chasing the bad guys from bare hill to bare hill, stopping briefly to pop off a few blanks at each other from a safe distance of several hills. It was stupid, wasteful training that served no purpose or taught a single thing about counterinsurgency, until the last day of the exercise when we were finally allowed to converge on a remote sheepherders' camp and "kill" the assembled bad guys. We caught them preparing their evening meal (store-bought food), which was much better than the rations we carried. We ate it all. My critique of this farce was unprintable. I recommended they send someone to Malaya as soon as possible, and they did.

Two years later, Lieutenant Mike Wyly changed all that at Camp Pendleton. Like me, he had read Mao, General Giap, and other guerrilla writings, and upgraded the course before he too went to Vietnam. He would also attend the Naval Academy and the same Army schools that I did. As a change agent, Colonel Mike Wyly, along with retired Air Force Lt. Colonel John Boyd, introduced "maneuver warfare" at the Marine Corps Schools in Quantico. This revolutionary approach of theirs was credited with the collapse of the Iraqi Army in Desert Storm and was also recognized as a departure from standard Marine Corps tactical doctrine. Wyly would later become the vice president of the Marine Corps University, where his visionary influence is still evident today. But his changes also were met with some serious opposition. Unlike my own limited influence, his contribution to Marine tactical doctrine still resounds in the minds of the students and faculty there. Unique recognition is also afforded John Boyd, whose statue stands there today. These men were successful in challenging and modernizing traditional concepts of amphibious warfare that still was focused on fighting an enemy that defended a beach, and on pursuing fixed World War II objectives once we came ashore.

Nevertheless, with the blessing of Commandant Al Gray, Mike Wyly became the father of the Marine Corps mobile desert warfare tactics that were used so successfully in Desert Storm. Marine units conducted amphibious feints and sent maneuver forces to bypass fixed enemy positions and then quickly "maneuvered" mobile units—the first U.S. units into Kuwait—to seize the Kuwait airport. But I can also hear the same old career Marines saying, "How dare he attempt to modernize *our* warfare? How dare he modify *our*

Marine Corps tactical doctrine?" Thank God we had visionaries like Colonel Mike Wyly. I knew I was in very good company.

In the summer of 1964, the first-large scale counter-guerrilla exercise, with a full Marine brigade taking on a 500-man guerrilla force, was directed by Headquarters, Marine Corps (HQMC). Our new commandant, General Wallace Greene, agreed with General Krulak (who had also been the counterinsurgency advisor to President Kennedy) that the Corps had better prepare for what was to come in Vietnam. Yet few senior Marines agreed with them.

By a quirk of fate and the timing of my arrival at Camp Lejeune, I was assigned to this unique guerrilla venture. My own rifle company was the only remaining company in my battalion that had not been "cadred" (that is, the other three companies were stripped of their Marines and weapons so they could be transferred to the other deployed battalions). That's how the U.S. Marine Corps played musical chairs in those difficult days, so the Defense Department would know we could meet all our readiness situations. In the summer of 1964, there were several serious emergencies erupting in the Atlantic, Mediterranean, and Caribbean areas that kept us very busy. The officers and men of Camp Lejeune's deployed (and overscheduled) battalions would meet themselves coming and going. They were home just long enough to kiss and visit their wonderful-but-lonely wives and kids before sailing off to another planned deployment and ensuring that every mission was completed. When yet another emergency arose, U.S. Marines answered the call. "Send the Marines," the saying goes, and they always did—but it was not my turn, at least not this time.

Instead, my India Company was assigned to the 2ⁿᵈ Force Reconnaissance Company, our elite parachute, scuba, and Ranger-like force. To form our new guerrilla battalion, another company was mustered from the division and base support units to flesh it out. Our initial training consisted of typical grunt recon activities: run, march, run, physical training (PT), and run some more. I really wished I could have been placed on jump status and made a jump with them. They also had scuba and small boat training from submarines that the regular Marines units did not receive. That's where the U.S.

military was in 1964, just *one year* before U.S. Marines went to war in Vietnam. That was hard for me to accept. Was I really one of very few that saw that war coming—and soon? What I failed to realize then, as a fairly inexperienced officer with less than 10 years of service, was the massive investment the Marine Corps had made in its amphibious doctrine and its successful use in World War II. Senior Marines paid a heavy price fighting this through the Navy, Congress, and against other service opposition. We were a bunch of seagoing grunts that knew we were a different breed. Many excellent Marine careers were compromised to fight this radical doctrine into existence. In 1964 a different war faced us, and our operating and maintenance budgets included zero dollars to train for it.

At Camp Lejeune, I realized that the challenge of Vietnam was a stretch at that time. Most of the officers and enlisted men knew only MEBs, MAUs, BLTs (Battalion Landing Teams), and amphibious doctrine. They were just beginning to hear about the guerrilla war smoldering in Vietnam, but it was "way over there" in Southeast Asia. So, there was considerable reluctance at Camp Lejeune to add this kind of training exercise to a heavy operations and training schedule that had Marines overextended just to outfit the deployed battalions in the Mediterranean and Caribbean. Most of the brigade units we would engage would be returning from those deployments to begin Grassroots '64, which would last two full weeks at Camp Pickett, Virginia. We had four weeks at Camp Lejeune to get the "guerrilla force" ready. I had a new company with only amphibious warfare training, and they were still employing World War II tactics.

The actual guerrilla-warfare tactics would be totally new to my Marines. Not one of my officers or staff non-commissioned officers (NCOs) had experience (or even a remote familiarity) with it. The returning brigade units would be the same, with zero counter-guerrilla warfare training. It was like asking them to step off their ships and try to chase the guerrillas. What kind of training would they get to prepare for my guerrillas? None, probably. I wondered if this would be another big exercise in futility, going through the motions just to satisfy a requirement and running around, popping off useless rounds. My own company liked the idea that they would be the "bad guys" and eagerly looked forward to the sneaky things they would pull on the "good guys." In their minds, it was much like a game of cowboys and Indians.

So, I had to wait until we got to our swamp camp to start actual guerrilla training. During the first training weeks, most of the guerrilla battalion was garrisoned right on the beach. It was a large, sandy beach, as Gwenny and the girls were already finding out. Since I was "bivouacked" with my company only a block or two away, I managed to join them for a swim every day and enjoy some real family fun. They liked Dad's neat new job; he was home a lot like he was at Fort Benning. Thank God it was summer and we all went to that family beach, but I knew it would be too good to last. No Marine remained at Camp Lejeune for long; BLTs loaded up and turned around quickly.

I approached the XO of the recon unit. Buzz and I had been to the same Basic School (officer training) course in Quantico, and I felt comfortable sounding off about the training curriculum. When he found out that I had just returned from Southeast Asia and had *really* studied the guerrilla wars in several countries, he asked me to brief the major and tell him what I recommended for our training. I brought only one reference book with me. A second one would have to wait, but it was equally important: the book, entitled *Anti-Guerrilla Operations in Southeast Asia,* was prepared in the 1950s during the British Emergency in Malaya. Their 12-year "emergency" took place well before the U.S. entered Vietnam. I was confident that less than 10 Marine Corps officers had seen the book, which was written by very experienced British veterans of several guerrilla wars, including even the Boer War at the turn of the twentieth century. It contained not only the settings for this kind of war in every Southeast Asian nation, but had other dimensions and insights into that different kind of war.

Even in 1965, these ideas would hardly be considered by any U.S. planner. In addition to the very unique guerrilla tactics, techniques, and the nature of their organization, it contained the political, economic, social, psychological, and human dimensions rarely planned into war games. It was totally different from what I had learned in military training as recent as my Fort Benning strategy and tactics courses. Their war games and problems had arrows that pointed to fixed objectives with many enemy unit symbols that we used to identify their specific organizations and capabilities. The British anti-guerrilla writings were totally different. Our traditional map and overlay procedures would prove useless after the first battles in Vietnam, when, as the British manual clearly stated: "The guerrillas have a special advantage." Rather than operate as ill-organized units, they were superbly organized from national to hamlet level. The guerrilla enemy had a head start. It would take years to understand and cope with it.

No longer would we storm up a beach to assault an enemy defender. This "other war" would be fought by an enemy that would frustrate and confuse us—as I tried to relate in an article I submitted to the Marine Corps Gazette in 1962, under the title, "The Forgotten Subject." Based upon what I was seeing and learning in Southeast Asia, it was obvious that we Marines would one day fight that different kind of war—and worse, we would be totally untrained and unprepared for it. But it was soundly rejected by the editor.

Then I presented my second book for the recon major, entitled *People's War, People's Army*, by Vo Nguyen Giap, a North Vietnamese army general and the philosophical leader of the Viet Minh. He had defeated the French at Dien Bein Phu. Later, Giap also directed the long war we would enter. We knew little about him and how he would fight us. The book was brilliant in its simplicity, defining organizations from the lowest hamlet guerrilla team right up to the large main-force regular army units, with their tanks, trucks, artillery, missiles, and airplanes. The rest is history.

Giap's book explained the advantages a guerrilla had by losing himself in the civilian population, "the fish in the sea." With them, a massive intelligence network was established. Kids riding on their water buffalos were as key to timely intelligence information as were jungle radios and operators who monitored our networks. Every villager reported all movements—or else! Then, the Viet Cong set their ambushes to wait for our patrols. Ignorant of this low-level capability, we openly discussed where we would be, and the exact

33

time and place. Then, *they* chose the time, the place, the size of their force, and exactly what they would do once we arrived in their kill zones. Ambushes hit quickly. Then, the guerrillas evaporated into an indigenous, friendly jungle where they hid in thousands of tunnels, trenches, pig sties, streams, and hamlets.

The guerrilla could wage war at three organized levels of engagement. At the hamlet level, a small unit war featured precise field intelligence collection. The peasants mixed with our own units at all time, even when we went out into the bush. At the mid-level of the guerrilla organization, fast, light-armed groups lived in dank, dark holes in the ground, for months if necessary. When *their* intelligence indicated that they had the advantage, they appeared from many hiding places. Each small team was guided to a muster point from which an attack of regimental size could quickly hit. Then, just as quickly, they dispersed and returned to hiding. They often left a bloodied, confused, frustrated, and demoralized U.S. military unit. At the top level of their "military" organization were Giap's conventional main-force units that local and main-force guerrillas still supported to "set up" the battle site and provide local intelligence. They rarely appeared until the enemy situation appeared unequal and favored Giap's well-dispersed forces. He "shifted the gears" of his war when his large, organized army—armor and heavy artillery forces—appeared. The French were dumbfounded when Viet Minh units fired artillery barrages from the steep hills above Dien Bien Phu, denying them air support and re-supply. It hastened their defeat. During the last stages of the Vietnam War, U.S. units turned over our old, dilapidated, and battle-worn equipment to the Vietnamese. While General Giap's phased, 10-year war cost many soldiers' lives, he still prevailed against heavy losses.

In the last gasp of South Vietnamese opposition in April 1975, Giap's large regular army forces swarmed into Saigon, virtually unopposed, and seized the palace. The war was over. In his calculated Phase III, the same conventional army that had defeated the French in their last days appeared once again at the Marine Corps base at Khe Sanh. Giap's weaponry included the latest Russian tanks, trucks, personnel carriers, mobile artillery, and everything a conventional force needed. Early in 1965, Marines and other U.S. military units first fought the hamlet and village local forces before they encountered the main-force units that would appear when Giap ordered them into battle. His ambush and harassment tactics would "set us up" with small local forces testing the size and strength of our ground units. They also gathered critical intelligence for the main-force units that quickly assembled when they held the location, size, and advantage. Giap was the chess master in his own ingenious game. In 1965, few Americans had read his book. In 1975, it was too late. He won the game.

I had previously studied a large number of guerrilla techniques and would teach a few to the guerrilla forces that would operate at Camp Pickett. Most of them involved deceptive and "baiting" tactics, where a squad or a platoon would pursue a very small guerrilla team only to find they had blundered into a well-laid ambush by a much larger unit. Later, in Vietnam, some of my good friends fell victim to the "collapsing horseshoe." When that ambush was executed, our point men would take fire from a few of the local guerrillas and then vigorously pursue them as they retreated into dense foliage. As the pursuing unit reached the woods or jungle's edge, they would find themselves encircled and receiving fire from the front and flanks, which then pinned them down and fixed them in a pre-planned "kill zone." Finally, their rear also was blocked—the horseshoe had collapsed around them, and they were totally isolated. Only another maneuver unit, heavy supporting artillery, an air strike or a weakness in the horseshoe could assist in extricating the unfortunate unit.

Many unwitting soldiers died because they failed to recognize the maneuver—or had no prior training in those guerrilla techniques. I trained our guerrilla units in as many of these tactical methods as I thought they could absorb, and there were plenty of them! But they wanted even more, so I also taught the use of dispersed spider traps that easily hid dozens of guerrillas along a route march. We added the night movement of teams and other guerrilla ploys and devices that outwitted our "enemy," and we took full advantage of a unit's apparent weakness. Most of my guerrilla tactical schemes were based on Giap's book and the Malaya Jungle School's documented guerrilla techniques. All of this was there to be read by the opposing brigade's leaders. But as they would soon find out, their amphibious warfare tactics were useless in the guerrilla environment. One year later, most of the brigade's Marines would be fighting a real guerrilla war in Vietnam—with very little training, except ours.

A guerrilla war is complex and well-organized. The British *Anti-Guerrilla Manual* did a superb job of presenting this difficult subject. Both of the training manuals I brought back from the Malaya Jungle School contained the comprehensive and in-depth treatment of the terrorist-guerrilla challenge, but for me to apply too much would have been overkill. So, I focused on what I knew the Gurkhas would do and decided it would be more effective if I kept our training very simple, but realistic at the lowest level. The British had wisely cautioned that too much study of the guerrillas and their unique capabilities could lead to a feeling that our own tactics and techniques were futile. They state, "While he is a cunning and a formidable, elusive fighter, a detailed study and understanding of this foe, his complex organization and unique tactics, could lead to his defeat." The British proved this in Malaya. Ramon Magsaysay, seventh president of the Republic of the Philippines, brilliantly accomplished it in the Philippines. The British also cautioned about this kind of war, "It takes a very long time to get results." And *there is a price we have to pay* if we expect to encounter, engage, and defeat the guerrillas in *their* own environment.

The British had another "ace in the hole" in Malaya: the Gurkhas. They were the pros, as all their enemies learned. The British knew from experience that Asians or locals should carry their own fight. Asians do understand Asians; locals do know locals. Unfortunately, we would not learn the key lesson except for Special Forces teams that *lived with* the local forces, whether they were regional forces, Hmong and Montagnard tribesmen, or the Vietnamese military units that helped man remote outposts all over the country. Regular U.S. Army units shunned that teaming, but U.S. Marines in I Corps would create their Combined Action Units. Our failure to learn and apply this lesson would plague us years later, during Operation Iraqi Freedom.

Finally, the recon major told me, "Okay, train this group of Marines as guerrillas." It was a good start, but because it was still a "recon" camp, we ran every morning, had a period of PT, and then at about 8:00 a.m. the guerrilla training would start—for Marines who had no idea what was coming. I followed the British training manuals closely and studied the enemy tactics they had used in Malaya. Again, I taught them just the basic tactics and techniques of the guerrilla, to the extent that they could be employed in a constricted exercise area at Camp Pickett. But it featured only small-unit operations, decentralized operations, and numerous well-laid ambushes. Unknown to them, we used their communication nets, where we could tap into their sound-powered phone lines that were scattered all over the objective area. Then, we would hide in our small "spider traps": a hole *always* was dug right under a fallen tree branch with a thatched lid we could pull over it. This ploy allowed hundreds of guerrillas to hide in an area of one square mile or so and not be discovered except in ones or twos, and never as a platoon or a unit that was much larger than a squad. Like real guerrilla leaders, we determined when it was the best time to employ them, waiting until the advantage was ours.

Without having even one day of training in basic counter-guerrilla tactics, I knew the opposing brigade would have a difficult time with us. Our small unit teams were turned over to our corporals who were delighted to find themselves commanding their own units. From day one, I insisted that my corporals (the lowest-level team leaders) were the key to *our* successful guerrilla war. Almost every night they were given a map overlay and a route to follow that always was along streams or rugged terrain and might require wading into the swamps. Their nightly route march was a minimum of five miles. They used a field compass and made designated checkpoints. Then, they also felt the supreme satisfaction of knowing they had led their teams successfully.

Morale rose sky high, as did everyone's professionalism. Within a few weeks my guerrilla Marines became experts at night movement, which is the guerrilla's time to move. They easily moved, hid, and dispersed. Then I taught them how to collect intelligence by preying on the weaknesses of the "enemy." While the real importance of this critical technique had to wait until we got to Camp Pickett, the basics of the "fish in the sea" were instilled. They learned how to monitor enemy radios and tap into their communication (comm) lines to listen and record. When they were sure no one was on a particular line, we re-laid it slightly so our guerrilla teams could sneak to it in the middle of the night and use the line for our own tactical plans and discussions. We used our own code, and very quickly! That way, we never had to rely on our own communication nets or lines, just like the Viet Cong did to us later in Vietnam. We also learned to set up ambushes and make diversionary raids away from the main part of a Marine unit to draw their forces to that disturbance. Finally, our "sappers" (with explosives) would sneak into unguarded helicopter pads, communication centers, ammunition dumps, engineer equipment sites, and other vulnerable targets we would find. Then we blew them up. Damages were umpire-monitored, and it was just like the Viet Cong would do to us—many times.

Just as the Viet Cong did in Vietnam, we built our own well-camouflaged camps just outside the exercise area at Camp Pickett. In Vietnam, we would continually find the North Vietnamese Army (NVA) and Viet Cong doing this along the Ho Chi Minh Trail and across the Cambodian and Laotian borders. In one more example of supreme stupidity by our commanders and U.S. President Lyndon Baines Johnson (LBJ), those areas were placed "off limits." In 1965 the enemy could fire at us, but we could not return fire. It was crazy! We could not pursue them. By 1971, President Richard Nixon had changed that absurd policy. Vietnamese units attacked Cambodia late in the war, but were badly defeated there.

In addition, I taught harassing and agitation techniques in which long strings of firecrackers were lit some distance away from an enemy unit. The long fuse we attached allowed us to be gone before uncontrolled and misdirected shooting began by frightened troops that saw and heard no one, yet feared someone was actually out there. The method worked in training, but unfortunately it was far too common in Vietnam. A maneuvering U.S. unit could use up most of its ammunition before it ever saw the enemy, every time that unit went out into Cong country. Until we came to know our enemy, there was little fire discipline by maneuver units. Many chose to employ "recon by fire"—a poor excuse when scared witless. This, and dozens of other simple harassment methods, sapped the resources, spirit, and physical strength of frightened men who slept very little. Little did our brigade Marines know what was in store for them—and little did they know how real we would make it for them.

To complete our training, before we engaged our Marine "enemy" at Camp Pickett, one platoon of each company was given the mission of being the guerrilla force while the rest of that company (three times the size of the guerrilla force) tried to find and capture as many as possible in a 24-hour period. I would rotate platoons so everyone had a chance to be a guerrilla. At first it was easy to capture "American" guerrillas. I had to change that habit with a scary punishment for anyone that was caught failing to hide in the swamps and miserable terrain at Lejeune. Unfortunately, it seems that most of my Marines were city boys, afraid of swamps, snakes, and the crawly things that they knew were out there. So, they just climbed a pine tree and were easily captured.

We had no time to dig the massive caves and complex tunnels the Viet Cong would use, but by simply running into the middle of a swampy bog, there were many creative ways to hide in the thick brush and reeds. I knew the Marines who would engage us at Camp Pickett would almost never go out into the murky waters of those big swamps, and they would be even less likely to venture into the ones at Swamp Lejeune. Worse, they would never go near places with snakes and scary things! This also proved to be true at Camp Pickett.

GRASSROOTS '64 – GUERRILLA EXERCISE CAMP PICKETT, VA.

BRIEFING THE GENERALS
Before exercise begins-Oct 64

-Gen. Van Ryzen: CG 2^d MarDiv
-Gen. Berkley: CG FMF Lant
-Gen. Robertson: Exercise Dir.

Captain R.L. Fischer briefs generals before Grassroots '64.

MY MUG POSTER
Wanted
Pablo Fronto
Guerrilla Leader
100,000 Pesos

POSTED
ON BASE

Guerrilla leader "Pablo Fronto" (AKA Captain R.L. Fischer). Posted at Camp Lejeune, NC, 30 days before Grassroots '64

Chapter 3: Camp Pickett, Virginia

Little did I know, at the time when I was assigned to be a guerrilla leader, that this large exercise would have such high visibility in the Marine Corps. Someone very high up, like the Commandant of the Marine Corps himself, was paying attention to what was going on in Southeast Asia—finally!

Two years earlier, in 1962, when I was still aboard the 7th Fleet flagship, I decided to write my observations about the guerrilla and insurgent threat I was certain we would have to fight one day. I composed an article for the Marine Corps Gazette that I titled, "The Forgotten Subject." The article documented my personal opinions and studies of four guerrilla wars and potential insurgencies, and how unfamiliar and untrained America's military was to cope with them. I was also brazen enough to claim that our current battalion training schedules did not have a single hour devoted to this different-and-difficult form of warfare.

Then I outlined the kind of training I had observed at the Malaya Jungle School and how it should be incorporated into U.S. Marine Corps combat training. The answer I received back from T.N. Greene, the Gazette editor, was a shocker in the least. He informed me that my thinking and opinions about the subject were warped and too far off-base. He quoted the current commandant, General David Shoup, a World War II Medal of Honor winner, who said, "Marines are already trained for any clime and place. All they need is the order, 'Saddle up and go.' They can fight and defeat any enemy, anywhere in the world." I took his rebuttal and rejection as the final word on that subject.

Fortunately, the next commandant, General Wallace Greene, had listened to other senior Marines like Lt. General Victor Krulak and Marines from our Military Assistance Advisory Group (MAAG) in Southeast Asia. They seemed to agree with me! So, in the early fall of 1964, he directed that a large-scale counter-guerrilla exercise be conducted at Camp Pickett in Virginia. There, a 2500-man brigade would face 500 Camp Lejeune-trained guerrillas, who would have two weeks at Camp Pickett to prepare for their arrival. Camp Pickett was a 74-square-mile Army post located just outside Blackstone, Virginia, which was used primarily for tank-firing exercises on its ranges. Its dense, almost jungle-like foliage was ideal for my large guerrilla force. We would have many observers and important visitors, including the Fleet Marine Corps Atlantic commander and the 2nd Marine Corps Division commander.

Major Carruthers briefs the Fleet Marine Corps (Atlantic) Generals (L to R: CG FMFLANT LtGen Bowser, CG 2nd MarDiv, MajGen Van Ryzen. Exercise Director BGen Robertson gives rules of engagement.

Before I began our actual guerrilla training at Camp Pickett, I obtained permission from the exercise director, Major General Donn Robertson, a veteran of Iwo Jima and World War II. He confirmed that he wanted the guerrilla operations to be as realistic as possible. I hoped the arriving brigade knew this would happen. Short of physically harming troops, anything went, including the Uniform Code of Military Justice (UCMJ) in case any Marine elected to press legal charges for the excessive training in the snake-infested swamps. We announced this policy to the men, and with that settled, I began Phase II of our training, with no holds barred.

At Camp Lejeune and later at Camp Pickett, I had my "country" kids catch every kind of snake they could find. Many were poisonous rattlers, corals, moccasins, and copperheads, as well as the harmless bull, king, gopher, garter, and rat snakes that also were in abundance in our swamp training area. The game of hide-and-seek took on new dimensions. If caught, one of several punishments awaited the Marine. First, he had to sleep between a few screen-covered barrels of snakes that swished and slithered right next to him. That was the first experience of a "puckered" Marine (one so afraid that he tightens the muscles in various parts of his body). A second capture left the hapless Marine wired to a tree and blindfolded. A long snake (harmless) was wrapped around his neck and tied there to wriggle and squirm until the captured grunt got the message that the swamp was much more attractive than this snake drill. My worst cases, like the New York Bronx kid who just would not (or could not) hide or play the part, I sent back to the battalion headquarters at Camp Lejeune, where they would have to face the derision of their buddies. There were other Marines there who quickly volunteered to replace this Marine. Being a guerrilla was an appealing choice for many.

At the end of our two-week training period, we had learned to live like guerrillas, ignore mosquitoes, crawl with the snakes, and have a unique confidence that we were superior in every way to those who dared to come after us. That "enemy" force would be a brigade of 2500 Marines in trucks, helicopters, buses, and tents. And we would be ready! Little did the brigade know what was waiting for them, mostly because these same Marines were training in the conventional way to fight Cubans, Panamanians, or even 10-foot tall Russians if necessary. They had extensive training in amphibious landings and charging up the wide beaches of the Caribbean. Unfortunately, Camp Pickett was a hundred miles inland, and a different enemy "guerrilla" force was waiting for them to arrive and try to defeat us. They would prosecute this guerrilla war with tactics they had been taught, and would employ the only things they had trained for—the same tactics we had used in World War II and Korea! I felt sorry for them, but the Viet Cong would not.

Five hundred guerrilla-trained Marines were flown north to Camp Pickett, Virginia, just outside of Blackstone. After four weeks in the swamps we were a seedy-looking bunch, filthy as dogs, with beards and long hair (which were allowed), just to get that "different" seedy look. All guerrilla leaders were given Spanish names, and "Wanted" posters were distributed all over Camp Lejeune with our pictures and a short description of our illegal activities. We looked much like a Castro and Che Guevara guerrilla band might look. I was given the name Pablo Fronto. My photograph showed a heavily bearded bandit, ammo bandoliers crossing my chest, and an Aussie slouch hat on my head—an image right out of the movie *Zapata*. I was the ruthless follower of one Retter (the recon major) and the commander of all guerrillas operating in the northern part of the District of MOB. This was the Camp Pickett exercise area (about 20 square miles), which would contain most of the 2500 Marines that would come to oppose us. I had a price of 100,000 pesos on my head, which seemed to me a paltry sum.

Guerrilla Leader, Camp Pickett, VA, Grassroots '64

After landing at the camp's airfield, we were trucked out into the fields of Camp Pickett, and then dispersed into two guerrilla regions that also were given Spanish labels. Finally, we were turned loose to familiarize our guerrillas with their operational area. We would have 10 days of training before the units from Camp Lejeune would arrive. My sector, the Northern Zone, was in the middle of Camp Pickett, where most of the arriving Marines would set up camp, their helicopter pads, and fuel, engineering and ammo dumps. There, my expertise as a guerrilla leader would be best employed. On the eastern side of Pickett, I found that a firebreak went north to south for several miles. East of that break put my guerrillas "out of bounds," just like the Viet Cong used the Cambodian and Laotian borders along the Ho Chi Minh trail. It was important to have a clandestine area to muster, regroup, and store our rations, ammunition, and water. These supplies had to sustain us for two weeks. Also, my guys had to have a place to retreat to like the Viet Cong did in Vietnam. There they could rest before returning to the murky swamps and their dark spider traps, which could be endured only for a day or two.

We explored our area to locate downed trees, creeks, swamps, road and path networks, and especially the terrain surrounding most of the defensive positions the brigade units would establish. That gave us well-hidden approaches and enabled us to retreat fast and unseen after we had set our explosives with exercise umpires approving it all. We would blow up aircraft, ammo, fuel, food, command posts, or whatever. Our mapping and surveying took several days, with my officers and staff noncommissioned officers (NCOs) preparing the maps. Every Marine became involved in a mission. Fortunately, one of my staff NCOs had (with my approval) driven his old Corvair up to Camp Pickett. I used it only during our preparation period, not after the brigade arrived. We were allowed no tactical vehicles such as jeeps, which guerrillas would not have. But our "command car" became invaluable for traversing the 74 square miles of the post, especially for meeting the scouting needs of my officers and monitoring our small teams.

When we ran over a six-foot water moccasin one night, I decided to pick it up and hang it on the car's antenna. Seemingly dead, it struck out and barely missed me—that was a close one! To continue "mapping" the whole guerrilla area, I sent fire teams out with the experienced corporals they had previously trained with at Camp Lejeune. *It was essential that they know the terrain!* Their teams would be the backbone of our guerrilla activity since they (not my staff or my officers) were the real leaders in this realistic exercise. I assigned them specific operating areas on their individual maps and ordered them to patrol there, day and night. They had to draw detailed maps by individual grid square and plot in every stream, swamp, trail, and the woods. This included heavy brush areas and fallen trees, especially the most heavily vegetated areas where spider traps could be dug and then covered up as well-hidden holes. These were the key to our ambushes.

Each guerrilla had to prepare three hiding holes that could be used as back-ups, much like a rabbit or gopher has holes to run to when the predator is at his primary den. To ensure that the teams had done their jobs well, fire teams from the other platoons would inspect each other's sites and try to find the holes and hiding places. That competition alone guaranteed they were hidden so well that we almost had to step into the holes to find them. I was extremely pleased at the progress and transition my company had made in thinking and acting like guerrillas. And they loved it all!

In the meantime, I had to locate my command post just outside the exercise area. We set up east of the firebreak and just 300 yards south of a main highway that crossed the post. There, in a thick and dense area of trees and high bushes, we built a big platform of logs from the southern pines that grew there. Like western lodge poles, they made a fine deck. It was several feet off the ground and also allowed us to hide our ammo boxes, water cans, and rations. We posted a guard so that even light-fingered guerrillas wouldn't be tempted to pilfer some of the goodies. Long pine poles formed the base of our canvas that covered the roof. Then, we lattice thatched the four sides with tall grasses, making our command post undetectable from the air or even from the patrols that might pass only yards away. The enemy helicopters would search for us almost every day, which is why we chose to neutralize *all* choppers as soon as possible—just like the Viet Cong would do to us. Blowing all of them up severely limited Marine mobility, and then we could fix the other units in places where we could easily get to them and keep their re-supply of food and water tied to truck convoys. Finally, we set up our ambushes at sites and times of our choice.

What we did not know prior to the exercise was just how successful our guerrilla training and preparations would be. We would find out in a few days. Our base camp was well constructed, and from a distance of just 50 feet away, was hidden so well that we had to mark our own path back into the thicket just to find it. An enemy search team would have to literally stumble on it to even find it. The sides were made of prefabricated thatch panels that we easily removed for more air at night, yet could replace in seconds if we had to camouflage it quickly. The first few days went by very fast, with exceptional results from the troops. Morale was extraordinary, and I only wished that such realistic training could be introduced into all Marine Corps field-training exercises. Most conventional training was unimaginative, and the men were very bored in a few hours. Most exercises required units to march from one hill to another, chase each other over the same old hills, fire some blanks, eat cold rations, and then go back to their barracks, totally spiritless and unchallenged by it all.

It was no wonder so many good Marines got drunk on liberty— they were truly bored to distraction. As a rifle company commander in the 4th Marines on my first tour of duty, I made sure that my platoons experienced as realistic an exercise as possible when we went to the field. Usually the first sergeant and my gunnery sergeant planned the enemy situation, basing it on their actual experiences in real combat. In the mid-1950s, training was strictly conventional warfare with objectives, bunkers, and an "enemy" we could see and hear and then shoot at right across a ridge line. A little imagination turned training into an exciting event, at least for us. There at Camp Pickett, Virginia, we had the opportunity to let it all hang out.

Until the brigade arrived, we set up a western-style camp with barbeque spits and ate food we bought at the local stores. We drank some beer and just enjoyed the life, camping beside the only lake in our area. The fish, frogs, and fowl (ducks) made some very delicious meals, every single night. The rations could wait for the exercise, a full week away. But water began to become a problem, since we had no way to distill it from local streams. Instead, the command car had its first mission: to haul dozens of five-gallon water cans to a gas station up the road and fill them. One day I decided to go up to the highway, just a short distance from our camp. Several homes were nearby. Modest, well groomed, three-bedroom ranch style homes, they were all situated on five-acre plots that provided some quiet isolation and remoteness.

I knocked on one front door of one house and there was no answer. I knocked again and there was still no answer, but I heard children crying inside, which told me someone was home. Just as I was about to leave, a terrified young woman appeared inside the front door. I removed my Aussie hat and told her that I was a Marine Corps officer (I wore no bars to indicate this). I hadn't looked into a mirror for some time, so I had no idea how I looked—but she did! I asked her for permission to use an outside tap to fill our water cans. I also told her that I was the commander of the guerrilla force and we were training to prepare for the large Marine brigade that would arrive in one week. I briefly explained what we were doing, just below her home, and that I had a camp over the hill along the firebreak. I told her I was responsible for the behavior of my Marines, on the post as well as off. Now we were off the base, I said, and were really short of water—would she let us have some of hers?

The woman walked carefully onto the porch and almost slumped onto me in relief. "Oh my God, Captain, you will not believe the rumors we have heard about you Marines! I am so happy—and relieved—to meet you. You can't begin to know what we have beard from the Army guys at Pickett. They told us you Marines were going to do the worst things to all of us, and we've been scared out of our wits!" I must admit that I also was relieved.

My XO was standing below the front porch, grinning from ear to ear. He interrupted with, "Have you looked in a mirror lately, Skipper? You'd scare the Pope." I had totally forgotten how unkempt all of us looked. Then, I pulled out my wallet and the snapshots of my own four little dolls, with a very pretty Gwenny just behind them. They looked like the most beautiful family *ever*!

The woman shook her head, laughed, and then sighed and said "Take all the water you want, anytime!" She was the wife of a civilian engineer who worked in Blackstone. Their home, like several others down the road, was really a country home site and quite remote. No wonder she had been so frightened! I told her that I would ensure that she would personally know each Marine who came to get water from her tap. We filled the containers and hauled off in a car full of cool, delicious water that must have come from a deep well rather than unpleasant city water. After that unsettling experience, I knew we had to be careful with any future contacts we might have with the local population. This proved to be much tougher than any of us expected. I should have remembered that we were in Virginia and racial prejudice was *in*!

My first sergeant, a Marine who had a gourmet appetite and hated C-rations, sent a group of our Marines out on that same road, several miles further away, to a typical country store. When I returned to camp that afternoon, he quietly advised me that we had a *major problem* and probably a racial incident. It could blow up in our faces and get all of us in a lot of trouble. It seems that our Marines had walked into the store when they were dressed like bandits. Fortunately, the first sergeant had the foresight to have them stow their weapons at our camp before going out. The store owner retreated in fear saying "Okay, guys, take anything you want, but I want no trouble and don't hurt anybody." The young sergeant in charge told him they were Marines at Camp Pickett for the guerrilla exercise and that they would not be causing any trouble. It eased the owner's concern, and he understood that everything would be okay. But then he really blew it by telling the sergeant, "I'll serve *you* in the future, but keep that Goddamn nigger out of my store or I'll call the local police." We had covered every base and every kind of conflict situation we had thought of, but had not considered that a racial incident could flare up after a comment like that.

At Camp Lejeune, many young blacks lived, ate, and shopped at all the Jacksonville stores, encountering no racial discrimination even though it was 1964. What we did not know, then, was that Virginia was the last state to relinquish its "Jim Crow" laws. Throughout the state, all the restaurants still posted signs that said, "No Service to Coloreds." In most public facilities and buildings, there were White and Colored bathrooms, fountains, and bus sections, strictly maintained and enforced by local sheriffs and police. One of the Marines with that group was one of my best corporals, who had never been subjected to such prejudice. He was probably a New Yorker, or may have been from Chicago. Even in North Carolina, he felt welcome. He was not about to be treated that way in Virginia! While no rifles had been carried outside the exercise area, most of my men carried a K-Bar knife in a sheath. The knife looked as lethal as it was. This corporal resented the insult and told off the owner in language that belongs in the barracks, but he did not threaten him in any way. My quick-thinking sergeant hustled the corporal out of the store, enraged, but he avoided the creation of a serious problem. Thank God for a cool sergeant! It was unfortunate that a fine young Marine had to experience such prejudice, which was something he never would forget.

The next day I visited the store to meet the owner, who was still steaming mad about the "nigger threat and insult." I quietly told him that 3,000 Marines would descend on Camp Pickett in one week, and not one damn Marine would set foot in his store. I was placing it *and him* off limits. I also informed him that the future son-in-law of President Lyndon B. Johnson was a Marine captain and native Virginian, and that he was stationed just up the road. (It was a bluff.) Finally, I told him that his own senator, John Warner, was a ranking member of the Senate Armed Services Committee and would hear from Marine Corps legal authorities just as soon as I could wire this incident to them. To defuse the mess quickly, I also bluffed that I had consulted witnesses that were present at the store incident. They would testify that they heard no threat of any kind from my Marine and that only the owner's sleazy name-calling was heard.

As I left, I told him he had the right not to serve anyone he chose not to serve, but he did not have the right to insult one of my Marines! I also told him that not one damn apple, candy bar, or peanut would be purchased at his store by one of my men. It was the nearest store to the exercise area. His insult and gross stupidity would cost him more money in one week than he probably made in a whole year. But the pride of a redneck, deeply prejudiced, Ku Klux Klan store owner mattered more. He could kiss 3000 Marine Corps butts as far as I was concerned! The word soon was passed to all the Marines, and the store was placed off-limits. President Johnson's future son-in-law, Chuck Robb, never was contacted, nor was any legal authority. It was 1964. Martin Luther King was marching, but he was not marching in Virginia even when it was as bad as Georgia.

For reasons I will never understand, I always managed to have a true "character" in every Marine Corps unit I commanded. India Company would not be an exception. This time it was my gunnery sergeant, who was right out of the Ozark hills and proud of it. Sergeant Hatfield was his name; he was a direct descendent of the Hatfields who fought the McCoys—and any other mountain boys who dared confront them. But gunny was more of a free spirit than a troublemaker. The troops never knew what was coming next.

When I needed short barrels for the live snakes to swish around in, Gunny Hatfield produced them within hours. He had a wonderful way with the troops, who also never knew what he would pull on them. Thanks to him we had great chow, ducks with no feathers, and any other delight he could come up with. He took to the guerrilla role like he had been doing it all his life. I'm sure his mountain life had many similarities. His biggest coup took place on our first Sunday at Camp Pickett. It seems that the local churches were quite concerned that 500 guerrilla Marines should go to church on Sunday. In pure Bible-Belt Virginia, what else would be emphasized by the locals? Sure as punch, both a Baptist minister and a Catholic priest showed up early on that Sunday, right there at our lakeside camp. They asked if we would separate the men into two church-party groups, one Baptist and Protestant, the other made up of Catholics. I told Gunny Hatfield to make it happen. He formed the company and then ordered the Protestants to take one step forward and assemble for the service. "Okay, all the rest of you guys are Catholics. Right face, forward march!" Off they went, right where the local Catholic priest had set up a makeshift altar for his designated "Catholic" guerrillas.

When the solemn service began, Hatfield pulled his next mischievous coup (that wily mind of his was always churning up something). Throughout the whole mass, he and a hundred grungy-looking Marines sang a lovely hymn, *Michael Row the Boat Ashore*— and they rowed it over and over and over! The shocked young priest said to me after the mass that it was one of the most unusual services he had ever held, but that he was sure that God enjoyed the lovely singing as much as he did. Hatfield went off smiling that smile of his, like the Cheshire cat that had scored again.

We all enjoyed his wit and tolerated most of his ploys. The troops rarely knew what was coming next, and they loved the guy for making their otherwise boring training something to look forward to. Some years later, after most of us had been to Vietnam, I was not surprised to hear that Hatfield was awarded the Bronze Star. I can only assume that a Viet Cong is still muttering, "That was one *dinky dau* Marine!" Sadly, in just one year, some of my best NCOs would earn the right to have their names carved on that black wall (the Vietnam Veterans Memorial in Washington, DC).

That week we began Phase III of our training. It was critical to have successful movement through the area, and this was the foundation for our intelligence collection. It began with that young housewife who I am sure told dozens of others that we were really nice guys and she was giving "them" water. Some of my kids had met local farmers near our area and began helping them to harvest, cut hay, and offer cheap labor for several hours a day. Our training back at Camp Lejeune had prepared the kids quite well for the Pickett exercise. So, at Camp Pickett we used our time to study and learn the area we would operate in and then prepare our positions and hiding holes. This also gave us a lot of free time. One morning several farm trucks pulled up to our lakeside camp. A few sheepish-looking farmers, who obviously wanted something, asked if they too could "borrow" some of my kids to help them for a few days. Shocked at my response, each one got some willing Marines who had already heard about the superb fried chicken the farm wives would cook for them (a few farmers' daughters no doubt inspired their work as well). A number of motivated Marines willingly loaded onto farm trucks early in the morning and had a ball doing farm chores that varied from threshing to harvesting their corn. Later in the afternoon, I explained to my men how critical they were in establishing our own "fish in the sea" relationship. We had become "friendlies" among *our* population, who in return would do anything to help us in the exercise to come. We became *their* Marines that were helping *them*. I also began to appreciate General Giap's cleverness when he described the importance of the people in his war schemes. We were the fish in the sea.

After a few days of hard farm work on the part of our Marines, several housewives found out that we were really "just like them." as the lady who gave us water also found out. They established a unique and effective intelligence network. The Viet Cong couldn't have set it up much better! In return, we asked them only to provide us with the best information they could uncover. Since they could drive, walk, or enter the exercise area on the same roads the brigade would use, we would have so much information that the brigade wouldn't stand a chance. They were the feared and unknown enemy, coming to Camp Pickett in a few days. The word went out that, "We have to help *our* guys." There were so many stories of the help the Blackstone locals provided that it would take me another full section to document them all. General Robertson could only mutter, "Amazing, just plain *amazing*!"

And so it went, until the lead elements of the brigade began to appear at Camp Pickett, driving slowly through Blackstone. Those 2500 U.S. Marines must have looked intimidating, as an endless line of trucks and buses rolled by the base, which was now being invaded by thousands of the "enemy." An alert third-grade girl ran from her classroom to call her mother as the brigade trucks drove by, shouting, *"Mom, Mom, they're here! Tell the guerrillas!"*

Within that first day we knew every unit, its location, how it was setting up, and where the ammo, artillery, and everything else was. We also knew where all the helicopters were located and staged. We even knew the distance in feet to each one from a hidden path that paralleled the airfield. At night, our farmers showed up with their trucks boarded up to haul us anyplace on the remote sections of the post where we operated, sight unseen and totally unchallenged. The brigade never expected such antics, much less the cooperation we received from the country folk.

Many ambushes were literally trucked into position when we sent false messages to various units. We used their own comm wire to communicate—they believed we were the command post ordering some platoon out to hunt guerrillas "seen out there." It worked too well and we were decimating confused Marines by the hundreds. Unfortunately, most were totally unsuspecting and fearful that they would be next. It also created some fear of us when the first trucks full of Marines passed under wriggling six-foot water moccasins tied to wires across the road, just above the heads of the Marines in the trucks. Did we let up as their guerrilla fears increased by the day? Did I feel bad? Hell, no! Try Vietnam.

If American guerrillas could train and prepare this well in just the few weeks we had, how well can a real guerrilla force prepare its own combat environment and ambushes to fight untrained and inexperienced Marines in a real guerrilla war? Unfortunately, we would find out too soon—I had only hoped they could learn it there. Retter, the recon major, had set up his own command post outside the exercise area where General Robertson could also monitor exercise progress from the guerrilla perspective. This area was off-limits to brigade Marines. And the major was really ready for the exercise. When he showed up in his fuchsia jumpsuit, we knew he had gone more than Asiatic. I know some of his officers were embarrassed by his bizarre, egotistical display. It had nothing to do with actual guerrilla warfare. I made sure I kept my own Marines as far from his "recon" camp as possible so they wouldn't get ideas. His concept of guerrilla warfare was obviously tainted by a brutal Escape and Evasion course he had attended. He had never studied a real guerrilla war like I did. When the major began to prepare the prisoner-of-war collection and internment area, it was apparent that he had slipped from the bonds of logic. I hoped his loony concept of a guerrilla war would not rub off on the rest of the guerrilla battalion. Since just a few of my Marines delivered prisoners, his influence would be minimal. There, right in the middle of his base camp, Commandant Retter had the hapless prisoners dig a large rectangular pit, approximately 10 by 20 feet wide and 10 feet deep. The only way out of it was to climb a ladder that was lowered to an unsuspecting Marine that was unfortunate enough to be captured. His fate was to continue to dig the deepening pit even deeper. Dozens of our prisoners would experience that pit after the exercise began.

An unfortunate division reconnaissance unit (not the elite Force Reconnaissance unit) was captured—all 30 Marines of the platoon were right out in the open. Their mission was to find our camps and provide early intelligence, three days before the exercise begin. We spotted the team immediately, away from the swamps and our cover, looking as inexperienced as they actually were. We quickly rounded up all of them and then broadcasted on their own radio net, using their shackle codes to feed false information regarding camp locations and numbers. They took the bait, continuing to believe that *their* recon team was proceeding effectively. Then we provided phony campsite coordinates, hoping to lure even more units into the elaborate lair we had prepared.

The last day before the guerrilla exercise was to begin, I sent a "personal" message to my buddy Cy Gonzales, the Division Reconnaissance Company commander, advising him that his whole team had been captured only hours after it had entered the exercise area. It enraged him so much that he personally mustered another recon team and came to Camp Pickett, taking charge of this unit himself. They never got close to us or even managed to locate a single guerrilla. It made him angrier when we hashed it over later, sipping good rum at my house. What enraged Cy and many others even more was the treatment of his men at the hands of Retter and the Force Reconnaissance Marines. All of Cy's men were given the "pit treatment." A captured man was lowered into the pit with several others, where he was given a shovel and a long stick. The shovel was used to dig an even deeper pit, but the stick was used to keep a couple of large diamondback rattlesnakes at bay, at the other end of the pit. The snakes apparently didn't enjoy their company either. When the pit was a foot or two deeper on one end, the prisoners played "switch." That meant they had to move to the other end of the pit, passing by those hissing snakes while keeping them *almost* 10 feet away. I'm sure there were some damp trousers as they eased by their enraged, scaly hosts.

It was little wonder that General Robertson stated that the UCMJ was not applicable for this unique exercise period. Fortunately, no one was bitten during the exercise, though hundreds went into and out of the pit as punishment for being captured. Although most prisoners were kept only for hours, they would never forget it. Afterward they were trucked the 200-plus miles back to Camp

Lejeune to tell their horror stories to all those that had remained behind, and to those that had survived the same terrifying prison pit. And how the stories grew! Cy would never forgive the insult, and he threatened to make charges against the Force Recon major, whom he already intensely disliked (a case of one recon type disliking the other type). There was nothing new there, but he would have to stand in line. Others also complained, but their complaints were rejected by the division commander, who agreed to the terms the exercise director had established.

From the first day the brigade arrived and settled in, it was obvious that they were like fish in a barrel. I felt bad that most of those kids had just returned from BLTs afloat, where they conducted amphibious landings on Caribbean and Mediterranean shores. When back on ship, they steamed from port to port, receiving a few classes in basic military subjects but *not one hour* on how to fight guerillas! Nor was there any real preparation for the Camp Pickett exercise. And, as in the ridiculous "guerrilla" course at Camp Pendleton, I am sure they expected to chase Marines who looked like bandits all over the fields of Camp Pickett, which is exactly what they did in *all* their other field exercises. It must have been disconcerting to find no enemy at all—except when we (the enemy) found them, usually in a well-staged ambush. There, the umpires tagged them as dead, or more unfortunately, as prisoners to be sent to Retter's snake pit. Within a few days, the brigade found that it was facing an enemy that didn't show its face, no matter how many patrols the brigade sent out or how many helicopter assaults it made throughout the exercise area. Word filtered back that another of their units had been ambushed, or a fuel dump exploded, or that several helicopters were blown up. All the umpire-declared casualties were quickly removed from the exercise area and sent back to Camp Lejeune, after which the brigade was "short" (depleted of its manpower).

Helicopters were the primary means of mobility that they employed against us. With the loss of this ability to move quickly, their alternative movement was by foot or by truck. It became much easier for us to ambush the hapless survivors or to execute a guerrilla attack. We had to employ realistic weapons and explosives. A simulated substitute for C-3 and C-4 (explosives), mines, claymores, and a dozen other destructive devices had to be rigged to look like the real thing. An umpire had to grant approval before we could use one. The brigade command post itself was eliminated one evening when two of my men, wearing uniforms we had captured, simply walked into that command post with a case of cold soft drinks. No one challenged Marines bearing such a nice treat. Then, as quickly as they came, my men left. Before anyone could begin to enjoy the soft drinks, the case "exploded." That is, the umpire in the command post, who had been briefed of the venture, announced that the whole post was destroyed and that everyone in it was killed. He turned over the case of soda to show an elaborate explosive rigging, bottle by bottle, with individual wires from an igniter to each soda bottle "filled with explosives."

And so it went, practicing our terror. When we sent the sapper teams into the helo pads at 4:00 a.m., each had to have a realistic explosive device and timer before the monitoring umpire chalked up another successful raid. In five days we had destroyed every helicopter and airplane as well as their food, ammunition, fuel dumps, their vehicles, command posts, and major communication centers. Brigade and battalion commanders were very upset—this was not how a field exercise was supposed to proceed. For too many years Marines expected to "win" every time, and the aggressors simply went through the motions. Not this time!

Out in the field, the infantry battalions had fared no better. We had reduced almost all their companies to platoon-size units. Up to day five of the exercise, they fell for the same ruses. By day two, most of their communication lines had already been tapped, and we had our men in their spider traps listening in. We had also "rearranged" a few miles of their wire so we could tap on and quickly lay our next plans in our own codes. No one could break our jargon. This allowed us to move, ambush, harass, and instill fear with no possibility that we would be surprised, since we knew every move the units would make. They knew this was happening, but could not do a darn thing about their own fate. By day six, with only a handful of men firing blindly at the "enemy" they could not see, the battalion commanders had virtually "lost" the war, their mobility, their ammo, and their food. Worst of all, it seemed that their troops had lost their confidence and morale when most of their counterparts continued to disappear. They knew they were next, and we showed them no mercy. Vietnam wouldn't show any either.

Even then, General Donn Robertson demanded that we continue to press on. The last night of the exercise (it lasted only six days), I drove into Colonel Peterson's battalion command post under a white flag and was met outside of their tight perimeter by the XO, Major Joe Giambardello. I advised him of his battalion's situation and that I knew exactly how many men he had left. Then I informed him that his supplies and most of his ammo were also gone and that his battalion had taken many casualties. He bristled at this truth. Realizing that I was pushing these veteran Marines a bit too far by continuing the pseudo-guerrilla warfare game, I asked if he would leave "our country," MOB, and leave us in peace. I knew I was testing his limits at that point, and he was obviously angry. Marines don't accept such demands, and I knew it. But he also knew that I was aware of his real situation. The point was made, so why press it? I also knew that I would have to deal with him and others back at Camp Lejeune—and I was aware that it might affect my career.

I left under my flag of truce, leaving a very upset major. He was not alone—the guerrillas weren't supposed to "win." Many others would also want a piece of me when we returned! Later, in 1972, I met Colonel Joe Giambardello again while assigned to his property-survey team at the Marine base at Twenty-nine Palms, California. I tentatively asked if he remembered me from the Camp Pickett guerrilla exercise. Expecting a blast, I was surprised when he said, "You know, Bob, we were not prepared for that exercise at all, and we couldn't begin to appreciate how good that training was." By then, we had both experienced and survived the real guerrilla war in Vietnam and had seen how the untrained U.S. Marines had to adapt very quickly to that different, difficult war. Training like we provided at Camp Pickett may have helped, but the war did a better job of it. But sadly, too few were ready for it.

With the exercise just one week old, we all were called to muster at a designated place in the exercise area. It was near our original camp, by the lake where we collected a dozen different kinds of snakes, some poisonous and still caged. The exercise director, General Robertson, wanted me to keep our guerrilla camp "alive" and just as we had used it. He wanted to show it to the Commandant of the Marine Corps (CMC), General Greene. The commandant would arrive at Camp Pickett that day, and General Robertson wanted me, the guerrilla leader, to brief the commandant and the entire brigade staff (all the commanders) as to how a rag-tag guerrilla force, on foot, accomplished this result.

Then, I learned that the commandant himself had terminated the exercise four days early, when it was obvious the brigade had not only lost its capacity to locate and destroy the guerrillas of our make-believe country, MOB, it had been decimated by the guerrilla force. Worse for me, I was personally ordered by the commandant himself (no doubt at the urging of General Robertson) to brief everyone on just how the hell this was accomplished by the guerrillas, who had little or no mobility (or so he believed). He wanted to hear the story from a guerrilla leader, and refused to be briefed by the brigade at all. What could they say after this outcome, when the commandant himself had to terminate it days early? No doubt he wanted to know what special kind of training the guerrillas had. Also, he wanted our brigade opponents to hear exactly how a small force of 500 had won against 2500 Marines that outnumbered them five to one.

After my ineffective counter-guerrilla training at Camp Pendleton until my moment in the sun at Camp Pickett, I cannot say that I hadn't wanted an audience to hear me out on this touchy subject. But this critique, before these hostile adversaries, was the kiss of death for my young career as a Marine officer. Yet I was ordered to brief the whole lot. As preparation I reviewed some of the training subjects, tactics, and techniques I had learned in Malaya, Borneo, and the Philippines. As I spoke, I referenced my earlier knowledge of the emerging Vietnam insurgency that was presently occurring. I told the assembled Marines how we had mapped and prepared the whole exercise area in just a few days, and shocked them by revealing how much the local population had assisted us. The look of disbelief on the faces of those officers is still vivid in my mind, and probably in theirs too.

The commandant, however, pressed me for more details. He had been to Vietnam only a few months before, and no doubt he remembered the helicopter pilots telling him of the difficult combat environment they were experiencing. What we had just done at Camp Pickett paralleled what actually was happening in Vietnam, right at that time. I reviewed how we relied on the brigade's weaknesses: unguarded helicopter ports, their fuel and ammo dumps, and the fact that *any* guerrillas who look like the people they mix with can move anywhere and do anything, including blowing up the brigade command post. Some of my listeners questioned how we were able to set so many ambushes and know almost everything the brigade was doing. I told them we monitored their radio nets just like the Japanese had done in World War II, where we used Navaho radio talkers to confuse them. I mentioned their very long and unpatrolled communication wire and how we had "rearranged" it to fit our own hiding places, but never cut it because it was too valuable. From wire-tapping that communication wire, we knew everything the whole brigade was doing.

I am certain that by this time, every one of the officers present had refused to believe that a guerrilla force could employ such devious tactics. We were the same Marines they were! No doubt they expected this exercise to be much like the lame Camp Pendleton version I had attended in 1962: send us "rabbits" out, let their dogs loose, and then chase us going "bang-bang" for 10 days, until they caught us all. Almost all of the brigade, regimental, battalion, and even company tactics were conducted in that same harmless way in our regular training. Sadly, most of the young, aggressive Marines were bored to distraction.

When I finished my talk, few questions were asked. General Greene thanked me personally for the realistic and beneficial training we had provided the brigade. He said nothing to the brigade officers present and simply walked away from them to return to HQMC—but not before he also thanked my assembled guerrilla team and was served one of Gunny Hatfield's guerrilla meals, snake and frog kabobs. I had to admit it took guts to eat it!

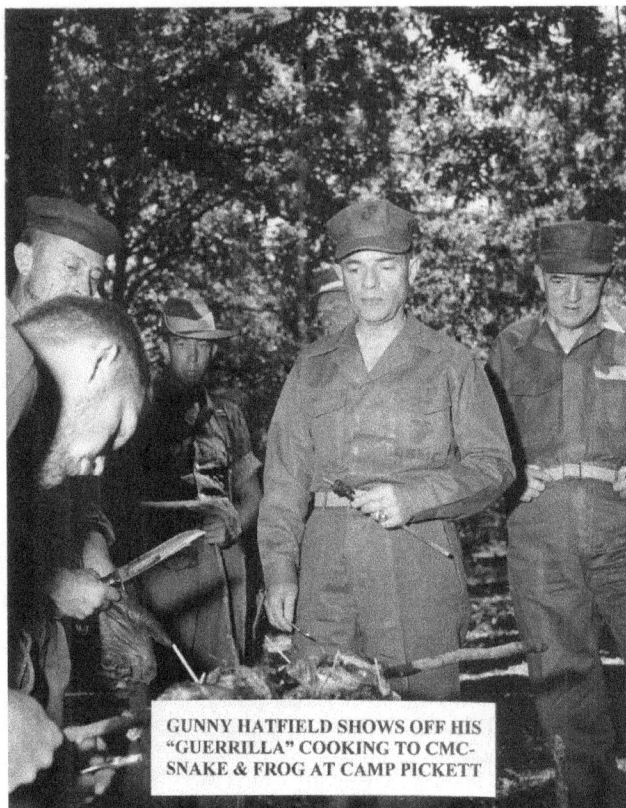

GUNNY HATFIELD SHOWS OFF HIS "GUERRILLA" COOKING TO CMC- SNAKE & FROG AT CAMP PICKETT

GySgt Hatfield and CMC Greene, Camp Pickett, VA, 1964

That afternoon my whole guerrilla force was trucked to the Camp Pickett airfield, where we would be flown (not trucked) back to Camp Lejeune. As we marched by the remainder of the brigade units awaiting their own rides, a scattered applause began, and then turned into a loud cheer by the Marines we had just beaten in a simulated guerrilla war. One year later, none of them would be cheering a real guerrilla army in Vietnam. Neither they nor their officers seemed to understand that Vietnam was looming on the horizon. As we flew back to Camp Lejeune on that cool October morning, I thought of all those young Marines who had been "exposed to" guerrilla warfare during the past week and what they must think of the exercise. Untrained and ill-prepared for it, they were sitting ducks for the 500 Marines that had trained my way. Would they learn from it? More importantly, would their officers?

When I returned to Camp Lejeune to resume my regular duties as a company commander, I also discovered that the exercise results had preceded us. First, I debriefed the battalion XO. With little interest or curiosity, he just wanted to know how we had pulled it off. There was no joy in Mudville on that day, and I was sensitive enough to know that I had put many officers' careers in jeopardy, including that of the brigade commander. One battalion commander, a singularly unlikable senior officer, prided himself on destroying younger officers' careers. He had "walked over the bodies" of many of my contemporaries, and made it clear that he would have relieved me of my command and mustered me out of the Corps if I were one of his officers. It was not the last time I would encounter him.

Fortunately I was subordinate to a better breed of men than this career crucifier. I had barely arrived at Camp Lejeune when I was given a difficult job to perform. Then, with the exercise director's mandate, I had carried out my unique orders "in an exemplary manner." Other missions with harmless tactical success might have earned a letter of commendation or some kind of recognition for even "playing the game." But as I would learn the hard way, never do your job that well, or you will pay a price! What I didn't realize at that time, less than one year before we sent Marines to Vietnam, was the smoldering opposition by many senior officers to any involvement in a guerrilla war. It included former Commandant of the Marine Corps, General Shoup.

The XO had heard enough and ordered me to get back to my regular duties. I would have just a few weeks at home before sailing off again. We began planning our battalion to ship out for a huge amphibious operation in Spain. Russia and the Cold War were still the top priority in 1964, so it was back to the beaches for me and my company. The operation, called Steel Pike, would be one of the biggest Marine amphibious landings conducted since World War II. All units of the 2nd Marine Division would sail to Europe to prove that we Marines could land a reinforced division on those shores like the Army had proven it could do one year before. Unlike the Army, which had the benefit of hundreds of Air Force planes to haul its troops, we had to rely on our World War II–vintage amphibious personnel ships and amphibious cargo ships. These, plus the brand-new Landing Platform Assault (LPH) carriers, could lift all the Marines and equipment. But the Navy didn't have sea-lift to carry the remaining logistic items needed to sustain the huge amphibious landing for one week. Much to the embarrassment of the U.S. Navy, we had a flotilla of beat up, rust-bucket freighters sailing in our convoy. It did, however, herald the need for new pre-positioned ships (roll-on/roll-offs) that we employed in Desert Storm—30 years later! It took that long for *that* important lesson to sink in.

I am sure the XO understood the existing Marine Corps missions better than I did. There were no deviations in his game plan, and certainly no guerrilla diversions at that time—that was not allowed! I would not recognize this character trait of his for some time. But then, that was how some generals were made: they stay the course, allow no innovation, and get the "right" tickets punched, one after another. The battalion commander was another classic example of playing this game. It didn't matter that he had none of the skills required to effectively lead men and Marines; he was commanding. The other officer present at that debriefing would become my lifelong friend, mentor, and when necessary, a solid defender of *my* faith. Major Tom Glidden was a very polished, professional Marine officer, a gentleman officer, whom I had always thought of as like one of the urbane Confederate officers who charmed Scarlett O'Hara at Tara in *Gone with the Wind*. But obviously I was breaking the mold of my traditionalist XO, who, like most senior Marines, did not support any deviation from their conventional Marine Corps doctrine—amphibious warfare. I also was an Academy graduate, and that was just too much for him. He truly disliked me!

One week after I had briefed him and Tom, he was looking at my officer's qualification jacket, which revealed that I was a Naval Academy alumnus. As I sauntered by his door I heard him shout, "Son of a bitch!" and saw the jacket fly across his office. "I didn't know you were one of those, Fischer!" That incident began a stand-off relationship with him that lasted until the day I retired, many years later. I also knew his attitude was endemic to the Marine Corps, just as West Pointers are disliked by many of the officer corps in the Army. It's a black day for them when an academy type is made commandant. That's why I obeyed an early order from Colonel Milt Hull to "shove the damn class ring where the sun doesn't shine." I never wore it for the rest of my career.

Major Tom Glidden, the S-3 (Operations and Training) officer, was a different breed of officer from the XO. He knew my performance at Camp Pickett had rankled many senior officers at Camp Lejeune. He also knew that Fischer was a unique officer and was to be admired for taking on a very big task, had completed it well, and looked forward to the next. His was the only faint praise I received, but it was sincere and I really appreciated it. Two years later, in Vietnam, Tom and I reviewed that unpopular moment in my career. We drank a bit, laughed a lot, and knew that I had been too gung-ho and too successful for my own good. This time we were sitting in the International House in Saigon and were experiencing "the real war." I just came in from the biggest operation of the war, Junction City (February to March 1967). My own Vietnamese Marines had chased down and killed real guerrillas on the rugged Ho Chi Minh Trail. We found their camps and destroyed many of them and all the weapons we could find, but we did keep their rice and the other available food. Our limited rations ran out after several days, and we were hungry when we came upon their well-stocked camps.

As Tom and I ate an excellent American dinner, we couldn't help but compare *then* with the *now* that we were living in Vietnam. Tom was with CORDS, a CIA-sponsored organization. He could tell me little about his work, but I could imagine it was very interesting. We wondered if *any* of the Camp Pickett brigade types and super-critical senior Marines from Camp Lejeune were serving in Vietnam, and what they thought of it now. Not only had I brazenly trained a Marine guerrilla force that decimated a first-rate Marine brigade, I also introduced counter-guerrilla training at that base for those fortunate Marine units that took the two-week course. But the majority of Marines went to Vietnam with no more training than how to shoot their weapons and make an amphibious landing on an empty beach. Even then, many senior Marines still believed an enemy would be waiting on the beaches, and they still refused to modify their former form of warfare.

About one week after the Grassroots '64 exercise, the brigade commander had all the brigade's officers and senior enlisted ranks assemble in the base theater to hear his exercise critique. None of the guerrilla force was invited. Obviously rankled by the abrupt and critical treatment he had received at the hands of Commandant General Greene, he solemnly rehashed all the events of the exercise, making no excuses but simply angered by the results. Then, he added this prophetic closing statement, "This could never happen in real life." The general was not the only senior Marine I would meet who refused to believe that the coming guerrilla war would be different. Very different! Exactly one year later, October 1965, when he was in Vietnam and stationed at Danang, Viet Cong sapper squads penetrated the Marines' Tactical Area of Operation (TAOR) at the newly built Marble Mountain helicopter facility. Six guerrillas destroyed 19 helicopters and damaged 35 (11 of them severely), virtually wiping out VM0-2. How those words of his, "This could not happen in real life," must have echoed in his mind!

Something similar occurred the same night at the Chu Lai base, where two A-4 fixed-wing aircraft were destroyed and six more were damaged. Two years later, in 1967, during another fateful October attack by Viet Cong sappers, the critical forward air support base and ammunition and logistic support base at Dong Ha was totally destroyed. All Marine Corps helicopters were exposed on its airfield, as were the ammo and fuel dumps. The infiltrators managed to blow up 20 helicopters! This time the base was so badly damaged that it would be abandoned. This couldn't happen in real life? But *then*, I'm sure the brigade commander wouldn't make the same comments he made back at Camp Lejeune. At that point, before Vietnam, who really knew anything about this future enemy, or even cared? A short training exercise was hardly the place to instill such lessons. But I am sure that brigade commander learned a lesson.

What amazed me more after Grassroots '64 was the lock-step return to the only thing we knew: regular field tactics and mindless, useless hill climbing. Training schedules still focused on the Russian and Caribbean threats, so we continued with our amphibious landings and the proven conventional tactics we had employed since World War II, giving no thought at all to what might be coming in that faraway place, Vietnam. I continued to take my Marines to the field; Grassroots '64 was just a memory. Yet I found myself in a difficult situation. The regular training schedules emphasized long marches out to the same training area where we had trained for Grassroots, but we used the same old tactics we would employ in conventional situations. The news from Vietnam, however, was not good. One of our first Marine advisors, Major Don Koelper, had just been killed while trying to alert a theater full of Vietnamese that a bomb had been planted. The bomb went off just as he tried to throw it out a side door.

Soon after that, on the last day of 1964, the war became very personal. My good friend Pete Eller, a Naval Academy classmate and the guy who introduced me to my Aussie wife Gwenny, lost many Marines of his 4th Vietnamese Marine Corps battalion in an ambush at Binh Gia by a large main-force Viet Cong unit (1800 Viet Cong). Pete fought his way out of it but lost his nose to a Viet Cong AK-47 round that amazingly split in two on the front edge of his helmet. For his heroism he was awarded the Silver Star medal. Half the bullet sheared off his nose and the other half left a one-inch dent in the helmet. Fortunately, there was an American plastic surgeon visiting in nearby Vung Tau, and he managed to create a new nose from other parts of Pete's body. At "Canoe U" (the U.S. Naval Academy), Pete's nose was something like a beak. Years later, his wife, Dee, confirmed that the new nose was an improvement.

Shortly after Pete's near-tragedy, Major Bill Leftwich, an academy graduate as well (and the "best advisor in Vietnam") took his Vietnamese Marine Task Force Alpha into harm's way and began the first of a series of major victories against the new, formidable enemy that back in America many referred to as "rag-tag guerrillas." Bill would almost lose his life to a sniper, as a bullet left a scar across his right cheek. He would also receive the Navy Cross for heroism during that same tour. He came home to tell us that it would take well-trained Vietnamese to engage and defeat the wily Cong. His Vietnamese Marines had just proved that. But like John Paul Vann (a U.S. Army officer who later served as a senior official of the Agency for International Development), he also would not be heard... for some time.

Almost as soon as we returned from Grassroots, my battalion would plan for a European invasion. It was the largest Marine Corps expeditionary unit formed since World War II. We would conduct a massive amphibious landing in Spain, with a full Marine division with supporting arms and equipment carried by a large Navy flotilla of helicopter carriers, troop ships, and cargo-carrying freighters. The exercise, Steel Pike (Oct. to Nov. 1964), enabled Marines to demonstrate the same capabilities the Army had just proven in its own large exercise in Europe. Thousands of U.S. soldiers were flown from the U.S. to man the pre-positioned equipment that was stored for them all over France and Germany.

Operation Steel Pike was an East-coast Marine Corps' priority. Just as the Army had been, we still were focused on fighting a huge land battle with Russia, on the atomic battlefield. That both Russia and China were manipulating another war for us to fight in Southeast Asia didn't matter to our current military leaders. The blinders were on—the attitude was, "Let's fight on in Europe!" The military wives, including Gwenny, knew that Camp Lejeune tours meant their husbands wouldn't be home for months. She and the girls were doing well in Northwoods. Soon, the whole 2nd Marine Division would mount out. I did have a nice Christmas with the girls, having been home for a whole two months before I shipped out again.

Tom Glidden had decided to have a New Year's Eve party at his home on the base. Gwenny and I attended with the other couples from the battalion. Little did I know what a tough night it would turn out to be! When we arrived, a bit late, there were many officers from all over the base. Most were senior officers, colonels and lieutenant colonels, as well as some other majors I did not recognize. Our battalion officers were also there in strength, including the XO. About 10:00 p.m., after a few drinks had loosened many tongues, several senior officers began to take me to task for the Grassroots '64 results. I stood my ground for a while, but the tone turned abrasive. I was getting angry and saw myself defending Marine training in counter-guerrilla warfare, which those at the party did not take as seriously as I did. Typically, my own battalion XO let me swing in the wind. After a few mild exchanges, one colonel, David Lownds, began to gently "counsel" me. He was a World War II and Korean War veteran and a superb Marine officer and one of the most respected in the 8th Marine Regiment. He had commanded the 3rd battalion just prior to my reporting in, and rightfully enjoyed a great trooper's reputation. What he said wasn't too insulting, but was more humorous than serious. A few officers surrounding us were jibing and sniping as he began to emphasize, "Marines have no business being involved in that Army Special Forces war in South Vietnam. We have a full plate already." It was very hard to take, from an officer I respected.

Colonel Lownds had experienced the Russian threat and their missile crisis in Cuba. As a former commander, that is where his priorities remained, and he was just reminding me of it. Tom Glidden sensed that I was heating up a bit too much and decided to break up the fun and games. He quietly told me to back away from them and hold my temper. Colonel Lownds gave me a final suggestion with a smile, saying, "Captain, why don't you take off that guerrilla jockstrap and rejoin the Marine Corps? Besides, it is just a Special Forces war and Marines will not get involved in it."

His comment managed to bring the house down, in guffaws, all around me. The very large chip on my shoulder fell off, and then I took aim at nearly everyone present by yelling my final comment: "Gentlemen, the Marine Corps will be fighting in Vietnam within six months, and you don't even know it." It is tough to be right when you're outnumbered! At this point, I grabbed Gwenny, who also had seen enough. "Can't you just let it go for one night?" she pleaded. "Why does it always have to be you in the middle of a conflict?" With that, I drove home quietly.

I'm sure my comments did not endear me to the other officers, nor did my reproving reminder the following May, at our Officers' Club Hawaiian party. I singled out most of the officers who had been at Tom's home that testy New Year's evening and brazenly said, "Sir, I made a statement to you on New Year's Eve. Do you remember what I said to you?" It was more than obvious that they knew I had been right, but it was hardly time to gloat. That March, just two-and-a-half months into 1965, the U.S. Marines had landed in Danang, Vietnam, to begin the longest war we would fight in the 20th century. The 9th Marine Regiment on Okinawa would spearhead the next war we would fight, and thousands were following, many from Camp Lejeune—men I had trained. I knew the focus would soon change, but I did not wait around the club to hear their comments. They could read, hear, and more importantly, know that their names would soon appear on permanent change-of-station orders. That meant moving and resettling families and then experiencing the worst part of it: having the kids see Dad go off to a real war. My prediction on New Year's Eve had hit home—but in one way, I was wrong in that prediction. We would be at war in much less than six months.

Very few of us knew *we would not be ready* for this war—not if our several prior war experiences were the norm. World War II took us completely by surprise; it took almost a full year to muster and train Marines for Guadalcanal. Then, the Korean War caught the U.S. and the Marine Corps totally off guard. We mustered the whole 1st Marine Division while it was en route to Pusan and Inchon! Even then, most regiments were still at half-strength.

For Vietnam, we would have well-staffed battalions and regiments. It was not the number of Marines that concerned me; it was the mental and tactical preparation that was lacking. If Camp Lejeune and the Grassroots experience was an example of our readiness for a Vietnam war, then we were far from ready for it! My guerrilla jockstrap would stay on, and I was going to pull that darn thing as tight as I could! Sadly, the Asian war was starting and I was heading off in a totally different direction to keep training for a (European) war we would never fight. Vietnam and guerrillas were virtually ignored. Even the U.S Army, with their Special Forces units warning that *that* war was heating up, still fielded the huge armored divisions to fight World War II all over again. It would take a very long time to change their minds.

After 1965 my Marine Corps would never be the same, nor would America be the same. I knew this would be different and unlike anything we had ever experienced. It still would be hard to convince most senior Marines at Camp Lejeune of that. But on December 31, I had something very nice to celebrate that took the edge off what had happened at Tom's house that night. We were late to Tom's party because December 31 was our little Kristy's birthday. It was our miracle baby's third one, and like always, Gwenny arranged a huge party for happy, giggling little girls to celebrate it. Very soon, there would not be a lot to celebrate. Dad would be going away again for another long, long time.

Note: My next book is entitled *Covan*. This is the special title bestowed on a Vietnamese Marine advisor, which I would become after my tour of duty ended at Camp Lejeune, North Carolina. *Covan* means "loyal, trusted friend." Yet it is a term I would hardly use to describe myself in my first days at Camp Lejeune, where I also considered myself to be an "advisor" of sorts, when I tried to open the eyes of those who could not see, would not see, and closed their ears (and minds) to the reality that was soon to overwhelm them: the Vietnam War. I was hardly trusted at Camp Lejeune, nor was I a friend at all when I provoked so much controversy in my own relentless quest to introduce them to Vietnam-oriented counter-guerrilla training. It was much like what I would experience later as a real *covan*—with my Vietnamese Marines. My Marine Corps would soon change dramatically but realistically, as we had to do in every other war we fought. Marines accept the challenge and then do the job! But that didn't apply to an East-coast Marine Corps that had other priorities in the early 1960s. The Cuban Missile Crisis and its near-nuclear exchange, plus the failed Bay of Pigs invasion, would certainly diminish any interest in Southeast Asia. Although we were already ordering our first troops to that distant war in Vietnam, it was logical that Europe and the Caribbean still came first. They were smoldering, and Marines put fires out. Gitmo (Guantanamo Bay, Cuba) and Panama were also *hot*, as was the Dominican Republic.

Chapter 4: Vietnam Will Have to Wait

In mid-October of 1964, we sailed from Morehead City in a large flotilla of U.S. Navy and Merchant Marine ships, as well as several chartered commercial ships that hauled everything we were taking for the big landing in Spain. I was on a brand-new helicopter carrier that was constructed from the keel up for that mission. It was designated as a Landing Platform Helicopter (LPH), amphibious assault ship, and it held most of my battalion on board. All our other companies would make their landings from the worn-out Amphibious Personnel Ships (APAs) and the old workhorses, the Landing Ship Tanks (LSTs). Our landing craft (the LCVP) carried both small vehicles and personnel, while the tracked landing vehicles (LVTs), our amphibious tractors, held barfing seasick Marines and plunged and chugged ashore through the heavy surf to disgorge them onto pristine Spanish beaches.

After five months in the battalion, it was obvious that my company could perform well in the field. My lieutenants functioned as platoon leaders and did not usurp the tasks and duties of NCOs, who enjoyed the duties their ranks required of them. Their Camp Pickett experience guaranteed this. Fortunately, Steel Pike and the division landing in Spain got me out of town and away from the Grassroots flap. I had become a controversial Marine, and that was the kiss of death for any young officer's career.

On a warm, pleasant morning off Almonte, Spain, just north of Cadiz, our large armada positioned itself for the Marine Corps' specialty, the amphibious landing. Several of my battalion's rifle companies would be helo-lifted from the new helicopter carrier, the LPH. It gave the proven, original amphibious doctrine a new dimension: vertical assault by helicopter-borne troops that augmented the waterborne landings of the landing craft and the amphibious tractors that slowly ground ashore in World War II and Korea. It was a "really big show," with many U.S. dignitaries witnessing it. Tom Glidden would accompany the Secretary of the Navy, Paul Nitze, who would go ashore to review the landing.

My friend Mo (Neil Moriarity) and I had our two rifle companies assigned to specific helicopter serial lifts. Each chopper could carry a dozen Marines. We had to stage our men in groups of 10 or 12, to be called by individual serial numbers to the flight deck and then quickly loaded. The choppers would fly off to specified landing zones in the "enemy" territory, miles inland. From my first days in vertical assault in the 4th Marine Provisional Regiment in Hawaii, we Marines had progressed to the first modern and very efficient carriers we would fly from that day. So there in Almonte, Spain, it made sense that if we were to engage Russian troops in Europe, the amphibious tactics we employed that day would be appropriate for that situation. My India Company was first off, and I boarded one of the first choppers to land with my first elements. Mo's company would then follow mine to a common objective area ashore. Everyone was excited and proud to be showing off the Marine Corps' vertical assault tactics and match the Army.

The 2nd Marine Division was going ashore en masse, and the Marine Corps was proving that it could project such a force onto a European shore as a counterforce to the Russians, who were still busily heating up the Cold War. Our Marine Corps landing, along with the Army's ability to put its airborne divisions inland in Germany, would give the Russians cause to pause if they got too carried away with their own plans in Europe. At 6:00 a.m., I jumped off a lead chopper and set up my own command post to await the rest of my unit. Then I assembled them and prepared to take an objective some distance inland. As I walked back to a small hill, I saw Tom Glidden accompanying a distinguished-looking gentleman in a Navy leather flight jacket. It was the Secretary of the Navy, and I knew he was in good hands with Tom. They beckoned me over to their position, and Tom introduced me to him. Damn, I had just landed and met the SecNav—what a day! It was great to be alive and well.

That I was alive was a matter of some concern to me only moments later. Standing with Tom and the Secretary, we were looking back toward the beach where a swarm of helicopters was approaching in the distance. It should be the remainder of my own company arriving, or so I thought. No sooner had I glanced back, than it happened: two Sea Knight helicopters flew right into each other. We could see the rotors smashing and the pieces of rotors and aircraft parts flying off into space. Since both choppers were miles behind us, we heard no sound, just the sickening, eerie sight of two helicopters in dire trouble, plummeting to earth. As the heart-stopping sounds began to reach us, both craft fell vertically from the sky and plummeted onto the beach. We saw the huge fireball rising above the wreckage. At this point in my career, I had seen two men killed during training. But the horrible sight of those two choppers smashing to pieces in flight was the worst thing I would see until I got to Vietnam. Tragically, the cause turned out to be pilot error.

Everyone in the objective area stood in mute, shocked silence, knowing that we had lost some Marines in that horrible crash. Tom and the Secretary whispered in a low voice that it was really bad. Tom would get a report as soon as one could be provided. Then, it struck me: I had the remainder of my company on those choppers. A subdued panic set in as I ran to Tom to ask him to find out as soon as he could who was on those choppers. I knew my XO and one of my platoon leaders was on the last of my serials, as were 10 or 20 of my men, depending on how many had made those lifts. I ran to the other choppers that were landing and frantically asked if anyone had seen the crash, but no one knew who was on those craft. There were too many choppers lifting off for anyone to know who had loaded on the two unfortunate craft. I could only mumble a few silent prayers.

To my left, Mo Moriarity had just landed the lead elements of his own rifle company, and he came running over to me."Anybody know what company that was?" he screamed. I told him it had to be the last of my serials and he said, "Damn, Fish, that's awful. I'm so sorry." Tom was anxiously trying to get a report from the ship. He was told that rescue choppers were on the way to the site, which was still pouring thick, black, funereal smoke into the cool, fresh Spanish skies. I returned to my own company area. A deep, sickening feeling was beginning to overwhelm me.

The first sergeant and my gunnery sergeant ran over to my position. "Geez, Skipper, did you see the crash? We flew right over it. It's really bad; there are some dead Marines in that one!" I told them it might be our own kids and my XO, Lieutenant Kelly. "Sir, I just saw him right over there," he responded, pointing to none other than Kelly and the Marines I thought I might have lost.

Then, I wondered, whose kids had crashed? It had to be Mo's. It took almost an hour for a reliable report to reach us; we heard it over the battalion tactical net. Indeed it had been Mo's company. Somehow, there had been some confusion in calling away and loading my last serials and the first of Mo's. The deck guides had misunderstood that one company (mine) still had a few serials that had not yet loaded. The confusion meant that Mo's first elements were led to the carrier deck and boarded while mine were still waiting on the ladders below, unaware of what was going on. Sixteen Marines of Mo's company were killed. In one chopper, the blades of the other slashed right through the cabin wall and killed a dozen of them while they were still in the air. The rest were killed in the thunderous crash. Unbelievably, four pilots survived.

I ran over to Mo. By that time, Tom Glidden, the XO, and others had arrived as well and tried to comfort Mo. He was inconsolable. If Mo had one weakness as a Marine officer, it was the extreme care and love he had for his men. He paid the awful price that it must exact. It was bad enough for a Marine commander to lose his men in combat, but to lose them in such an unfortunate accident was too much to take. Finally, we were given word to move out toward our objectives. We could do nothing for the dead Marines. Somewhere back in the U.S., their parents would soon hear the tragic news. It was much more tragic because we were not at war, but were just training for that eventuality should we have to face the Russians in Europe. There in sunny Spain we faced no real enemy, just the pretend enemy that we usually imagined. Mock enemy units were marked on our maps, but we had just lost living young men, exceptional young Marines.

My route march took me through two small towns, where we could see that olives and grapes were the principal crops. As we entered one town, I noticed that the natives kept away from the armed Marines, who moved in a column along the main street. Later, I called a halt to our march so we could buy soft drinks and some of the local foods that were laid out on the tables in front of the modest shops. I looked forward to this Spanish venture, not only for the military exercise, but also for another opportunity to practice my Spanish with the real Spanish folk who lived there.

Because I had learned Castilian and even how to use the tongue-tied version the Sevillianos speak, I felt right at home. That alteration of the language was an artifact from the days when their king, Phillip II, had a lisp. They all adopted that lisp in their own vernacular, in respect and deference to their king. I was delighted to find out that I was easily understood. Unlike the crude, bastardized Spanish spoken in the border towns of Mexico and throughout the Caribbean, this crisp, distinct language (Castilian Spanish) was easy to speak and understand. I was going to make the most of it, and they respected my ability to speak it.

Yet the first question that I received from a shop owner floored me: "Señor, what country are you from?" Obviously, no one had briefed them that a large American exercise would be taking place in their own front yard. I told him what we were doing there, and he was sad that we had already lost some of our men in the "battle." Having survived the Franco war when they were assaulted by the Germans some 25 years before, I am sure he wasn't surprised at another strange army showing up on Spanish terrain. As I was leaving, he whispered, "We have the very best wine in Spain. You must return and drink some." I sure would! But first we had to attack the empty "enemy" just up the road. Here we were, in another foreign land, and the shop's puzzled owner, who had obviously experienced real war earlier in his life, asked me that startling question. It was amazing!

Ten years earlier I had landed in Spain, just 30 miles from this place, and had visited the famous Bodega Tierry winery not many miles away. Too many *vino* samples at that time had reduced a bus full of Naval Academy midshipmen to *borrachos* (drunks) when we emerged from the cellars into the blazing hot sun. I was ready to try the samples again. The shop owner was right—the wines were very good. That afternoon, we finally arrived at our company objective. It was on a low rise above the olive groves of a farmer. The battalion was ordered to dig in for the night and start no fires, although it was beginning to get quite chilly even for Spain.

Our battalion umpire was Major Andy Anderson. He was a stocky, tough Marine who had acquired a reputation for his daring and unpredictable ways. I had met him on the LPH and enjoyed the bizarre tales he told us each night in the wardroom. A trained recon Marine, Andy had picked up the nickname "Recon Andy." It would not be the last time I would meet or serve with Andy. In fact, I would relieve him in Vietnam when I reported to the Vietnamese Marines, two years in the future. Andy and I were paratroopers, so we shared a kind of brotherhood as risk-takers—and in my case, as a change agent as well. The little I knew of him indicated he was a no-holds-barred Marine who tried anything.

Shortly after we landed, Andy stopped his jeep to tell me that it would be wise to have a few counterattack plans ready. Our pretend enemy force would have heavy tanks. At the Army Infantry School I had studied tank attacks, their penetration of infantry lines, and the best way to fall back, absorb the attack, and then conduct our own counterattack. So had Tom Glidden, who had also been to the same school. Later that evening, I decided to mention this to Tom at the battalion command post. Never one to miss an opportunity, Tom sat me down at his field desk. "Draw one up for the battalion, Bob." I did, and we distributed it to all the rifle companies that night. Tom thanked me. As S-3 (Operations and Training) officer, he had the responsibility for planning our tactical schemes. Later I would thank Andy for the tip. He already knew he would receive orders to Vietnam, and we talked about the difference between what we were doing in Spain versus what we would be doing in a real guerrilla environment. I told him about my earlier experience in Southeast Asia and the Grassroots results. He was all ears, agreeing that East-coast Marines just didn't get it.

Later that night, all the company commanders were informed that there would be a memorial service at 10:00 the next morning on a lovely Spanish hill near our exercise area. Every commander, including an admiral and his staff, would be present. Mo had arranged 16 rifles with their bayonets stuck into the ground. On top of each rifle butt was the helmet of one of his lost Marines. A simple wooden altar had been constructed just behind them. Several division chaplains held an inspiring service on that sad, sunny day in Spain. It would be an appropriate ceremony for our fallen Marines, and one that had been held many times during the history of our Corps. It was our final battlefield salute.

After the simple Marine Corps service, all the officers went over to Mo and his guys to offer their sympathy. I kept looking at my own two officers and my kids (who should have been on those helos) and thanked a merciful God that they had survived, even though other Marines had to die. Then I walked off the hill with Mo. I was his best friend and also roomed with him on the LPH. I really understood this complex, very intelligent Irishman and was probably the only one he would listen to at that terrible time in his life. Then, we parted and headed off to our own operation areas to continue the tactical assault at noon. Marines bury their own, and then we salute them and march on to continue the business of war. It was the best way, and the only way! We learned to do it many times in our Corps' long history.

So there we were in Spain, in 1964, with the Russians lined up on their Warsaw Pact's buffered borders throughout Europe. We were somewhat ignorant of the mischief they planned in Southeast Asia. Huge amounts of military equipment, military advisors, the latest anti-aircraft missile technology, and the expansion of communism propped up their Vietnam allies Ho and Giap, where they were already sucking us in to test our political and military resolve. We were about 10 miles inland, in open terrain with few towns, as we swept over the hills. We moved with companies on line, spread across several kilometers as we moved to another set of empty enemy objectives with no enemy aggressors, just an "enemy situation" that the umpires imposed by messages to the command post that we had to adjust to.

That night at about 9:00 p.m. we received a flash message, the worst-case situation. Enemy infantry had penetrated our outposts with armor units leading the way. The battalion had to fall back, muster our own tanks, and then employ our anti-tank weapons and rocket launchers. We had to execute the planned fallback to specified phase lines, hold our lines, regroup, and then counterattack right into the enemy's point of attack. While the whole event was just a command-post exercise paper drill, it worked pretty well. Tom just smiled at it all—it's very simple when you have no enemy! We would also have to execute several other counterattacks during this operation. The current European situation required it.

At Fort Benning, nine of us Marine Corps students had to operate as the enemy forces with a small group of tanks and several armored personnel carriers. I never will forget the sight of 100-plus tanks racing over the hills and chasing us. Even in training, that sight alarmed me, though I would never see it for real. Recon Andy was highly complementary of the battalion's tactics that we used to counter his "night attacks." Tom, true to form, passed on his "well done" to me for my help. I didn't know it then, but I had already worked my way into his S-3 shop as his assistant operations officer. Finally, I had a staff job. It was a key job that involved staff planning many of the tactical operations and competitions that we would use in future battalion operations. Tom was already looking ahead to our next deployment, two months away, when 3/8 would become the Caribbean BLT. It meant four more separation months for all of us and our families, even though it was a stateside tour.

Our last night in Spain, while still in the field, we had a stand-down. It was okay to light fires and eat some grapes. "Hang loose," we were told. But Doc Hanlon and I had other ideas: we decided we would *drink* those grapes. With the aid of his ambulance, a corpsman driver, and me wrapped up on a stretcher in the rear of the vehicle, his chief corpsman and I headed into Almonte, the biggest town nearby, which was off-limits to all Marines on this operation. Military police (MPs) guarded all the roads into Almonte, so we had to figure out a ruse so we could enter. Since the only hospital for the exercise was set up there, it was logical that an ambulance and a patient could pass those MPs, and we did. They didn't notice that my stretcher rested on a dozen five-gallon water cans, all empty, waiting to be filled with wine.

It was after 9:00 p.m. when we drove into the city. The streets were filled with the local populace walking through the town in the evening custom Spaniards have practiced for centuries: *Dar El Paseo* (Take a Walk), meeting and greeting each other every night. This hour-long walk made their late dinners taste even better. In my best Castilian Spanish, I asked where the nearest *bodega* (a production winery that sold its wares) was located. We were told that all the bodegas had closed for the night. "*Tan lastima* [what a pity]! How sad for you, gentlemen, because we have the finest wine you can imagine." We were drooling by then, so I asked if they would tell me where one of their best wine merchants lived. They pointed to a two-story home at the end of the street and it was obvious their dinner was already in progress.

Dinners last for hours in Spain, but we didn't have hours. I knocked on the downstairs door. No one answered, so I stood on the hood of the ambulance and shouted up to the open windows, *"Hola, Señor. Tiene vino para nosotros comprar? Lo mejor de todo?"* ("Have you wine to sell us—your very best?") After a few minutes, a portly man leaned out of the upstairs window, amazed that a military ambulance was waiting below. Finally, he appeared at his front door. I explained our plight and that we really needed to buy some good wine from him. It was our last night in Spain. He smiled at me, apologized, and said his bodega was closed. I protested that we would pay his best price and that we really needed 100 liters of his best wine. "How many liters, Señor?" That did it. He whistled at my dozen big cans. We drove off to his bodega, just a block away, where we discovered many large, oak casks filled with every kind of wine in Almonte. He gave us each a sampling ladle to dip and taste from each of the generous casks. We all did, except for the driver, who of course had to drive. The chief and I decided to fill up the cans with five of the best wines we had tasted. It turned out that he had additional10-liter containers, so we loaded up 13 heavy containers into a sagging ambulance.

Price was not even discussed until after we had filled up all the cans. I misunderstood his price quotation. He used a business term I did not readily translate. Thinking he wanted 5 dollars per container (about 65 dollars total), I eagerly pulled out my U.S. dollars, which we both knew were in great demand in Spain (and all over Europe in those days). We had previously been told that our U.S. money could be exchanged only at banks. There I was, alone with a wine merchant, with not a bank in sight. Just as I was handing him the 65 dollars, he protested that the amount was not correct. Whoops! I felt the heavy hit coming, and I was prepared to give some of his wine back if the price was higher. To my surprise, he told me that each container was only *two* U.S. dollars! We felt as if we had died and gone to wine heaven.

The overly generous wine merchant asked if we wanted some of the excellent bread and cheese they also sold in their fine *tiendas* (shops), which also were closed for the day. No sooner had I agreed than he had a more-than-eager brother merchant on the phone, and off we went to load up the long rolls of bread and rounds of tasty cheese. Again, the price was right for both of us. With blankets covering our bountiful booty, we slipped out of town just as easily as we had entered it.

What a fine feast we would have that night, for just $40 US! Wine, bread, and cheese—*caramba*, a *gran fiesta*! I dropped off a five-gallon can at the battalion command post, to their delight and amazement. Then, I invited Recon Andy to my company area for one heck of a party and more of Andy's sea stories that night. The hot, crackling campfires warded off the cold. My troops, Doc Hanlon's medical unit, and our visitors felt no pain that night.

Sometime during the night, Big John Ryan, our battalion adjutant, had sipped a bit too much of the grapes and made a call of nature on the edge of a very steep hill that turned out to be a mini-cliff. He would not be found until later in the morning. When he finally was located, at the bottom of that very large chasm, he was snoring and blissfully asleep in a huge ball trying to keep warm. His bare butt was almost blue in the chilly morning air, and his pants were down around his knees. We would laugh often about that bizarre scene for many months to come, but our laughter wouldn't continue—Big John's name would be carved in the granite of the Vietnam Memorial in Washington, DC, just one of our 3/8 Marines.

The morning after the party, we flew back to the carrier, somewhat hung-over and saddened by the loss of so many fine, young Marines in this land that Marines had never known, much less invaded. I met Mo in our stateroom; he was in no mood for conversation or anything else. Tom Glidden and I stayed close to him. It would take Mo a long time to get over his tragic loss.

On our way back to the States, we made two short port visits, one to the historic city of Marseilles, France. While we felt uncomfortable in a country that didn't like Americans, I wondered how such a country could forget all that we Americans had done for them, not just in one war, but in two very large, bloody wars where we buried thousands in graves in that same unappreciative country. That they still had a nation was in large part due to the sacrifice of Americans who fought and died on their soil. This antipathy would not change; years later, their hostile anti-American disdain would challenge us politically and militarily.

The only high point of our visit was the timely rescue of a young girl who had fallen into the river off a walking bridge. One of our young Marines saw it happen and quickly dived into the icy water to bring her to shore. This unselfish act inspired the French people, and their newspaper *really* found time to appreciate him. He was given local honors by the mayor and the city's dignitaries, as well as a huge kiss from the grateful young girl. My God, these folks did like Americans! I had visited France almost 10 years earlier and had not experienced the open arrogance we found in Marseilles. Brest and Paris had not shown us the discourtesy that this city had. We left them with a bad taste in our mouths, vowing to let them go to hell.

Our next stop was in Plymouth, England, the city the pilgrims had left on their way to North America, where they landed at Cape Cod and our Plymouth Rock. I looked forward to visiting London on an overnight pass. There, we stayed at the former home of Lady Astor, right on Hyde Park. She donated it to the U.S. military for use as an officers' club called the Columbia Club, where visiting officers could stay. The food and entertainment was the best in London, and we saw a legitimate theatre play for a meager $2.50 US. We made brief stops in Soho, Piccadilly Circus, and Buckingham before taking the train back to Plymouth, where the Royal Marines were our hosts. Their training center was located there, and a small number of our U.S. Marines had cross-trained with them like John Ripley, P.X. Kelley, Duff Rice and a dozen other fortunate Marines.

On our final night, they invited the 3/8 officers to a "bash." Lieutenant Kelly, my XO, already had been adopted by one of the Royal Marines who liked the quick-witted Irishman. As he drove to the officers' club with his new friend, a huge excavation ditch appeared "right out of nowhere, right in the middle of the stupid road." The car, Lieutenant Kelly, and his buddy disappeared from sight. Not to be diverted, the buddy simply climbed out of the pit, brushed himself off, and said "C'mon, Kelly, we'll be late for the bash. I'll collect it later."

And what a bash it was! Indeed, the Royal Marines are royal. It reminded me of my earlier drinking "bash" with the British officers at our embassy in Kuala Lumpur, Malaya. Somewhere in their training, heavy boozing is a mandatory event. Most Marines drink, but not to the degree and with the capacity that those British officers could. But they were openly challenged by the Australians, who also were there in force that night. No one was feeling any pain. About 11:00 p.m., the "Tarzan and Jane" event began. This activity involved an upside-down drinking event where the competitor was hoisted upside down to a 24-foot wooden beam that spanned the drinking room. This weird chug-a-lug involved moving along the beam by only the calves of the legs while hanging upside down with a schooner of beer in one's hand. Then, the competitor gulped the frothy brew, upside down, without spilling any—or, if there was a spill, several "whippers" with rice-filled canvas straps smacked the contestant's butt to make sure the next gulp did not splash on the floor. A few Royal Marines traversed the beam and felt the straps.

The Aussies, who had introduced the game, were next to go. They zoomed across the beam, beating all that had previously tried it. None of the "Yanks" would give it a go, and were subject to the derisive jibing of the crowd. Finally I said, "No Aussie is going to beat me at *anything*!" So, across I went, quickly, with my leg action trying to outrun the butt smacks, but very sloppily—and with a sore butt, I got what I deserved! I tried my best to "leg it" across, stop, pull up in a tight kip, and then try to gulp the brew. Unfortunately, the drink still slopped—and I got hit. When I did make it across, saving face for the Marine Corps, I received boisterous applause, which made me feel pretty good. As I got down, a cute little blond was hoisted up, locked the backs of her legs on the big beam, grabbed her beer, and just seemed to zip right across the long beam, skirt down over her face and panties at full show. She didn't spill a drop of beer! It was obvious that she had performed this tricky feat more than once at this club.

It turned out to be a heck of a night, and the Royal Marine hosts were the greatest. I had spent other nights drinking with the Brits and the Aussies in Malaya, Hong Kong, and the pubs of Sydney, but this drinking bout topped them all. No wonder so many U.S. Marines eagerly sought exchange tours with the Royal Marines. We left merry old England in great spirits, with many fine memories to rehash back at Camp Lejeune. Except for the tragic helicopter accident, which would sadden all of us for days to come, the Marine Corps had just demonstrated that it was ready—for the last war! Mo was somber all the way home, and had hardly enjoyed the fun we had. His heavy loss obviously had hit him extremely hard.

No sooner were we back home when 3/8 had its orders to prepare for a Caribbean tour, which would last four months and include several weeks in Vieques, Puerto Rico, for tactical exercises and live-fire drills. Tom Glidden saw to my speedy transfer to his S-3 shop. I'd had only six months as the company commander of India Company, but with my other two company commands in Hawaii, it was obvious that I was well qualified to command one. It was logical that I move up to learn staff work. We would spend two full months getting ready for the afloat tour. On Vieques Island we would conduct company and platoon tactics competitions, and I also laid out plans for a counter-guerrilla exercise in Panama, where the steamy jungle terrain suited it best.

Gwenny and the girls were happy to have Dad home for two months. Unlike Fort Benning, where I was home all the time, this afloat tour would take me away again for an awful long time. It was the Marine Corps and I was part of it, like it or not. My days at the S-3 office also became very long, with Tom and the XO ensuring that every facet of our future operational plans was detailed and accurate in every way. I appreciated the fact that I was learning staff work from one of the finest staff men I have ever served with. Together, we developed plans for an amphibious landing on Vieques and a platoon raid on a missile site with rubber boats. Finally, we would hold our realistic, company-sized tactical exercises to test both the company commanders and the companies. The somewhat barren island was best suited to routine Marine tactics, and the platoon raid I was planning would create a competitive environment for some very competitive officers. The 9th Marines had just landed in Vietnam as we were loading our amphibious ships to go the other way! With its bare hills, open terrain, and its small exercise area, Vieques wasn't appropriate for me to plan a guerrilla exercise.

Tom had delegated the field tactical exercises to me, since he knew I had an intense desire to develop these competitive grunt areas. With the war in Vietnam just beginning in March 1965, I had no trouble convincing him or the XO that we should conduct jungle based, counter-guerrilla training in Panama. I laid out detailed plans for an actual counter-guerrilla exercise. The two attached recon units would serve as our "live" guerrilla force, which our companies would try to encircle and outmaneuver in the dense Panamanian swamps. Shortly after loading out of Morehead City, we were deployed again. This time we had only a three-ship Battalion Landing Team which held all of our companies and their equipment. Attached units such as motor transport, artillery, engineers, recon units, supply, and other teams augmented us to complete a fully independent fighting force that is unique to the Marine Corps.

Our first stop was Vieques, where we would make a full-scale BLT amphibious landing. This included heli-borne and amphibious tractor landings—vertical and surface assaults that were *the* latest tactical techniques of the Marine Corps. Tom and the XO had planned the ship-to-shore phase, when the amphibious tractors and small boats made their landings over the beach. True to the plan, it went off with absolute precision, like a professional amphibious landing should. Had it been graded, it would have deserved a solid 4.0! Next, our first unit competition included all 12 rifle platoons, which had to make a night raid on an enemy radio site to capture a guided missile that was needed for an intelligence study. The raid would start from a small island (our ship or sub equivalent) just a few hundred yards off a wide sandy beach and about half a mile from the objective.

I had prepared a detailed, colored raid plan that showed the radio site layout, guard posts, roads leading to it, and finally, a separate photo and technical description of the "missile" that each platoon must capture and carry off. The raid plan stated that this missile weighed 300 pounds and that each platoon must prepare its own vehicle to carry it off. Back at Camp Lejeune, the Operations chief and I had managed to scrounge a 500-pound practice bomb case from the air wing. We painted it with all the tactical markings we had taken from an actual Russian manual, and it looked very authentic with its white color accented by red, black, and orange markings, exactly like the Russian photo we had. Then, to add a more realistic touch to our "missile," we filled it with concrete to ensure that it would, in fact, weigh 300 pounds. We had to use a big forklift to put it into the heavy shipping crate we had built. It was loaded as a "training device" box. When we finally had it off-loaded on the beach, the Operations chief and I commandeered a tractor and bucket to move the monster up to the "radio site." What a load! We constructed a missile ramp, painted it to look very authentic, and then put a large, white squad tent in the middle of the site. We also rigged battery-powered lights on the four corners of the site, as well as inside the "command" tent. There, a mock Russian missile team dressed in white coats.

Lastly, we set up a missile radio station and a mock control system. At night the Russian site looked as authentic as a real one—our training would have reality added to it. It was an eerie sight, especially at night when the competitions took place. There were no lights on the beach or on the craggy roads leading up to the missile site. While stealth and speed were important, a key competitive element soon would separate the winners from the losers. It was obvious that each platoon was really charged up. A dozen of the enemy, including the guards, were to be captured along with the missile. If the raid was delayed more than five minutes after it was discovered, the missile team had to blow up the missile, and the raid would be a failure. Each platoon had its briefing at 9:00 p.m. Then, in rubber boats, they rowed to the island to begin their raid at about 9:30 p.m. It would take 30 minutes to sneak up to the radio site. I had specified an attack time of 10:00 p.m. and a maximum of 30 minutes to return to the ship (island). Then, the raid would be over.

I had several staff officers acting as umpires, one with the raiding party and two at the radio site. As I had expected, at least half of the platoons had not planned to haul the 300-pound missile, undoubtedly not believing the details of the raid plan. And I knew exactly which lieutenants would have prepared to haul a heavy missile. One platoon had only two medical stretchers and others had nothing at all—believing, no doubt, that this exercise was just another "goat rope" and that no heavy missile would be part of a training raid. Little did they know what they would find there! Hiding a heavy, cumbersome "enemy" bomb on a Navy ship took a lot of imagination—and crating. I debriefed the first platoons that had finished their test to keep quiet about the missile's size and weight, since it was a competition and was graded. It is why I didn't use company commanders as umpires—they might pass too much information on to their own platoons. It was a competition, and it was obvious that they all took it seriously.

It took two weeks to complete the raids, with only two or three platoons successfully approaching, capturing, and moving the missile back to the "ship." Reality training had just not been part of their former field experience. Six or seven platoons could not even move it from the site. They tried to hand-carry the missile with two boards, with canvas slings, an Indian travois, and other rigs that would not work. When it was obvious that they could not move it, we gave them the alternative to blow it up in place with "dummy" C-4 blocks and take a lesser grade. True to form, the three best lieutenants in the battalion produced fold-up and quick assembly, in-place carts. The best of their rigs was a wooden platform with its axles mounted. Two other Marines carried the rugged bicycle wheels, which they snapped to the cart's frame in seconds. A pull-tongue was also attached, and away the missile went, as easy as a 300-pound load could move. Once a platoon carried the missile to the beach, I stopped the raid there rather than lose it in the water. The last platoon dragged it there, and we left it in a clump of bushes. It served its purpose. Later, the raid was the subject of stimulating conversation at the "O" club. "Imagination, imagination!" I yelled at the losing platoon leaders.

The training was realistic, and was enjoyed immensely by Marines who long ago tired of a "dummy" enemy and the endless empty hills. As long as I was the training officer for the battalion, all our competitive exercises would include as much realism and real opponents as I could muster. It was a job I had a natural talent for, and I enjoyed the exercises as much as the kids did. The "missile" had another life, which we would not know about at the time we left it on the beach. We were finished with it, so I didn't give it another thought; it was left in some bushes near the beach.

Sometime later, when we were sailing off of Panama, a message came to the ship asking if we knew anything about a Russian bomb that was discovered on the beach. Since it was 1965, and a short time after the Bay of Pigs confrontation with the Russians, this discovery seemed to be of great importance. Was it possible that the Russians had landed on Vieques or had dropped it there as a lesson to us? It really caused quite a stir. An explosive demolition team had even been called in from Guantanamo, Cuba, to check it out. They quickly identified it as a harmless, 500-pound bomb case full of concrete, but its origin was still in question. We never acknowledged that we knew anything about the "missile." I didn't realize my training device would cause such a ruckus! Tom was amused and jokingly told me that the damn "bomb" almost caused an international incident.

With a few days left on Vieques and company tactical tests also completed, we spent more time in the officers' club. Arm wrestling, chug-a-lugs, and our very loud "aroogahs" consumed most of our evenings, interrupted by lengthy urination stops outside. Since the urination tubes were located way down the hill, we did the next best thing and urinated down the very steep hill, knowing it would all go to the same place, one way or another.

With my bricklayer arms, I did pretty well in the arm-wrestling competitions and had conquered almost all the battalion officers. Just as I was beginning to enjoy my new fame, a huge football type showed up from the attached artillery battery. In a split second, this Neanderthal slammed my arm to the bar, and he was the new bar champion. So be it! Another conflict involved our condescending grunt attitude toward attached units. We held them in disdain, since we were the ones who made the marches, ate the dirt, and lived like dogs in the field. Tough bastards we were—or so we thought. Careful, the mighty are often mice! Tough mice.

One evening, a slightly built officer from a supply unit had a few drinks too many. I overheard him challenging two of our best young lieutenants to a midnight run. Drunk or not, he would whip their asses. They took his challenge seriously, and the bet involved a road race that very night. I acted as the "ombudsman" and would hold the money. First, the challenger said that since he had challenged the lieutenants, he had the right to pick the distance they would run. Our two "studly" lieutenants were egged on by all of us, since the very drunk challenger said he would match any amount of money that *any* of us would bet. Quickly, a few hundred dollars flashed onto the table and I picked them up. We were really enjoying this! Our two battalion guys were our best runners and jocks—and they were sober, having imbibed little that night. After 30 minutes, the three officers lined up outside the club." How far is the run?" I asked.

"Five miles," the supply officer mumbled. I told him I would drive down the main road for two-and-a-half miles and have the jeep lights on so they could see the turnaround point. That plan was okay with everyone. How, I wondered, could this guy even run a mile in the shape he was in? Holding all the bets, I drove exactly to the two-and-a-half mile spot to wait for my guys to show—and probably to drive back to pick up the sotted carcass of the inebriated, boastful officer. When I saw the sole apparition in the headlights, it was the supply officer! Where the hell, I wondered, were our officers? My two men were nowhere in sight. This officer in the glare of the lights had just run four-and-a-half-minute miles, according to my watch. No sooner had he zipped around my jeep than I asked him where the other two guys were.

"They're way back there, Captain. I'll pick up my money in about 10 minutes, if that's okay with you," he said.

A few minutes later, my two haggard young officers also appeared, saying. "That son-of-a-bitch conned us, sir!" I told them to move out. He was at least three or four minutes ahead of them, and they were gasping so hard that I knew there was no chance of them catching him. As it turned out, Lieutenant Con Job was a first class, All American cross-country runner from the University of Kentucky. Even half-bombed he whipped our best. I paid up, handing over all of the money, then watched him return to the club and resume drinking like he hadn't even left it that night. The demeaning treatment by our guys quickly diminished. That event formed a new, respectful bond among everyone in the BLT.

That same week we had a joint U.S. Marine–Army Airborne exercise. The operation began with a simulated landing by us and a real 82nd Airborne drop with tanks, trucks, and self-propelled artillery parachute drops. I had tried my best to be assigned as a Marine liaison for the jump. No doubt, another 110 bucks would have helped too. But the planes had been loaded back at Fort Bragg, and there was no way I could join the jumpers there. Still, I hoped I could perform some liaison job to get near the jumpers. The air drops went well, with huge cargo chutes letting M-60 tanks and heavy trucks drift down to a dusty landing. One drop, however, was a very heavy, self-propelled, 155mm gun. Its chutes failed and we watched as the large vehicle dropped, almost in slow motion, hit with a deafening sound, and exploded into pieces. It left a big hole in the drop zone. They dropped no food or water, relying on us for basic sustenance, which we joked about later—we had their chow! For years, this had been a bone of contention between soldiers and Marines. They could get there fast, but then what? Yet joint Army-Marine exercises always went well. Paratroopers and Marines seemed to share a common bond as best of the best.

That evening, before the Airborne brigade would return to Fort Bragg, we had a joint-service blast at the officers' club. To cap off that hilarious evening, we managed to burn down the club. No one knew how the fire started, perhaps it was due to a bad propane line or some booze spilled too close to an open fire. Someone near the bar yelled, "Fire!" and we all tried to exit through the single front door. It was a riotous mob scene at its very worst! I am sure the airborne group thought Marines really were as crazy as they had heard—and they saw flaming proof of that claim that night. I can imagine them saying, "They even burn down their O club as the finale to a good operation!" This fiasco did not endear us to future Marine battalions that came to train and found no officers' club standing. But it certainly was a good party!

We had a great week in San Juan, Puerto Rico, and the wives came to spend it with us. Most of the battalion officers reserved rooms at the Naval Station, Roosevelt Roads, which was located near the big hotels and fun spots. Gwenny and I were delighted to spend this quality time together. Our separations had become too frequent at Camp Lejeune. That was the life of a BLT Marine and she accepted it, as a great service wife does. We danced, gambled, took tours of the island, and ate wonderful food. My relief officer and his wife appeared to have a great time, but they rarely came out into the light of day and preferred to stay honeymooners. How we kidded them! It would make my memories of him even sadder when I recalled how close they were that week and what a huge loss his death in Vietnam would be. But later, we would lose many more fine officers as well.

Chapter 5: Panama Jungle–3/8 Guerrilla Warfare Exercise

I saw Gwenny off at the airport and told her I would see her in a few months. We still had Panama to go, where I had planned a battalion-size counter-guerrilla operation that would last most of one week in the dense jungles along the Chagris River and a nearby canal. But first we would stop at Guantanamo Bay, Cuba, where we would go ashore, refuel the ships, and see what that bastion against Castro's Communism looked like. The base lay on the eastern end of Cuba, and its common border with the mainland was a heavily guarded fence line with tanks, artillery, and hundreds of angry men looking at each other. We expected an incident every minute of the day. You could smell the tenseness.

The commanding officer (CO) called Doc Hanlon and me into his office to let us know that the two of us would fly ahead to Fort Sherman, Panama, to set up a medical center for the battalion and receive their briefing about snakebites and malaria. We had been shot full of several serums before we left Camp Lejeune, but there would be several more, as Doc found out when we arrived. My tasks involved making arrangements for an exercise area and then scouting out the whole region so I knew where we could maneuver, bivouac, and heli-lift at least one rifle company as a reaction force. I also had to find the most advantageous places to set up and phase our own "guerrilla" units into the exercise. The recon unit would go into the jungle as "my" guerrillas. Many had been to Ranger School at Fort Benning and would (I thought) be familiar with the swamps and dense jungle. How I was tempted to join another guerrilla force!

Off we went to Panama, as sort of an "odd couple." Doc was enjoying it immensely; he was like a school kid who was let out early. We flew in the same type of Beechcraft airplane that World War II Corsair pilot, Colonel "Maggie" McGill, taught me to fly during my two years aboard the Saint Paul. At Fort Sherman, an Army liaison met us and took us to the medical center, where Doc was briefed on the many bad bugs we would encounter in the jungle. There was a very long briefing about the poisonous snakes. One of their briefings recounted the thousands of men who died digging the canal. Hundreds were killed by the *fer-de-lance*, bushmasters, the bamboo and tiny, striped coral snakes. The boa constrictor was considered harmless and not large enough to harm a man, as a python of Southeast Asia could. While Doc learned about serums and such, I took off with my liaison sergeant. He knew the jungle since he was an instructor at the famous Army Jungle School. There, my battalion would spend a few days learning about the flora, fauna, and jungle survival. It was "shades of Vietnam to come," but at least we were now training for the right war in the right environment, with the same kind of snakes, bugs, and oppressive jungle heat.

Our Panama jungle home, "the Bohio"

We scouted the whole training area, which had few open sites. Finally, I selected the battalion campsite where we would have to construct shelters when the rest of the troops arrived. Initially, every Marine would have to build his own *bohio*, a lean-to made with poles and a floor just off the ground, where he would place his air mattress. The roof of this jungle hut would be covered with the very large leaves of the fern, banana, and the elephant-ear plants that were there for the picking. It would be our home for the whole time we were training there. I located suitable helicopter landing zones near the canal, where I positioned the guerrilla force for a final assault.

Map reading would require real skill—and the men would be separated from the boys, as I would soon find out. I drafted a map overlay for the exercise that included the landing zones near my designated "hot" zones where a wily guerrilla force might be found—where I had placed them. Since we had very little time in the exercise, this had to be simple. My plan employed counter-guerrilla techniques right out of the British manual I had obtained at the Malaya Jungle School—the one we used during Grassroots '64 and we employed search-and-destroy methods, encirclements, and decentralized patrol bases instead of two-up-and-one-back, standard company tactics. By positioning the units in counter-guerrilla formations, I hoped to make their job much easier. These were the same formations the brigade failed to use at Camp Pickett. The officer in charge of the Panama Jungle School was quite impressed by my extensive knowledge of guerrilla warfare and the operation plan I had for the exercise we would be conducting. When I told him where I had learned it in the past few years—hands-on in Southeast Asia with the Gurkhas—he was all ears. At his Jungle School, only jungle survival was emphasized. They were hardly focused on Vietnam; Cuba was enough.

The Army's own Special Forces units and several friends of mine who were Vietnamese Marine advisors were already fighting in some of the provinces in Vietnam. Because things were heating up there, I told the officer in charge that it was time our battalion be exposed to counter-guerrilla tactics. Many of our young Marines soon would need them for real.

Doc Hanlon and I found that we had two days to travel across the isthmus, visit the canal, and shop at Colon and Panama City. There, we would ride the peppy little narrow-gauge railroad train in a scene right out of *Tarzan and the Apes*. We had a ball, and in the evening we visited the officers' club to find "No Women, No Wives"—nothing but other officers quietly drinking at the tables and missing their loved ones at home. Doc was having a blast, being free from his wife and his medical responsibilities at the battalion. He drank quickly and not very quietly, shouting and yelling out "aroogahs" and various Irish epithets, embarrassing me and also bothering the Army officers present.

After a few too many drinks, Doc decided that I would make a good punching bag. When I wasn't looking, or was talking to someone at the bar, he would sneak up (guerrilla-style, as he called it) and slug one of my arms—hard. While he was having his own boozy ball, the rest of us no longer found it funny. Finally, after I decided he had slugged my arm for the *last* time, I turned on him before he could get the next punch off, aiming to hit his left arm. My aim was poor because my right-cross glanced off of his shoulder and hit him square on the jaw, dropping him like a sack of flour. He was sprawled out on the floor, out cold! The officers that had endured Doc's juvenile actions and seen my own frustration with him all evening gave me a loud cheer.

We revived Doc, who looked at me in total amazement, as if his best buddy had just betrayed him—and his jaw was swelling up real fast. I only hoped that I hadn't broken it. I took him to the medical facility, where they confirmed that he had a bad bruise and should put some ice on it. "How did it happen?" one guy asked.

"Fischer hit me," he retorted. And he would tell everyone we saw for the next two days that this damn Marine had beaten him up! My real concern was the CO's reaction when he saw Doc's swollen jaw, especially if Doc told him "Fischer hit me." Fortunately, Doc was a much better friend than I had expected. We met the first heli-lift as it landed on Fort Sherman. On it was the XO, accompanied by Tom Glidden. Sure as blazes, when the XO saw Doc's puffy face, be asked about it and Doc said, "Fischer hit me—but I won't tell the colonel." I could hardly wait to hear exactly what he *would* tell him. I had the impression that both Tom and the XO *knew* the Doc had likely deserved it—that mouthy little Irishman! To the colonel, his swollen jaw was passed off as being due to a swollen tooth, which Doc said he had already taken care of. I warned Doc that if it ever happened again, I would slug him again, and harder. He just smirked and said, "I'll tell the CO!" The next time, he probably would. Sometimes it takes a fist in the mouth to maintain a friendship.

The battalion arrived in force, off-loading at the Panama Canal docks near the Jungle School. Everything we owned was brought ashore except for one essential training item: the blank ammo. The CO decided he did not want any kind of ammo in the hands of the troops because it could cause an injury or some other problem. He felt it was better to be safe than sorry—to cover his ass and let his Marines yell, "Bang, bang!" in the dense jungle. My appeal to the XO fell on deaf ears. How the heck do 1200 Marines and a realistic aggressor force run through the jungle for a week and just yell, "Bang, bang" when they contact each other? Fortunately, I had an ally in Skip Fisher, the Battalion S-4 (Logistics and Supply officer), who saw my predicament immediately and told me not to worry. The ammo would be there for the exercise, he assured me, despite the CO. How could we train without it? I wondered. And worse, did we mistrust the men that much? He was acquainted with the first lieutenant aboard ship and those in charge of the ammo holds, and he assured me that they would help me out.

But first, we were to attend a day's lecture at the Jungle School, where all of us had to eat the various products of the jungle and learn how to distinguish the good stuff from the bad. The monkey and snake meat were quite delicious if eaten in small amounts. Then, we were shown the cages of the most deadly snakes in Panama. The best example of our training came when an eight-foot boa constrictor, Old Molly, was passed up and down the rows of Marines from lap to lap. She was well-fed and had made this trip many times before. The snake was docile and even looked a bit bored with all of us. That afternoon, I had to prepare for the exercise so I jumped into my jeep to head back down to our bivouac site. Skip had off-loaded the C-rations, water cans, and—*the ammo*. God bless the Skipper!

It would be a realistic operation after all. But on the way down to the bivouac, what did we spot ahead of us on the winding jungle road? An eight-foot boa constrictor crawling across it! A young officer, Lieutenant Jim Dastugue, the communications officer, was in the backseat. I jumped out of the jeep, grabbed the snake's tail, and pulled the squirming monster back on the road. The snake was heavy—and angry. Enraged, it flashed back at me and almost got my arm. It seemed like I had a tiger by the tail—worse, I had a mad eight-foot boa by the tail! I yelled to Das to find me a piece of wire or a rope, anything I could tie to its tail to keep it on the road. He was looking at me desperately and yelling, "Are you sure we want to catch it?" Heck, I had just been to the snake training and handled their snake that was almost as big as this one! But Old Molly obviously was on Valium; this snake obviously was on uppers, and it was getting madder as I hauled it back on the road a fifth time.

Das managed to find a four-foot piece of communication wire. I told him to tie a loop in it and slip it over the end of the snake's tail, and he did. Then, the slimy bugger almost got him too! He dropped the wire, and the snake tried to escape into the heavy growth again. Just as it cleared the road, I made a desperate grab for the trailing wire and caught it, pulled on it, and found that the extra three feet really helped. I yelled at Das to hold the wire while I cut a six-foot tree branch with a fork at its end. "Just pull and drag it back, Das. It can't get you then," I tried to convince him. A pale Das managed to keep it on the road, dropped it once, but got the feel of the drill and pulled it back again. I trimmed the branch with my handy K-Bar knife, cutting off its smaller branches and then quickly cutting a V at its end. A forked, six-foot weapon was my only defense in catching this squirming, slimy monster that now really hated me.

While Das pulled hard, I began the difficult walk up along the snake's back up to its neck. I quickly shoved the fork onto the middle of its moving body, but had to jump away again as it reared back to grab me, which it almost succeeded in doing. Finally, I managed to get a good tight hold about three feet from its head. I knew I couldn't turn back after that. There, for all to see, was an overheated communications officer lamenting, "Why did I have to be riding with 'Guerrilla Bob' this day?" This overconfident training officer had been with snakes for too long at Camp Pickett and now in Panama. Our dusty, sweaty struggle had not gone unnoticed. A jeep pulled up, and then other vehicles pulled behind it. Tom and the XO were returning from the school and wondered what that loony Fischer was up to. Thoroughly amused, they continued watching for awhile. A few had cameras out to record the altercation, probably hoping the snake would win.

Finally, I managed to get an even better hold on its big neck while easing the fork up inches at a time until I could grab it just behind its ugly head. If the snake-school teachers were right, this grab would subdue that furious descendant of Adam's demise. To my surprise (and relief) the big snake stopped as if it were dead and just lay there—all eight feet of it. We had just been taught that constrictors will stop moving when caught by their neck, an instinct that probably came from knowing that its death was imminent. Now that I had proved it was true I still had to convince a quivering Das.

Das was totally exhausted, mostly emotionally, and we had conquered the smelly one. It stunk to high heaven. Our jeep driver, who had witnessed the whole thing, looked at me in mortal fear, knowing that I was planning to pick that thing up and haul it into the jeep. My plan was to carry it back to the school and give it to the snake handlers. We understood that they gave them to the Panamanians; the snakes were a delicacy they would otherwise pay for. That big mamoo weighed more than 100 pounds, so we slowly lifted it up and then sat on the back of the jeep with it lying across our laps, with my hand tightly holding the neck. Thank God that "Hands" really had big hands! The growing crowd clapped appreciatively for the show as we drove back to the school. A few Marines and the CO were still there, but there were no snake handlers in sight. We were stuck with a real problem.

Das and I staggered toward the main enclosure just as the CO approached us. He had remained behind to take a Public Information Office picture with Old Molly drooped over his shoulders—a photo that would appear in the Camp Lejeune newspaper some weeks later. For reasons I still cannot explain, the next event would become almost tragic. Had it played itself out, my career would have ended that day and I could still see myself in Fort Leavenworth. The CO thought Das and I were carrying around Old Molly and he came over to us, smiling and saying, "Oh, there's my old girlfriend."

With that, the CO reached out to grab her from us. Das said, "Let him have it." My right hand almost released the thick neck—boy, how I wanted him to "have it"!

Thankfully, my better judgment prevailed. I told the CO, "It's a real wild one, sir. We just caught it on the road." He reared back in stark amazement that his training officer would dare to catch a live one. What I still ponder, these many years later, is what would have happened if we had actually given it to him? I had a vision of this furious monster grabbing his arm with a deep bite and then winding and twisting around his neck to suffocate him—with no snake handlers around to pry it off. I could also see the prison at Fort Leavenworth, where I'd rot away for years as a prisoner sentenced for the attempted murder of his CO! Fortunately, we created enough of a commotion so that two snake handlers finally showed up and took the big snake away. They commented that this one was particularly vicious since it was a female and probably pregnant, and that even the best snake handlers would have had their hands full capturing one like this. They also gave us a "well done." Now, it was time to focus on what we came to Panama to accomplish. Here, Marines would get a first taste of what the dense Vietnam jungles would be like, and I had another opportunity to train them for the different, difficult war to come.

Our major training event was the counter-guerrilla exercise that began the next morning. I briefed the two recon units and gave them map overlays for the phasing of the operation over the next few days. It was their job to maneuver in the areas designated, and we would have to locate and contain them there. In the dense swamp and jungle terrain, they had a great advantage because there were so many places to hide like real guerrillas would do. I set some boundaries (daily areas) to let us have better odds in such a short time. Skip issued the blank ammo. I had briefed Tom on our ammo situation and he said to tell the CO we borrowed it from the Jungle School, which had more than enough. That's what we did. I am sure the XO had already convinced him that we had to have the ammo. The first thing I had to do was to outline to the CO and the XO what counter-guerrilla operations were. Neither really understood that the battalion wasn't moving out with two companies up, one back, and hot chow in the rear—the standard old hill-by-hill grunt tactics. I patiently explained to them that there were *no objectives*, no enemy positions, except in this case where I'd actually put them.

To plow through the jungle aimlessly would waste a battalion and exhaust and frustrate the men, and we would capture none of the 100 guerrillas. Our exercise would last only a few days, so each tactical event had to be accelerated. The men were, however, going to maneuver and hide in the same small units and *almost* the same way we operated at Camp Pickett, like real guerrillas do. This meant that we had to employ the British counter-guerrilla tactics, right out of their book—and that's exactly what I briefed the CO, XO, and all the other battalion staff members that we would be doing. We would "counter" this guerrilla force in *its own* environment. Tom suggested that the staff monitor the exercise (staying out of the way), while I initiated the decentralized saturation patrols, patrol bases, and the quick response by our helicopters when a full company-size reaction force was required.

The rifle companies sent squad-size patrols out. We monitored their exact positions and movement through the dense terrain. In this way, we soon "saturated" the whole exercise area by assigning companies to their own areas while still coordinating all patrol activity. In the rear, near the battalion command post, the fourth company waited to be called out as the heli-borne reaction force. They would fly to the enemy site and surround it from three or four sides to trap the guerrillas and eliminate them. Well, that's what the book said! What really happened was very different than we had anticipated in the planning phase. First, we set up the battalion command post and our logistics area in a large, grassy field near the canal. As we tried to set up tents, food, and water sites, the first Marines to enter the area came running back toward us with short striped snakes impaled on their bayonets—a lot of them. It turned out to be a deadly coral-snake breeding ground, much like the cobra field I had experienced in Borneo where we carefully backed off and surrendered to the snakes. We chose discretion here as well, and we left! A well-used campsite was found a few miles away.

Our battalion patrols moved out and saturated the areas. Water would become a major problem; our first helo lifts were to transport dozens of water cans to company command posts. A Marine needed to drink a minimum of four full canteens a day—a lot of water. Jungle reality was proven in this exercise. Vietnam would be no better—but there I would have to dip my canteen into a filthy stream with village waste, animal waste, and everything else imaginable in it. My sister sent me many small packets of concentrated lemonade. With a heavy dose of Halizone water purification tablets, I managed to survive not just the days, but weeks in Vietnamese jungles. Many of our young Marines would experience those same jungles in less than a year after the Panama exercise. In Panama they would become familiar with just a few of the many problems the jungle would present, much like the curriculum that had been offered at the Malaya Jungle School at Johore Bahru. Unfortunately, few of the Camp Lejeune battalions would ever receive this kind of training. In their training, they would still hit the beaches (two-up and one-back, hot chow in the rear) and remain untrained for the real thing they would find in Vietnam.

On the second day, we (literally) lost the elite Force Recon Marines. Their studly, six-foot-five lieutenant who could run, jump, scuba, push-up, and do every other kind of physical exercise, could *not* find his way into or out of the jungle. We received his muffled call—telling me that he was lost and did not have a clue where he was. Unfortunately, he had managed to lead his team into the very tall saw-grass in the huge swamp. He said he was walking in circles and could not seem to get re-oriented. I told him to hold his position and drop a red smoke in a cleared area so he did not start a fire and burn himself up. He was to douse the fire when my helicopter spotted the smoke. He did as I said. Then, I gave him a map vector to come back in, instructing him to follow it straight out, with no deviation. He did as I said and led his Marines out of the swamp in a few hours. To augment his Ranger, airborne, and scuba training, I suggested he brush up on map-reading.

The exercise finished with the heli-lift of two companies in a frontal assault, while the other two rifle companies were already in their blocking positions near the canal. The guerrillas, who were repositioned and pursued for several days, were only too happy to exit the hot jungle and be clobbered by the encirclement. They did a very good job, but it was humorous to see the puzzlement of the CO, XO, and all other staff types. This was far from what they had learned or experienced in their traditional tactics, and also was a major departure from amphibious doctrine. Maybe it was too much for them! Their resistance was endemic, and I could sense an impatience to end this strange "guerrilla" thing. Yet I was given an opportunity to debrief the exercise and hand out kudos to the aggressors and our own rifle companies.

The Panama experience was a harbinger of things to come—and much sooner than we would imagine. It was like Camp Pickett all over again! I wondered what it would take to get the rest of the Marine Corps to understand this. Everyone looked exhausted—but then, no one could imagine how exhausted they would become in Vietnam when that war would not end for eight years, until 1973, with every kind of mental and physical strain that challenged us all. Had we (the CO and XO) learned any lessons in Panama? I seriously doubt it. Reality hits hard, especially in minds that continue to reject any new or different tactics. It was a hallmark of the U.S. military: *we continue to train and fight the last war,* and then ignore any thought of the next one! We did the latter quite well. But Camp Pickett and Panama just didn't set well. Vietnam wouldn't "take" either, until it was too late.

By the time we had completed our Panama training, we had operated in the Caribbean for over three months and were preparing to return to Camp Lejeune. A Barbados liberty call would help us restock our booze supply. Doc Hanlon had another trick up his sneaky sleeve and labeled a number of shipping boxes as "Medical Supplies." They held 10 gallons of the best Caribbean Rum I could find, and that was *my own* shipment. Dozens of these boxes would be off-loaded at Camp Lejeune right under the noses of the Treasury Department inspectors that roamed all the beach landings to try to spot contraband. Mine made it through.

In Barbados I had Shore Patrol duty our last night in port. It was an easy watch since there was only one big nightclub in town, with the usual attractions. Harry's was a big open bar and dancehall, yet it could not hold all of our Marines, and that presented my worst-case situation that evening. By midnight, I had several Shore Patrol wagons running drunk and boisterous kids back to the duty boats. But the most unique drunken escapade occurred right in front of the most prestigious hotel in Barbados, which was frequented by very prosperous senior citizens. A phone call was made by the angry hotel manager, who reported that there were drunken Marines in the nude. Sure as I feared, there, in the huge fountain in front of the hotel, were six or seven naked Marines frolicking like kids at a fireplug, jumping in and out of that fountain—to the cheers of the seniors enjoying it immensely from the balconies above. When we finally got them in tow, raucous boos erupted from the balcony audience—the floorshow was over. When we loaded the last duty boat that night, I breathed a sigh of relief.

There also were nicer memories of that lovely island. The whole population was amazing. The British did a superb job in their teaching and training of very poor, common people. It was a delight to see a large group of natives singing like an *a capella* choir on every street corner. The voices were clear, resonant, and polished by superior musical training. One could pick dozens of concerts from the many groups that sang for an hour or more. It was simply beautiful and unforgettable. What was, however, by far my most impressive experience occurred along a country road where I had become disoriented trying to find a club on the other side of the island, where a formal reception was being held for all officers. In my Marine Corps uniform, I stopped to ask a cane-cutter where I was and how I could find that club. In my best Spanish, quite slowly, I asked him where it was. In the English language as spoken by British royalty, he replied very clearly, "But of course, my good man, if you will follow the road to the clearly marked intersection some three kilometers distant, you will turn to the north and then proceed for two more until you reach the island's main concourse. The club is but a block or two south. Is there anything else I may help you with, sir?"

Certain that my mouth was hanging agape, I muttered in my inferior English, "I don't think so." The ragged, dirty man in the tattered straw hat turned away briskly, flashing a toothy smile. I am sure he laughed about this experience for days. You certainly can't tell a book by its cover!

We sailed back to Camp Lejeune, landed our equipment, smuggled booze to our homes, and then learned that the battalion that had relieved us had just landed in the Dominican Republic, live ammo and all, in a real shooting war. The 1st Battalion, 6th Marines and the 82nd Army Airborne brigade had been air-lifted ashore, where they would rescue American civilians. They soon were taking enemy fire from rooftops, from heavy 50-caliber machine guns and mortars. Darn, we had missed it by only a few days! Skip and I would ponder if the CO would have let us take live ammo ashore— probably not, since he obviously did not trust his own Marines to handle even blank ammo.

We were lucky. Colonel Peterson's battalion, the same one we had opposed at Camp Pickett, was in the thick of it. It was a real war, with real bullets and real casualties as both Army and Marine units tried to marry up forces in the center of the capital city. Thank God that Marines were trained in our own combat towns for combat in built-up areas! It involved a house-by-house and building-by-building clearing of snipers and dug-in units, the kind of combat we were already trained for. It was little wonder that Vietnam wasn't a priority! Marines and the Army Airborne troops did it very well, and the revolution was suppressed in days. It also confirmed why Colonel Lownds counseled me at Tom's home. We still had real problems, there in the Caribbean.

After we had landed back at Onslow Beach, where my girls went swimming, I was called into the CO's office. He handed me a set of orders to the Army Special Warfare Counterinsurgency course at Fort Bragg, North Carolina. It was just a two-hour drive from Camp Lejeune. Months before, and just after the Pickett exercise, I had requested a school to get out of town, I wanted one that emphasized counterinsurgency; it was at Fort Bragg. But I had not expected to receive the orders on the day I was getting off the ship! Boy, I wondered, how do I tell Gwenny this one? Home for the next week and then off to Bragg for three more weeks! Ben Dean, a member of the division staff, also had been ordered to attend. I had very mixed emotions. A part of me really wanted to further my knowledge of guerrilla warfare. The U.S. Army Special Forces were the only U.S. military unit emphasizing it—they sure wore the "guerrilla jockstrap," as Colonel Lownds had called it. Ironically, only a few months after Tom's party, the colonel was assigned to the Counterinsurgency desk at Fleet Marine Force Atlantic in Norfolk, Virginia. I heard via the grapevine that he had put out feelers to try to get me assigned to his staff. How the whole scenario had changed!

Three years later, Colonel Dave Lownds would receive his orders to Vietnam. In 1968 he was the Marine Corps regimental commander at Khe Sanh, where besieged Marines beat back the overwhelming assaults of a massive NVA that was determined to repeat Dien Bien Phu. Colonel Lownds received the Navy Cross for his regiment's tenacious stand in one of the toughest battles fought there as well as in the annals of Marine Corps history. Like so many senior Marines at Camp Lejeune, Colonel Lownds had to shift gears rapidly to adapt to the war in Vietnam. But his regiment did not fight a classic guerrilla war like most of the Marine battalions and companies had been doing in other parts of the country. In many ways he was almost right in what he had told me at Camp Lejeune that New Year's evening in 1965: "Take off your guerrilla jockstrap, Major. It is a Special Forces war."

He was right about the first part, but like too many senior Marines in 1965, he just could not believe that Marines would ever get involved in Vietnam. Instead, Giap attempted to turn Khe Sanh into another Dien Bien Phu, with virtually the same tactics. Khe Sanh was ripe for Giap's third phase of the People's War, which he had defined as the final conventional warfare phase that follows the earlier local guerrilla and main-force guerrilla phases. Like the French in 1953, Marines were located on their remote and difficult defensive positions at Khe Sanh. It was too much like the French airborne were isolated at Dien Bien Phu. So, it must have been too tempting and worth the heavy risk to annihilate a major Marine

Corps unit, a whole regiment. Had he succeeded, America may have done the same thing France did—sue for peace and quit the war. It became a set-piece battle, with the Marines fixed in their battle position like the French paratroopers had been while they were pounded by artillery and mortars for weeks. Giap did not know U.S. Marines—they never surrender or quit!

The elusive NVA units remained well hidden in the heavy undergrowth and jungle-like terrain adjacent to the Marines. Though outnumbered about ten to one, Colonel Lownds' regiment fought off assaults and tunneling right up to their lines and murderous fire by Chinese and Russian mortars and artillery. Finally, the Air Force saturation-bombed every square foot of enemy ground while Marine artillery ''walked" up and down the trench lines. General Giap terminated his futile, bloody assault. Now, I had another tough decision to make. Should I keep my "guerrilla jockstrap" on and attend the course or plead with the battalion commander to send someone else in my place? I soon learned that the billet required a parachute-qualified officer. Tom Glidden chided me, "That's what happens, Bob, when you go to jump school at Fort Benning." Like it or not, I was qualified! On the personal side, I felt bad that I had barely seen my family since I had arrived at Camp Lejeune one year ago. When would this end? After the Fort Bragg training, it was probable that I could be reassigned to the next deploying BLT going to the Mediterranean.

The Marine Corps had other problems involving our budgetary survival. Amphibious ships, Marine air wings, fleets of helicopters, and the operations and training dollars associated with them were real Capitol Hill survival matters. Not one U.S. Marine Corps funding item had "attacking guerrillas" in it, which is why so many of the older Marine Corps veterans were vehemently opposed to the Marine Corps' involvement and commitment of troops in Vietnam. The leader of this opposition was the former commandant himself, General David Shoup. He saw the Vietnam War as a limited Army (and possibly Marine) advisory effort, with Special Forces training Vietnamese to fight their own war. Higher political powers, however, already determined that it would be a full-scale American war, and that U.S. Marines would be fully committed—but they lacked the training.

The real disconnect involved our readiness for that different and difficult war, especially at Camp Lejeune, where such a war had a very low priority, considering other real contingencies the 2nd Marine Division faced. So, we continued to meet them as previously scheduled—until our heavy casualties began to change that priority. At Camp Lejeune, playing musical BLT chairs and the troop-juggling game would have to end. Until 1965, that was how we maintained our force in readiness and kept Congress from putting the U.S. Marine Corps out of business. We still had many devious enemies, including our competitor, the U.S. Army. We strained resources on back-to-back deployments, with Marines never staying home for long. I didn't tell the girls right away. And I managed to dent my new rum supply for the whole weekend. I needed that time! I didn't have the guts to tell Gwenny that day. She was so happy to have me home.

Kim, Kerrie, Kristy and Kathy in Camp Lejeune, NC

Chapter 6: I Begin My Own Guerrilla War

I was delighted to return home. Since reporting into 3/8, I had been gone for most of the 12 months that first year. Now, the orders to Fort Bragg would add three more weeks. It was mid-summer, and we were finally scheduled to move onto the base after waiting a year for quarters. Gwenny did not take the school news very well, and its timing could not have been worse. My Marine wife and mother had been playing "daddy" a bit too long. Still, she understood what a military career involved. She also knew how important the Fort Bragg counterinsurgency training was, and how much I had already committed to this "guerrilla" business. When I finally convinced her that I would leave early on Monday mornings to make the 90-mile (hour and a half) drive to Fort Bragg, and would be home for dinner on Friday evenings, she felt a bit better. I promised the girls that we would spend the whole weekend at the beach when I got home. The Camp Lejeune beaches are some of the finest on the East coast, and my girls believed the Marine Corps owned them. While I would spend the heart of the training week away, I spent the weekends with my family. It was better than other lengthy separations.

The week before I had to report to the counterinsurgency course at the Special Warfare Center, Fort Bragg, we made our move into a spacious Capehart home on Timmerman Drive. The girls liked this move because there were many playmates living nearby, and the beach was much closer. Since I would be taking the Pontiac station wagon to and from work, I found a cute little red Fiat that had a stick shift, and Gwenny could drive it. One of my greatest treasures and memories is the photograph of that little red car with my four little girls posing beside it, with the reliable station wagon parked just behind them. An even better memory is of my five ladies in that neat, tiny car "choofing off" (scooting or driving the car) to the beach, as Gwenny usually called it with her typical Aussie expressions. What a picture! Four little blonds and my beautiful Aussie redhead all packed into the Fiat.

That fall we added another blond beauty when Gwenny's kid sister came to visit us from Australia. This 20-year-old knockout, Joy, attracted most of the young officers at Camp Lejeune, and

Gwenny had her hands full sorting out the good ones from the "bad sorts." Her own trip around the world had honed her female ability to spot the insincere types. Gwenny was a keen "sorter" of the suitors and did most of the telephone screening as well.

Having completed almost a full year at Camp Lejeune, I paused to consider that I had been almost totally separated from my family, except for a week or two at home before we were ordered to another Marine venture. This was a stateside tour? Hardly! It was more like an overseas tour—again.

The battalion began its next phase-down, losing troops to a sister battalion that was preparing for its BLT departure to the Mediterranean or Caribbean. As it turned out, it was an excellent time to go to Fort Bragg. Since I was a qualified parachutist, I would be placed on jump status and receive pay for that period, but I ended up making no jumps. There was a jump scheduled in the exercise in the last week of the course, but it was made only by Special Forces troops who then swarmed into the bills of North Carolina. I would remain a non-jumping grunt for that part of the training.

Also, the present CO was relieved by a new battalion commander, Lt. Colonel Robert Lucy. He was a sharp Marine officer and a stark contrast to the commander he had relieved. My first battalion commander in Hawaii had it right when he said, "You'll like only half of us." My new colonel also was a Marine Corps lawyer who had previously been an infantry officer in combat in Korea. As a first lieutenant, Bob Lucy had been with Ray Murray's 5th Marines, commanding his 4.2-inch mortars. While I would have to wait to actually begin working for him, I immediately liked what he said (or didn't say) with his quiet-but-impressive demeanor. I had a brief discussion with him before leaving, and he advised me that since my officer's jacket was full of command time, I would go a staff job when I returned. As a captain, I knew that meant taking my pal Skip Fisher's job as the S-4: moving trucks, ammo, and chow. I would become the logistician. The next Monday, a very hot July day, I was off to Fort Bragg and the eagerly sought counterinsurgency training at the prestigious Special Warfare School that President John Kennedy had inaugurated just before his death in 1963.

The Army recognized the need for such specialized training to counter a number of unique conflicts in various parts of the world. Many of these were Communist-inspired and were initiated by the Russian, Cuban, and Southeast Asian insurgents who had formed revolutionary cadres to overthrow their existing governments by political, economic, and even military force—whatever means they might have to employ. The Special Forces teams had been organized from the late 1950s, when the Special Warfare School was ordered into existence by President Kennedy. It was the first formal, official recognition that specialized training in countering guerrillas, insurgents, and revolutionaries was needed worldwide. It also prompted the U.S. to send military advisors to countries worldwide. This unique training encompassed counterinsurgency and special operations, psychological warfare, language training for advisors, and several other courses the U.S. military would need to prepare us to fight enemy forces in a unconventional war. But it was also shades of Camp Pendleton all over again: soldiers chasing soldiers who looked like soldiers! For me, it was a timely assignment and I was still pleased that I could attend it.

Later I would learn that the Special Forces was a novel experiment that many regular Army officers seemed to oppose and questioned. These traditionalists couldn't accept this departure from the conventional Army career paths. So, it wasn't only the Marine Corps that was struggling with this specialization to fight guerrillas. According to the syllabus, we would spend two weeks in the classroom learning about the insurgent's multidimensional way of waging war, and one week on an actual field exercise, chasing guerrillas in the hills of North Carolina. At the Special Warfare Center, the old World War II and Korean War strategy and tactical methods were considered passé and outmoded. I thanked God that someone in our U.S. military had begun to think outside the box and comprehend the reality of Vietnam!

The first returning Special Forces teams had an even better insight into this different war. They, and our first in-country U.S. military advisors, had small-team and even local experience with remote border outposts manned by the loyal Montagnard people and the small hamlets and villages all over Vietnam. But I felt that the British Anti-Terrorist Operations manual would have been a much better text. The Brits dealt with the entire population and employed all of their military and police in fighting the guerrillas and terrorists. Unfortunately, this book was also ignored. The Army wrote its own material, so we studied various insurgencies like Vietnam, the Philippines, Malaya, and even the Cuban revolution. There also were a number of foreign officers in the course, some that were actually living real insurgencies and would be heading home to face more.

I enjoyed the course, taking pleasure in knowing that someone was focusing on that new, different war that few commanders at Camp Lejeune had felt was important—even when East-coast Marines were beginning to receive orders for that real war. The situation was unbelievable—and it would get worse. I still was a lone voice harping for a major change in Marine training, and it would stay that way for months. Just a few months earlier (in March 1965) an SLF, a battalion of the 9th Marines from Okinawa, landed on an empty beach at Danang to secure the airfield while our helicopters supported Vietnamese in the emerging Asian war.

Like my buddy, Gerry Devlin, who wrote *Paratrooper* while sitting at our shared desk at Fort Benning, I began to formulate my own proposal for a Counter-guerrilla Training Center at Camp Lejeune, and I had an outline in process. Most of my ideas were from the British Jungle School's curriculum; a few more were from the course materials at Fort Bragg, especially the Viet Cong structure and its cadre training that was ongoing at that time in Vietnam. This included many lessons the French had not learned when fighting and being defeated there. I also used General Giap's book, *People's War, People's Army,* as my background. Why not quote the source that defeated the French by employing what he had actually written for us to read? In my proposal, I emphasized a block-training type of course, first for squads, and then evolved up to platoons and finally to rifle company. But most importantly, the individual Marine was given hands-on training because so much depended on his skills, and these alone, in many enemy situations.

The guerrilla war was a jungle-based chess game that pitted the wills, the senses, and the basic instincts of these adversaries against each other in a brutal, dirty, and often unfair environment. Those who fought the wily, treacherous Japanese and even the masses of Chinese in Korea were not exposed to, nor did they experience, anything like we would face in Vietnam. Our Marines would encounter lethal booby traps, ambushes, tunnels, and an enemy that looked like everyone else in any hamlet. He had to learn that *everyone* was his enemy—that was the genius of General Giap in *People's War, People's Army*. It also was much more than a *military* war and would involve political, economic, psychological, cultural, and even social dimensions that we would initially ignore, actually believing that these "rag-tag" guerrillas could be mopped up militarily in a very short time. Sadly, thousands of untrained American kids wouldn't learn these skills as they were surviving a very different and difficult war. They paid a heavy price to learn it. It was this complexity that senior Marines refused to understand or evaluate, and was the challenge I had to accept if counter-guerrilla training were ever to survive.

Undaunted and somewhat undeterred, I proposed that a training cadre be established. It would consist of the Officer-in-Charge (captain), an XO (first lieutenant), a senior staff NCO or a first sergeant with rank enough to handle all the enlisted men in a rifle company, and a savvy staff NCO who would be a combat specialist who was experienced in small-unit operations such as ambushes and squad patrols. A demolition expert and other junior training NCOs formed the remainder of the CGWC training cadre.

To illustrate the training environment we would utilize, I drew up plans for the classroom, a Vietnamese village with animals and rice paddies, guerrilla camps, a booby-trap trail, and a pop-up target range for fast-reaction firing. Subjects like the Viet Cong and Communist revolutionary warfare also flavored my syllabus. I had thought of most of this proposal while we were still hunting guerrillas in Panama, so it was just a matter of writing it down on — and what better place for it than at *the* Special Warfare Center?

I had the proposal completed by my second week and would submit it as soon as I got back to the battalion. But that was a week away, and I had the field exercise to go through. I had to hand it to the Special Warfare staff, who had decided to have this guerrilla war in a real town, Troy, some 40 miles west of Fort Bragg. The citizens of Troy had volunteered to help train their neighbors and had turned over several buildings, including the local high school and an elementary school, to serve as administrative headquarters and supply/logistics sites. Since it was mid-summer, there was no problem with the schools being used, and I'm sure the school boards were well compensated for their "rentals." Those of us participating in the exercise had a "tent city" outside the town proper. While we students were considered as part of the exercise, we were just a small part of a larger brigade exercise, much like our Marine Corps' Grassroots '64 exercise at Camp Pickett. The brigade was mostly comprised of Special Forces teams and the 82nd Airborne Division guys, who had jumped in Vieques and were amazed when we burned down our officers' club. They thought it was routine.

Right behind Vieques it was the 82nd that went into the Dominican Republic revolution and joined up with Colonel Peterson's battalion. It was his BLT that had relieved us just weeks before. It seemed much longer, but it had been only four weeks. Now they were back home and part of this counter-guerrilla exercise. On the night before we trucked out to Troy to start that operation, I went out to a local McDonald's for a Big Mac. Seated near me was an Army staff NCO in his utilities (camouflage uniform). I introduced myself and moved over closer to his table. He had returned from the Dominican Republic conflict just a few days earlier, and I was eager to hear what he had experienced.

His platoon was the point unit that had to clear the way to a bridge in the center of Santo Domingo and link up with our Marine company. He was very proud of the job his platoon, especially its young lieutenant, had done. A West Pointer, the lieutenant really knew his stuff. But just as they had neared the bridge, the sergeant saw his lieutenant almost drop in his tracks. On the officer's PRC-25 radio a familiar voice was heard asking, "How is it going, son? I want to know." It was LBJ, the President of the U.S. The young officer had handled the tactical situation with no problem, but he was never the same after he heard directly from LBJ himself—right from the White House Command Center. Talk about overkill and over-control! But there it was, and there it would be throughout the Vietnam War, when the same pushy LBJ would call General Westmoreland daily *and tell him where to place a combat battalion and run that war as well—right from his office!* Hell, what did Westmoreland know? He was just the senior commander of the whole war in Vietnam! LBJ wasn't the last senior to micro-manage.

Almost every general, admiral, and even some of our bothersome and ignorant politicians pulled the same stupid tricks. Lieutenants just could not be trusted to run their own units in *that war*! Because it was a different war, young officers couldn't be expected to understand the "big picture." Actually, there was a lot of truth in that. I later saw this overkill many times during my tour in Vietnam. It was just one more instance of sheer ignorance and total mistrust by those who were in charge of our military bureaucracy. This drill reminded me of French President Georges Clemenceau's prophetic comment in World War I:

"War is too important to be left to the generals."

Amen to that! I could imagine all the North Vietnamese commanders monitoring our radio nets, and how they must have chuckled gleefully—the brass, not those who were on the ground, were running the guerrilla war. How they must have relished the extra time the field commanders had to waste trying to implement those higher-level orders. Setting Viet Cong ambushes also took time, and our U.S. geniuses made sure they had it. Even the President couldn't trust his own military leaders. It is well known that Secretary of Defense Robert McNamara refused almost any advice or input from the Joint Chiefs of Staff, electing to follow his own advice. It was, essentially, the fool fooling the fool. This behavior by him and LBJ is documented in an excellent book by H. R. McMaster, *Dereliction of Duty: Johnson, McNamara, the Joint Chiefs of Staff, and the Lies That Led to Vietnam.* It uses staff memos, field orders, and directives as proof.

McNamara himself had an "inspired" change of heart, years after the debacle was over, and his name was plastered on most of the stupid mistakes made *at the top*. The Joint Chiefs, in turn, did not trust their subordinates. More than 30 years later, during the Kosovo "war," we would see the fruits of that same misguided leadership, as squads and platoons would again be micro-managed and our once-very-capable military rank structures would almost disintegrate. To reemphasize and reflect this bad judgment, I have to modify Clemenceau's prophetic comment into: "War is too important to be left to the *lieutenants*." Why trust those young idiots? Heck, they were just out there in the field fighting the war!

The counter-guerrilla exercise began with a guerrilla force like I had employed at Camp Pickett, taking to the hills of the redneck country outside Troy. But there was one major difference: they did not act like guerrillas and didn't even look like guerrillas! Most of them drove their four-wheel-drive vehicles and were dressed in Army fatigues, with a random civilian sweater—but their clean-shaven heads did little to distinguish them from the locals, who *really* had the seedy look of an enemy. The experience was to be like Camp Pendleton all over again: grunts chase grunts, then go "bang-bang," run over some empty hills, and then muster to attack a conveniently grouped enemy on the last day of the silly exercise. Why many of the senior officers continued to relate this activity to any reality was a mystery to me. Yet that was our standard training for the Vietnam War. We, the U.S. military, just did not "get it"! It appeared to me that we refused to even *want* to get it.

Was our knowledge of Vietnam and other insurgencies too remote for us, geographically and mentally? It sure seemed to be. Just one year before, I had been a student at Fort Benning, where we had learned how to fight massive Russian divisions in Europe with long, sweeping arrows that depicted divisions maneuvering against the Warsaw-pact countries. It was like *World War II, all over again.* There was no mention of Korea at all, and we had just four hours of an oversimplified counter-guerrilla exercise that was almost from the Boer War. I wondered if the soldiers that fought in World War II began their training with World War I manuals. They probably did!

What we actually needed in the exercise was the advice of recent Vietnam returnees, or even combat-experienced veterans of Malaya, the Philippines, or any guerrilla experience. We didn't receive such training. Nevertheless, I was grateful to be part of the first military training that focused on Vietnam, and I was confident that this part of the Army military education would expand upon their actual Vietnam knowledge they would soon experience.

Like most of the counterinsurgency students, I was monitoring "the war" from a warm, clean command post at the Troy high school. We were there to study it, not really to be a part of it. How I would have loved to contribute my "two cents," but I knew that attempting to do so would be as futile as the New Year's Eve confrontation at Tom Glidden's home. I told myself to back off, shut the hell up, and try to understand why it was so hard for them to just "get it." Was the problem the lack of experiencing that war in faraway, non-European jungles? Were we still fighting the Civil War, maintaining a lock-step mentality permanently branded in our minds? Were these outmoded and obsolete tactics simply all we knew and had ever experienced? In the battles of Antietam, Gettysburg, and the bloodiest of the Civil War altercation, we lined up and marched forward right into the enemy's battle lines like ducks in a shooting gallery. Powerful rifles and artillery slaughtered them by the thousands. World War II Marines can also relate to this carnage, losing thousands attacking a beachhead.

Tacticians who study that war *ad nauseum* still focus on how a particular tactic could be better employed by knowing that the frontal penetration of each other's lines was much too costly. But their alternative was nothing more than another type of the same assault—like massing on a flank, but still finding a concentrated enemy force and experiencing the brutal slaughter all over. Can it be that the same men who fought in our American Revolutionary War—as guerrillas, using the unconventional "move, ambush, shoot, and then fade away" techniques—really did get it? If so, how did we revert back to the worst way to fight a war? Is it the lock-step mentality of a military mind that cannot even begin to change? *"Yes, sir, I have my orders. I'll walk off that cliff, but watch those ranks, keep that line tight, and look military! Don't ask questions."* This mind-set led to sending a million men into the guns, which General Haig did in World War I—a million Brits fell as they ran into the German's deadly machine gun fire. That military mentality was locked in the "man against man" struggle, to move head-on and let the chips (and the bodies) fall where they may. This attitude focused on fixed position, set-piece battles set in mental blocks—and it would barely change in the war to come.

Midway through the Troy operation, the counterinsurgency students were called into the school auditorium to hear a resident FBI agent speak about his own experience with the local "insurgents": the Ku Klux Klan (KKK). In the hills of North Carolina, the Klan had one of the most active and aggressive branches in America. This was in the mid-1960s, when Martin Luther King was just starting to march. The KKK burned the black churches, ran blacks off roads, invented reasons to hang innocent black men and women, burned crosses, and then spewed their gutless hatred from behind childish, idiotic, white dunce caps and masks— even when young black soldiers were being ordered to fight in Vietnam. Klan members were too cowardly and probably too ashamed to show their hidden, pathetic faces to us. This agent had his family harassed, his dog poisoned, and his car run off the road. A false bomb was planted under his house. The agent, however, had stood his ground and told us that evening what it was like to live a real insurgency. He was living in one—the hidden, sneaky enemy lived in Troy and other towns in those hills. I would have loved to have hunted those gutless and pathetic bigots—to expose them as the real cowards they were—but we had to learn about this one through the sad experience of a brave and fearless FBI agent who stood his ground. I also wondered how many Klan members owned stores in Troy and were "good old boys" who had little more going for them than persecuting blacks.

My four-day separations from my family went by fast, and I was glad to get back home. That summer I would make up for some of the long tours away from them. And I got only one speeding ticket as

I drove 80 miles an hour to and from Camp Lejeune, eager to get home with my girls.

When I returned to the battalion, I had a new job and a new battalion commander. Lt. Colonel Bob Lucy was the epitome of a Marine commander. He advised me that I was now his S-4, the Logistics and Supply offer. I was the logistician, in charge of the trucks, the beans-and-bullets guy who supported all troop movements, tactics, and training. The job, however, would not last long because I submitted my proposal for the Counter-guerrilla Warfare Center (CGWC), its training team, the syllabus, and even the site where it should be constructed (a dense, heavily treed area just inside the main gate).

My first obstacle was our battalion XO, the same guy who threw my officer's jacket across his office This two-up, one-back traditionalist found my proposal unnecessary, and it greatly upset him. Like many of his rank, he felt that Marines were trained to fight in any clime and place, reflecting the same party line of the Marine Corps Gazette editor: *Why did we need this specialized training center?* When I tried to explain and review the results of the Camp Pickett exercise by still pointing out that we were totally untrained and unprepared for the *coming war*, my words fell on a deaf ear. Fortunately, Tom Glidden came to my rescue, in that smooth staff style he had developed. He told the XO that he should forward the proposal, endorse it, and critique it if he had to, but send it forward anyway. Thankfully, Lt. Colonel Lucy signed it off without question and recognized many positives in it. Lucy had seen Korean combat with Ray Murray's 5th Marine Regiment—he knew real war. Although he knew little about this kind of war, he was smart enough to know that we were already committing Marines to our next war in Southeast Asia. And one of his captains had some very good ideas for how to train for it.

So, off the proposal went to the regiment. There it encountered another delay—ironically, it was interrupted by the same battalion XO that had tried to stop it at battalion level, months before. He had been transferred since then. So I resorted to the old "end-run" ploy I had used a few times before. It required a sympathetic and supportive person at the next headquarters level, in this case, the division commander. A person who dared to facilitate and move a proposal along had to be creative and maintain an aura of personal innocence, as in, "Who, me? Why, I didn't know a thing about that!"

Such a facilitator was Colonel Ken Clifford. He was a full professor at Fordham University and a Marine Corps historian. He served at the division for his two-week reserve requirement. I had briefly met him at our officers' club and he seemed genuinely interested in my proposal, especially when 2nd Division Marines were already on their way to Vietnam. He knew we were ill-prepared for the war, so he had a ready ear (or eye). I gave him a copy of my syllabus to read, asking him to critique it if he thought it necessary. Prior to Colonel Clifford's departure from the division, he penned a note to me that commended my paper and recommended that I "gut it through." He also "mentioned" it to the division G-3 and the chief of staff, a brilliant colonel who soon became a general and supported my proposal. He would serve as General Westmoreland's Marine staff assistant in Vietnam (something Colonel Clifford was not aware would happen).

I sat back and waited for a reply—any reply; I just wanted to know that my proposal would be read and understood, especially by the 2nd Division's commanding general, Ormand Simpson. His own recent experience in Southeast Asia, where he commanded the 3rd Marine Expeditionary Brigade, a force of 5000 Marines, landed in Thailand in May 1962 to counter a border incursion by the Pathet Lao. North Vietnam's military assistance had created this situation. What only a few Asia-based Marines knew at that time was that North Vietnam was already expanding the Ho Chi Minh trail inside Laos as early as 1961. To accomplish this strategic and tactical goal (which later would assist North Vietnam and the Viet Cong to overthrow Diem's government and also become the most important strategic reason Giap would "win" the war), they provided 12,000 advisors, weapons, and support troops. This helped the Communist Pathet Lao overthrow the U.S.-backed Laotian government. When this expansion into the Laos panhandle threatened Thailand and South Vietnam, President Kennedy approved a Marine "show of force" that lasted two months. My admiral and our 7th Fleet flagship also were there at the time.

I went back to work moving troops, chow, ammo, and water to the training areas. Our battalion was replenishing its lost troops; at this rate, we would be ready for another deployment. Yet I feared that the GCWC idea would go down the drain. In September, a new regimental commander took over. He also opposed establishing the GCWC, and even was firmly against that type of training. Nevertheless, he forwarded it to Division for a reading. The G-3 was a gruff, gung-ho veteran of Guadalcanal in World War II, and of other island battles against the Japanese. He immediately called for a briefing where I would present my ideas to members of his staff as well as to the staffs of the regiments and others that would undergo such training—if and when it might be approved. At least I would have a hearing by those who still had to be convinced of its merit before this kind of training could begin. Colonel Clifford's supporting comments were attached, along with a positive recommendation for approval and some staff comments that were required for forwarding.

Yet I knew I had to "sink or swim" on my own, so I readied myself for the briefing at division headquarters. Everyone except the division commander was present. I spotted some of the Camp Pickett participants, expecting them to be hostile to anything the guerrilla victor might say. Once I got into my pitch, I found that I was plowing new ground and was confident in what I presented. I had been to Southeast Asia to see and study this kind of warfare for myself. Lt. Colonel Bruce Meyers a battalion commander stationed at Camp Lejeune, had preceded me in Malaya and had written the article, *Malaya Jungle Patrol*. His opinions already were known to many Camp Lejeune officers who also had read his article. In addition, we were receiving weekly "situation reports" from Vietnam and these reports detailed the problems Marines were having with patrols in jungle terrain, identifying the enemy in the villages, and extensive use of Viet Cong mines and booby traps like the deadly punji stakes. It was General Tran Hung Dau's war all over.

I continued my presentation by emphasizing that *it was a different war and we were not ready for it!* That was my own motivation, but by then, the facts were pouring in to support what I had been saying. I tried to minimize my success at Camp Pickett, but the subject had to surface. It was still fresh in the minds of those that were present. Still, I tried to suggest that the wrong tactics were used there and that countering guerrilla units required a very different kind of tactics. Surprisingly, it was the G-3 who shot me down when I said Marines desperately needed this training. His response was as gruff as his reputation: "Dammit, we fought the Japs and licked them in the jungles!" The others agreed with him.

My reply was a respectable, "Yes, sir, but these kids did not fight those Japanese. The Chinese guerrilla tactics always defeated the Japanese in China." One battalion commander, "Wild Bill", already despised me because he knew I had led the "successful" guerrilla force at Camp Pickett and thought it unforgivable to "show up" any senior commander like I had done. In his narrow view, I should have employed Camp Pendleton's "guerrilla" tactics and run happily over the hills, letting their grunts "shoot us" and win. Didn't I comprehend that? But he just sat there, glared at me, listened, glared some more, and then quickly left before I had even finished my presentation. I knew I would encounter him again and that it would be unpleasant. Finally, the G-3 thanked me, dismissed me, and put my proposal back in the "forget it" file.

Chapter 7: HQMC Asks All Marine Organizations: "Where Is Your Counter-guerrilla Training Program?"

That year, a former boss and the new commandant would play critically important roles in rescuing my novel proposal for a 2nd Marine Division Counter-guerrilla Warfare Center. First, Lt. General Victor Krulak, my former CG at San Diego Recruit Depot, became the Commander, Fleet Marine Force, Pacific (FMFPAC). The Marines in Vietnam were within his purview, and he took this responsibility seriously. Prior to his becoming commanding general of FMFPAC, he was the counterinsurgency advisor to President John Kennedy when few senior Marines were even interested in it. General Krulak had been rescued by a young Lieutenant John Kennedy after his Marine Corps Raiders attacked Choiseul Island during the early Guadalcanal invasion. They were stranded on an island that Kennedy and his PT boat patrolled.

Krulak and Kennedy had become very good friends and remained so until President Kennedy personally asked him to advise what should be done in Vietnam. This was in 1963, when advisors were among the few other Americans that were trying to make sense of that unique insurgency. General Krulak had visited the future war zone and proposed a similar solution to one the British were using in Malaya. It was an ink-blot technique that emphasized "safe" zones throughout Vietnam, which would be expanded outward as we trained, supported, and aided the Vietnamese to take control of their whole country. It was the same strategy the Malayans used to finally take back their country and win their war with Communist terrorists. Krulak, a brilliant mind and a well-read Marine, would have been among the very few who actually read the British manuals I was promoting. At FMFPAC he published weekly lessons-learned about our mistakes and proposed solutions that Marines should employ in our training programs before going to Vietnam. He had them distributed all over the Marine Corps *to educate U.S. Marines*! Then in late September, the Assistant Commandant was touring all Marine divisions and wings. The general asked only one question of the 2nd Marine Division G-3: *"Where is your counter-guerrilla training syllabus?"* Ironically, we had one—mine—but it had been collecting staff dust for several months. A frantic search through their old files uncovered my proposal, including the syllabus I developed. They quickly found it and presented it to the assistant commandant as if it were a living document. A quick phone call to Colonel Lucy informed him that I would be receiving my orders to the division G-3 office—immediately!

And so it began. The commandant, General Wallace Green, the same general that had me debrief the brigade staff at Camp Pickett, was asking for our syllabus. In short, he wanted to know what the 2nd Marine Division was doing to get ready for Vietnam and *that kind of war*! Finally, it seemed, someone really cared—and that person happened to be at the top of the U.S. Marine Corps. Otherwise, the training I had proposed and outlined never would have happened. General Krulak and General Green were both Annapolis graduates. They saved another graduate: *me*! As if nothing had happened to oppose the center, I was ordered to get moving—to find and propose its training site, advise the division engineers as to construction requirements, define by rank and military occupational specialty the training staff I would require, and flesh out the syllabus with lesson plans, outlines, and details for each course of study. Then, I would lay out a schedule for company training, with starting dates.

A month earlier, my proposal had been in the trash can. Now, it suddenly was the *prime training subject* of the 2nd Division! Within a few days, I reported into the Division headquarters company. "That's the fastest set of orders I ever processed," noted the Personnel officer. I was given a single desk at Division. A working party of one, I was *the* counter-guerrilla warfare staff that day. My big mouth and my pen had gotten me this far. Now, all I had to do was just get the job done! It was my "tar baby"—and what a sticky one I was holding! But it was a start—a good start.

Before I could get my desk seat warm, the G-3 told me that the next counter-guerrilla exercise (like the one at Camp Pickett) was to begin at Cherry Point, North Carolina, at the Marine Corps Air Station just a few miles up the road from Camp Lejeune. A Camp Pendleton type of "guerrilla" war was to begin in the fields and forests behind the airfield. Lt. Colonel "Wild Bill's" battalion was assigned as the primary counter-guerrilla force. The guerrillas would be a company unit like ours had been, but they would have no prior training by a Captain R.L. Fischer—and positively none of the latitude we employed at Camp Pickett. Wild Bill made sure he would not have the same fate his predecessor had. And I wished that I could have led that guerrilla force against him—and busted his butt, which I would have loved to do. But I was ordered to just monitor the exercise and offer any assistance (if sought) that I could, now that I was *the* counterinsurgency officer of the division. My role lasted one day—actually one hour, which was long enough to walk into Wild Bill's command post and tell him who I was and what I had been told to do. Wild Bill told me what I could do—first! His suggestion would have been a bizarre act to perform on a rolling donut. Immediately, I knew that my advice wasn't desired, so I got out of there as fast as I could.

It was already October, and I knew there would be only a few good weeks left to build any kind of basic training center. Would the CG really want to wait until the following spring, when the war in Vietnam would be one year old? And, I wondered, were my orders to the division C.P. only a diversion, since the syllabus now existed and an officer had been assigned? I could see myself as a staff "pogue," writing meaningless memos and directives to "All Commanders," recommending "these subjects" for training.

Like before, Marines could run over the hills yelling "Bang, bang," and then give the exercise the label "Counter-guerrilla Training." Why not, when that was all that Camp Pendleton, Wild Bill, and almost every other unit was doing? The CGWC could wait. Certainly, the 2nd Marine Division could spare one lowly captain to get HQMC off its back. And for sure, the day before the assistant commandant's visit, there would not have been a single vote to start such training. I had a desk and a G-3 boss who felt that Marines *already* knew how to fight guerrillas. In their eyes, the Camp Pickett results were a fluke—such things did not actually happen, and the exercise should be forgotten as soon as possible. On the personal front, at least daddy was coming home at night now, except for the days when I had the officer-of-the-day watch. I could just imagine all the "additional duties" piling onto me. I was an available body, assigned to do all manner of things—except training. My S-4 job had been a lot better than just sitting at a desk waiting to get started.

While I was the S-4, I added up all the monthly training requirements a Marine had to complete, in order to find out if there were any hours left for the counter-guerrilla training I was proposing. My results surprised Tom Glidden when we saw that a rifle company Marine could not begin to fulfill all the training hours that were imposed by the three higher levels of command. It was no wonder that "Bull Hull" (the nickname of Lt. Colonel Milt Hull, my battalion commander for my first USMC tour in Hawaii) got into trouble with the Marine "martinets." He skipped the parade-field crap, where we spent too much time polishing our shoes and marching around. Such activities left too little time for the boondocks where we could learn what real Marines do—in war!

The Bull trained us for real combat. Unfortunately, too many officers were promoted for their starched and polished parade-field look. When they tested in the field, they usually got lost—in more ways than one. Careerists skip the hard, filthy field stuff and make sure their units complete just enough for the checklist. They never excel in company tactics competitions or combat-type training. In fact, they seem irritable and uncomfortable when their shiny boots and starched utilities get scruffy and dusty in the field. But you will see them on the parade field every day, practicing the spit-and-polish look, making sure they catch the colonel's eye with their sharp performance. They seek visibility, like "poster Marines." *Hup, two, three, four... look at me score!*

My poster Marine was the kid in Vietnam carrying an M-60. His uniform and flak jacket were in tatters, and his helmet cover revealed the many days he had spent in the trenches and filthy foxholes. He was covered with caked mud, dust, and the grime of real combat. His eyes were sunken pockets, but he exuded a gut-wrenching pride—no enemy son-of-a-bitch was going to whip his ass or the asses of his buddies if he was there. *He was a grunt!* There were no written tests where he proved his superiority in attacking and destroying his enemy, but his solid battlefield skills ensured his survival, as well as that of his buddies. That's why my Corps is the greatest—and all I wanted to do was train our grunts.

The Army colonel on the USS Saint Paul had it right when he advised me that "Nobody loves you—take care of your own career." How true, and how prophetic! But I really believed that every officer had to make this choice at some time—to make the "unpolitical" decision. How many risked it, that is, to do the ethical and right thing? Too few, in my observation. Careerists take zero risks! But that day and that month, I was faced with just such a decision in my own career. Should I roll over and play the game, and how important was my next rank *if* I had to compromise and back off? I knew very well that many young kids would soon go to Vietnam, totally untrained to fight that kind of war—and worse, knowing *only* "two-up and one-back, with hot chow in the rear." The Viet Cong would relish that situation, but the Marines' mothers would not.

Fortunately, things began to improve when my training team grew by one member: a corporal who had just reported in. He as a nice kid with a fresh face who looked good in his uniform but was dumb as hell. I knew why I got him; it was because nobody else wanted him. He probably flunked his interviews or basic skill tests at some other battalion, so naturally he was passed on—to me. But he certainly was a body! Right then, I needed anyone who could perform simple, basic work tasks; there was no need for brains. But this Beetle Bailey would prove me wrong, and very soon.

Just inside the front gate of the Marine base there was a level, forested area that was suitable for the "jungle-like" operations we had to simulate. There was also a very large clearing along a meandering stream, an ideal place for the Vietnam village that I had already designed and laid out on paper. Most importantly, the site was only a short marching distance from each regiment. It was the ideal place for the center! Companies could march out to training in 30 minutes and be back in garrison within minutes when training was completed. It seemed too good to be true.

I submitted my request to the base commander, Major General Herman Nickerson, with my proposal and the CGWC layout schematic. His reply came back immediately: *Rejected.* That area was planned for the Marine Corps Base's horse stables and riding trails. Only about 50 riders would ever use the stables. The general also rode horses. I hoped he would see the importance of counter-guerrilla training for *thousands* and weigh the options. When, I wondered, will I ever get my Marine Corps priorities right?

This general, however, had much bigger problems. Exposé reporter Jack Anderson had just put him in the national spotlight for unauthorized use of military funds to build an expensive dog run in his backyard, and for other priority home enhancements. I would eventually build all the CGWC training sites and structures for 10 percent of the cost of his dog run. But he may have done me a big favor in spite of himself. The eventual CGWC site was near a swamp with snakes, ants, bugs, mosquitoes, and even the unsanitary living conditions reflective of …Vietnam! It would turn out to be the best of the worst-possible locations.

My new boss reported in and we had a good time rehashing Vietnam, from which he had just returned. He had been on a staff and briefly saw our Marine Corps build-up at Danang. Before he left, he had made a few forays into the villages just outside the base. But our mission was only defensive at that time, with a few patrols protecting the large airfield. In those early days, Marines encountered their first booby traps, a few minor ambushes, and harassment fire by the Viet Cong, who were just welcoming us to Vietnam. Besides that, he had little more to offer than had the senior officers at Camp Lejeune. But at least he had seen Vietnam and had actually been there! He too confirmed that this war would indeed be quite different. He shrugged his shoulders when I told him that my request for the main-side training site had been rejected. His look told me that he already knew it.

Finally, I was told to start looking out near the Infantry Training Center, near the swamps and coastal area by Sneads Ferry. It was 20 miles distant from the base and ideal Vietnam-like terrain. But I knew a major problem when I saw one. Every Marine engaged in my training, his chow, ammo, and so forth had to be trucked out and then picked up after we completed training. I really liked the remote location and jungle-like terrain that was full of snakes and streams—

a great place! It also let me have the training company full time, day and night, just like the real thing. To heck with the general's riding stable. This was reality!

This was *the site*, and I had to get started right away. I ordered my one-man troop to check out a rowboat from Special Services and also get a machete or big knife and then tow the boat down to the swampy area above Sneads Ferry. There we had endless miles of reeds that we would use to thatch the village structures. I had designed thatch huts, marketplace, cattle pens, and other buildings as prefabricated structures. With pine log poles measuring 8 feet by 10 feet, we would build panels and thatch them in an assembly-line method. Then, by building frame structures, we would attach the panels to the sides and roofs. We could vary the size of the structures as long as our 8-by-10-foot panels could be employed and assembled into the final item.

The not-so-swift corporal asked how much reed-thatch he should cut and pile on the beach. I told him more than be could possibly cut in a year—just start cutting and piling, and I would tell him when to stop. I was working at my desk that afternoon when a drenched, sodden corporal dripped water right up to my chair. He said he'd had an accident. When he tried to reach out to cut the reeds, the boat, which was all metal, tipped over and sank. He had to swim back to shore and damn near drowned. So, there was no boat, no machete, no reeds, and no village!

I called Special Services and tried my best to explain what I had the corporal doing. The NCO on duty didn't believe a word I said, but told me that if the corporal would come to his office, he and his team would go out and rescue the boat—if the corporal could tell them where it went down. Fortunately they found it, but not without major problems. The corporal thought be knew where it had sunk, but they gave up on him and took a long boat hook and probed the bottom for hours, finally banging the hook-end off the metal boat. My first venture had been a disaster, and I didn't have a clue as to what I could ask "my" new corporal to do next. Whatever it was, it wouldn't include a boat! No one noticed my soaking-wet corporal.

My next major task was to formally request base engineering support I knew I would need. A Naval Academy classmate, Bobby Goins, was in the Division Engineering Battalion and counseled me that Vietnam villages were not the things they did best. Major military construction, airfields and their matting, pontoon bridges, roadways, and conference-room paneling were their normal daily projects. He also said I had to formally present my request to their operations officer, an obese, bureaucratic Marine major that I vainly tried to brief and convince of my engineering needs. I needed tunnels, pens, floors, and sides for the village huts, and a marketplace. I had laid more concrete than this in a week with my dad, and knew I could do the job with just a few Marines and one concrete mixer. It was no big deal—but he made it one!

The major's response was classic, and not unexpected. Paneling the division conference room, framing a wash shed, extending a road, and other trivial jobs were first on his work calendar. I told him that the CGWC had *some* priority too. It was not a part of his schedule, he said. This interaction was going nowhere, but I was. A week later he finally told me that they could not get to my jobs for at least six months or even longer. He looked at me like I was an idiot that just did not understand engineering priorities. By the time they completed this job, the war might be over! My boss told me to back off; he would see what he could do to help. I had a site, but no engineering support. I had a training syllabus ready to go, but no training team. And I had a Marine Corps commandant who wanted Marine training in counterinsurgency—*now*! At that point, I almost requested orders back to my former battalion so I could forget the whole mess. I wondered: did anyone really care? Instead, I elected to employ an "end-run" and just do whatever I had to do to get the job started—to hell with fat majors, priorities, and "can't do" attitudes. This approach would become my modus operandi from then on.

I recalled my earlier visit to Fort Benning's counter-guerrilla training site, where I heard Army Captain McCarthy relate the same problems and the same opposition from the same types. The Pentagon Army had the same opposition as did senior Marines. Vietnam was not in their budget. With no funds, McCarthy had managed to build a mock village and a booby-trap area. Trainees would fill the stands around the village, and a rifle company would helicopter in, surround the village, and take the "enemy" (soldiers in black pajamas) as prisoners. There were no villagers, just other soldiers. When the Vietnam War began in March, he was struggling to keep the place alive. A few months after the war began, he had to train dozens of companies—*they had orders to 'Nam*! Suddenly, this kind of training had become a priority even if it was just a demonstration with the trainees watching from the stands. He told me later that when the training became a priority, every senior officer above him took credit for it and tried to run the site. McCarthy later left the Army in pure frustration—who wouldn't have felt that way? Since my return to the U.S. two years earlier, I also knew that there was no realistic counter-guerrilla training like I witnessed in Malaya. There, a real insurgency was still underway, and Gurkha troops trained the next generation in this type of war.

I was undeterred, even brazen, and my next initiative was to canvass the battalions for anyone who had even been to Vietnam or had any training or experience in a guerrilla war. I had the general's approval to screen all of the 2nd Division's personnel records, so I began there. I also had permission to interview any interested Marines, if they applied. But my first response was a huge disappointment. Commanders were eager to let their problem guys go, and this was what I got on the first canvass. None of the first applicants had a remote idea of this kind of training, and it was obvious that they were just looking for another "soft" job or a way to goof off. I quickly rejected the first bunch of applicants.

Next, I scrambled to review personnel records of new arrivals before they reported to a battalion. I did manage to find a corporal with demolition (and even some booby-trap) experience. Corporal Harrington would turn out to be one of my best finds. Then, my "spies" told me of several Marines that had returned from a tour in Vietnam. When I approached one battalion commander about them, he told me to get lost. To ensure that I would get none of his men, he sent them to Guantanamo Bay, Cuba, as replacements on the line I had visited the previous year. My real finds in this endeavor turned out to be two staff NCOs. The first, Staff Sergeant Bob Atkinson, had spent a full year as an advisor with the Vietnamese Army of Vietnam (ARVN) and he also had extensive experience in search-and-destroy missions in the villages. I had to have this well-qualified combat veteran, who was an experienced staff NCO. It turned out that he was from my former battalion. I was determined to have him assigned to me, even if I had to resort to the old "end run" tactic.

Since canvassing to create my team had not worked, I knew I had to resort to other devious guerrilla warfare methods. These were sneaky, backdoor tactics. I used any kind of excuse, device, or ploy—whatever it took to get me the best-qualified Marines. So, I went after Bob Atkinson. Fortunately, I had a CG, Ormand R. Simpson, as well as a *new* G-3 who believed this kind of training should be made a priority as soon as possible. They would support my search for, and selection of, the best Marines I could find. First, I met with his parade-field Marine boss, who flatly rejected my request for Bob Atkinson. I told him that the needs of the Corps at that time came first. He would have none of it; his attitude was that *his* needs came first. So I briefed my boss, who briefed his boss, and so forth, until a call from a higher-up expedited Bob Atkinson's orders—and the survival of my training team. Colonel Bob Lucy, who then was Atkinson's battalion commander, knew how badly I needed real experts with Vietnam experience. I am sure he "advised" the parade-field commando to let me have him. Boy, was that spit-and-polish guy ticked off! I would encounter this Marine some years later at the Naval War College. He never forgot what happened.

My other find was Staff Sergeant Harry Jordan, who was no-nonsense and hard-nosed. He came from division recon, thanks to my neighbor and good friend, Cy Gonzales, who understood and supported my frantic search. Harry, who had just reported in to the division, had successfully conducted a number of small unit ambushes in Vietnam and was *the man* I needed for my small unit training staff. With these two experienced Vietnam veterans, I had my two key training experts. Better yet, both were more than eager to move on from their units and employ what combat knowledge they had learned in Vietnam. They were also puzzled as to why so many at Camp Lejeune opposed this timely, critical training when the real war was just beginning in Vietnam. They had been there to see and experience it.

This was great! I had three of my key men, and it had not taken long to ferret them out. At that point, I sent my half-drowned corporal back to the division; he would not fit into the kind of team I was mustering. Finding my guerrillas also proved to be a difficult job. I wanted a squad—12 men. With the division, still shuffling Marines among battalions, I was asking the impossible and I knew it. But I received a huge surprise when the officer in charge (OIC) at the Infantry Training Regiment (ITR) unexpectedly gave me a call and asked if I would be interested in taking on several Spanish-speaking Marines—that very day. These kids had come into the U.S. from other countries and had found their way into the Marine Corps. They spoke little or no English. Most units could not fit them in. Would I like to have them? *Would I?* Almost instantly, I had my own team. What great guerrillas they would make! Fortunately, I spoke Spanish passably well, so I went to interview them. These men were perfect for the job. I was told they had grown up on the land, with no running water and in the very environment that most guerrillas originate from. I told the personnel officer that I would take as many of these men as I could get. He told me that I could have this group, but no more.

Now, I had most of my team except for a couple of NCOs who could speak Spanish and act as team leaders for these new Marines. Division Personnel found me two NCOs who had just reported in. Sergeant Sanchez was a goldmine. He knew how this unique, select group should be handled. We found a solid leader in him. I was on cloud nine. Other training NCOs would be added as we added more subjects to our schedule. But initially that was my guerrilla team, and I could not have asked for a better group.

The last position I needed to fill was that of my assistant, a lieutenant. He turned up one day, out of the blue. "Lieutenant Willie," I called him, but there are many more names I would later call him. I wondered why any battalion would give up one of their officers, as tough as it was to flesh out most platoons. It turned out that he was on light duty for some ailment that kept him out of the field and off future deployments. He had been in the battalion that went into the Dominican Republic, where he had duties as an interpreter and liaison officer between the Dominican forces and our Marine units. For this service, he was awarded the Navy Commendation Medal in recognition of the exemplary "linguistic" duties he had performed. I was impressed.

No sooner had Willie reported in than the trouble started. I had been writing the individual courses for the syllabus and needed help to format, edit, and publish each course. His first input was to let me know that those courses would not fly. My Communism and Insurgency introductory course was to provide an insight into the Viet Cong, an organization inspired and led by Communists. The course was right out of Bernard Fall and Douglas Pike's superbly researched and documented study of the Viet Cong, naturally entitled, *The Viet Cong*. The high quality of the course material didn't matter, because Lieutenant Willie was a product of an Ivy League University that I will refer to as "Pinko Junction." There, many young men like Willie were badly warped by Communist-leaning professors. They were anti-American liberals, and he spouted *their* rhetoric openly. Sadly, Willie had learned his bad lessons too well. At first I thought he was kidding, but he truly was the epitome of "pinko" teaching and an avid convert of the socialist garbage that some of his Ivy League professors had warped his mind with.

Much later, I encountered my own brand of rabid pinkos at Rensselaer Polytechnic Institute in Troy, New York, right after my Vietnam tour. At Quantico, I had already met a few Willies—like the idiot who managed to get our Basic School Company 4-55 labeled the worst company to ever go through Quantico. Then, we had a few too many Willies. I asked this one why be had joined the Corps, and *how* the Marine Corps had let him join? My comment went right over his head; he was that dense when it came to understanding that he didn't belong in the USMC with that negativism. Finally, I told him I would handle all the course material. Most came straight from those who actually fought the Communist-inspired guerrillas in

Southeast Asia. Since I had been there, studied it, and brought it home, it was my responsibility.

Willie became a distraction, and I was too pressured and busy to engage him in his obvious game. So, I told him to take the Anti-Guerrilla Operations Manual and translate it into short lessons for our Spanish-speaking Marines. Then came shock number two: he didn't speak *that much* Spanish, but knew only a few catch-phrases that I'm sure must have impressed his seniors in the Dominican Republic. It certainly did not impress me, or any of our young men. It was very clear why he had been assigned to me; it was for the same reason I rejected the other division castoffs and the goof-offs the commanders were only too eager to get rid of.

What the heck could Willie do? Not much. Finally, I took him to the training site to work with Bob Atkinson and our kids. I told him to supervise clearing the only open area that was not heavily overgrown or swampy. Then, I went back to writing my lesson plans, feeling that a big load had been taken off my mind. Atkinson soon told me that the lieutenant was totally useless. He philosophized right in front of the troops and was completely inept at any kind of leadership. Clearly, he had not comprehended what I had tasked him to do: to lead as a Marine Corps officer when I was not present! I knew I had an emerging problem. I also knew that Pinko Willie wouldn't last long on this team.

Our next major project was to find a site to construct the thatch panels and store them until we could haul them to the village site. There, we would assemble the houses, cattle pens, and village marketplace buildings, just like Atkinson had seen them in Vietnam. Our thatch was abundant, and the Spanish-speaking Marines were naturals in collecting it. Staff Sergeant Jordan solved the pine-pole problem when he spotted firewood logs (and tall poles) that the prisoner details had cut. He "cumshawed" (borrowed) a truck from a motor-pool buddy. And, as we would do many times that fall, we made midnight runs and staged our booty at a hideaway right inside the main gate. There were all kinds of poles, roof spans, and cross beams, just for the taking (at night) and for the "unofficial" hauling we became so adept at. A nearby military housing area, just outside the base, was in the midst of being torn down. We loaded good pieces of wood, some roofing material, some bricks and stones, and a few window frames on our trucks. Then, we hid all of them as well. It was mid-October, and we were just starting to build the CGWC with two officers, two staff NCOs, two NCOs, and a dozen young Marines who spoke no English at all. It was a "Spanish Coxey's" army, but I really liked what I had inherited. And a wonderful guerrilla team they turned out to be, every one of them. Only Willie remained a problem. Staff Sergeant Jordan asked me if I could keep Willie far away from him, as he could no longer guarantee the lieutenant's safety. I knew he meant it—not as a threat, but Harry had eliminated (killed) Viet Cong in a businesslike fashion, with no rancor or emotion. I knew I really had to watch Willie.

We began to receive the first actual reports from Vietnam that told of ambushes, booby-trap injuries, and the shadowy enemy that Marines could not find. But at Camp Lejeune, it was seen as just another war fought by *other* Marines. The Camp Lejeune mission was still in the Mediterranean and the Caribbean. That was the priority and the *only* mission—unless, of course, the Viet Cong attacked Camp Lejeune.

My woes had just begun. Every initiative I took was met with some kind of opposition. The clearing for the Vietnamese village brought out the Department of Forestry. It seems they had just planted hundreds of pine tree seedlings right where we were clearing a spot to put our village houses, marketplace, and so forth. That it was the only clear place for a Vietnam village made no difference. The base commander had to have the other good location for his horses. Ironically, their horse fertilizer would have made those trees grow like mad—in the swamp I inherited. But the swamp was perfect. Fortunately, our CG made a firm decision to continue the village work. He *was* reading those terrible combat reports from Vietnam. Our booby-trap casualties were increasing; 80 percent of our dead and wounded were caused by them. The trail and village soon became our most important sites.

Next came the Medical Department's inspection of the site. Where, they wanted to know, were the Marines going to eat, sleep, and relieve themselves? During my former swamp and field training at Lejeune, I lived and slept under a poncho, ate field rations, and found nature's bathroom just fine. All grunt Marine units operated this way, without such luxuries as the medical guys demanded. But since this was to become a full-fledged training center, it had to have tents to sleep in, latrines, and even a separate place to prepare the meals. I was beginning to wonder if he expected the Waldorf Astoria! But we had to have a washing site, with a generator for lights and a place for stoves and the wash tubs.

Where would I get a budget to support all this? It would take years to requisition what we needed. I had just two months to get ready to begin training and I didn't have a dime appropriated for this CMC-stated priority. Obviously, counter-guerrilla training would take its place with the other training programs. Fortunately, my staff NCOs came to the rescue. It seems we had a big Property Disposal Office right there at Camp Lejeune, which happened to have dozens of unserviceable tents in their lots. These were the big, spacious squad tents that held a dozen Marines each. They also had beat-up wash cans, food-service property, and used latrines that I could have. The tents had some cuts and slashes, and the cans had dents, but overall this "junk" would work out well for us. It was perfectly suited for a USMC swamp site. All I had to do was sign for the stuff and haul it away. I had a pen, and Jordan had the truck. Little did we realize how many truckloads it would require. These were big tents, poles and all, but we managed to drag them into our hiding place, just inside the main gate but hidden from view. When we finally put the last item there, it looked like a staging area for World War II. It was massive and looked like a huge pile of military junk, but it was salvation for us and the CGWC. I had to wait for Bob Atkinson and his gang to clear the bivouac site before moving that mountain.

After two weeks, I was called to the division command post where my boss asked me if I knew anything about a huge pile of military equipment that was found by someone right inside the main gate. I said I did, and explained the agreement I had made with the Property Disposal office. He winced at first, and then told me to meet the same fat, insulting engineering major that had discovered the hiding spot. This would be a tough one to explain.

When I arrived at our huge stash, the major was incensed that I was taking construction into my own hands and said he was going to have my butt right there. He obviously did not appreciate my guerrilla solution. By this time I had suffered every delay, obstacle, and insult that I was going to take—and most of it came from him. To this day, I can't believe I didn't fire a punch at him. For some reason I can't recall, I held back and chalked up this butt-chewing to another step I had to take to make the CGWC a reality. I had learned that to succeed in this important venture, my butt had to become fodder for anyone who wanted it. I had to step up and around these obstacles if the Marines at Camp Lejeune were to get the most basic training in meeting and defeating guerrillas in that real guerrilla war that was going on in Vietnam.

When the major finished his tirade and told me I would not receive *any* engineering support from him, he ordered me to get that junk out of there as fast as I could. "Yes, sir," I responded, but could not resist commenting, "When are you leaders at Camp Lejeune going to understand that we are *now* in a real guerrilla war in Vietnam? Your own Marines are completely untrained for it and they are getting orders there as we speak!" The major reprimanded me and walked off, as perturbed as the first day I had met him. He was that way until he received orders to Vietnam, where his own men would face that same devious enemy he never understood. But he would find out, and may have looked back and wondered if that insolent captain (me) had been right. Being right can be wrong—and that day he was certain that I was very wrong.

My last major hurdle involved constructing prefabricated sections for the village walls and roofs, 8-foot by 10-foot panels that we had to thatch in an assembly-line method. It became obvious that we could not do this on a parade field, or even at our field site. Since it was rainy and cold at Camp Lejeune in early November, I had been given the use of one of the empty offices right next to an empty mess hall that a Marine battalion had vacated while they steamed in the Mediterranean. Ironically, that large mess hall belonged to

Lt. Colonel Bruce Meyers, author of *Malaya Jungle Patrol*. I'm sure he would have approved what I was trying to do. Forty years later, he did, when I accidentally met him at a car rental agency in Washington, DC, and told him the whole story. He was glad his mess hall had helped.

My office was small, with space for my XO and the two staff NCOs. There, I wrote lesson plans and nothing more. But when we noticed a huge empty mess hall, we envisioned our factory for assembling the panels. My demolition man also spotted the empty ovens, where he could bake his booby traps from plain old mud. Since the battalion was far away from Lejeune we expanded our territory from a small mess cook's office into the whole mess hall.

When most of the panels were thatched, completed, and stacked in piles 10 feet high, we had a visitor. Piles of grass and pine poles were scattered all over that big room when the worst possible visitor arrived: the fire inspector, who was checking fire extinguishers. He almost dropped in shock when he saw the massive fire hazard we had created. But when I explained to him what we were actually doing, the Almighty must have told him it was all right. He simply said, "I did not see this stuff today. I was not even here today. But tomorrow I will be here, and then I will not see what I think I saw today. And I had better not see then what I am seeing now, okay?" I'm sure he had been a Marine. I was relieved to have just escaped another general court martial! How many "lives," I wondered, would I have with this endeavor? We moved that potential fire risk all day and night, until not one piece of straw remained. Ovens that had been packed full of baked mud were bright and shiny, as if never used for baking Viet Cong booby traps. I am certain the fire inspector blinked twice the next day and probably doubted he had seen what he thought he saw, if he saw what he thought he saw at all.

By then, the stuff was hauled way out in the swamps, and my Spanish-speaking kids had already started to assemble the buildings with the panels and poles. Most of these kids already knew how this was to be done, no doubt having seen some of their own homes constructed in the same fashion. What a talented bunch of savvy guerrillas they were! And I never understood why my kids rarely

141

stood division watches. Maybe my boss realized that we worked 12-hour days, 7 days a week and that we needed the time. By Thanksgiving Day, we had managed to construct most of the new Vietnam village, which we called Tri-Me ("try me"). It had a tall, imposing front gate that looked authentic. Bob Atkinson had copied it from one he had seen during his own Vietnam tour as an advisor. He also managed to locate authentic bamboo right there in North Carolina. For a small price, we cut and hauled tons of it with our cumshawed trucks.

A few of our Marines handled machetes with great skill, just like they did at home. This talent was a real find, and it gave an authentic look to our Vietnam village. We worked all Thanksgiving Day, and Gwenny was kind enough to cook enough turkey for the whole crew. She was relishing the job as much as we were, and later she would even decorate the hut interiors. During a very cold December, the CGWC team continued to fabricate and build the entire CGWC. It seemed incongruous to be building structures like Marines would find in Vietnam, where temperatures are often above 90 and 100 degrees Fahrenheit. We were near freezing at Camp Lejeune. Wearing our field jackets, hoods, and gloves, we thatched the huts and chopped the frozen land. Our freezing fingers were too stiff to perform other tasks.

Yet the Vietnam village went up well ahead of schedule. I had not received one dime of support from the Marine base, or even from my division. Instead, I paid hundreds of dollars from my own pocket to buy the bamboo and pay the other miscellaneous expenses, which included hamburgers for the troops on many occasions. I never heard a discouraging word and never found my kids too tired to build one more hut or another guerrilla camp. When most Marines were sleeping and enjoying warm barracks, my guys we were out in the cold, bitter winter of Camp Lejeune, building a thatched Vietnam village and the other training sites.

The following photos of the CGWC village and troops were taken by Public Affairs Office staff photographers at Camp Lejeune.

The 2nd Marine Division Counter-guerrilla Warfare Team

The front gate beckons at Tri-Me (or "Try Me")

Tri-Me village

Bamboo "booby trap" exploded by Cpl Harrington

Featured in a *True* a magazine article by war correspondent Malcolm Browne, "Devil Weapons of the Viet Cong":

Pole grenades for helicopters

Homemade grenade

**Paddy scene by GySgt Bob Atkinson—
so authentic, with ducks and pigs, that visitors
asked, "When do you harvest rice?"**

Cordon-and search village operation (photo 1)

Cordon-and search village operation (photo 2)

Cordon-and search village operation (photo 3)

Typical village home interior with eating utensils

Searching suspicious areas

Searching everything suspicious—including cattle pens

Interior village search

Interior village search of hooches, shrines, and tunnels

CMC inspects booby-trap trail

CMC inspects village house

Officer in Charge demonstrates a homemade device

Village complete with flag

In the last week of December (we took off only on Christmas Day), we had tacked up the last scrap of canvas. It was a huge canvas cover made of tarps that sprawled over long wooden frames for our "classroom." We added some large pieces for the sides. We also had managed to scrounge a 500-kilowatt mobile generator from Property Disposal that was inoperable (Code H). That is, until Sergeant Jordan "found" a generator repairman who got it running again. What a find! It provided all the power for the classroom lights, film projector, my office tent, and the exterior lights for the mess area that we set up below our "tent city." There, we had constructed enough tents to house a whole rifle company of 200 men. Exhausted, we looked with pride at a huge Vietnam village with its dozen buildings, cattle pens, market, and so forth. Later, real animals would be added.

There were seven other training areas as well, including the authentic booby trap trails, ambush sites, guerrilla camps, a pop-up guerrilla target range, the Gurkha 360-degree reaction drill site, and other outdoor training sites where small, squad-size classes were held.

What had been a remote site that was too far from the main base turned out to be exactly what we needed for an authentic counter-guerrilla training environment. The main-side location would have been overrun by too many unwelcome visitors. Here, we would have the training company all to ourselves. Finally, in a roaring sleet storm on January 2, 1966, we held our first guerrilla rehearsals, where my kids became the guerrilla enemy and learned to employ *their* tactics just as we had learned in Malaya and the Philippines. We also relied on the lessons that Gunny Jordan and Bob Atkinson had already experienced in actual jungle and village operations and ambushes in South Vietnam.

The village looked like the real thing. Gwenny helped to set up basic tables and furniture with Oriental plates and other decor items she had found. But the most realistic area was the rice paddy field that Bob and his "guerrillas" had constructed. They were so authentic looking that I thought I was back in Southeast Asia! Later, in the spring, we would have borrowed pigs and geese rooting around to add more realism. They were loaned by the local farmers for a few months. Every cattle pen and every hooch (house) had secret hiding places and escape tunnels out to the heavy growth behind them, so our guerrillas had a way to escape. It was left to the ingenuity of the rifle company to ferret out *all* of the enemy and find those escape routes. We knew the Viet Cong also dug extensive tunnels and that every village had ingenious hiding places to hide snipers and sapper teams. But little did we know how extensive they would be in Vietnam.

It was hard to find our "counter-guerrilla school," which was well off a country road near Sneads Ferry, a sleepy little fishing town about 20 miles southwest of the main base. To help find it, we ordered a very large sign to be constructed by the division carpenter shop. They fabricated a beauty! It measured 10 by 20 feet and was anchored by two posts at each end. The paint shop had also put extra effort into the very attractive Marine Corps scarlet and gold emblem and lettering. One could hardly miss our almost-hidden entrance with such an impressive "billboard" that pointed out our remote location. Just as importantly, I had another sign in front of my office—a dirty, smoky, canvas tent that simply stated our CGWC mission: *"To instill in the Marine the senses, suspicions, reflexes, and reactions that will enable him to defeat the guerrilla in his own environment."*

The mission statement was simple, concise, and focused on *that* enemy and his unique battlefield. No more two-up, one-back with hot chow in the rear! This was another kind of war, and our training had to prepare every Marine to fight it a different way—or the guerrilla would win. While we could not turn our U.S. Marines into real Gurkhas like they had at the Malaya Jungle School, we employed the same training that would instill *senses, suspicions, and reactions.* This gave the Marine a chance once he was on the guerrilla's own turf.

It was very different, but it was not well-accepted by the "Old Corps" Marines. One former commandant bluntly stated, "This is not a Marine Corps war, and we should not get involved in it." It was too late—we were in it up to our necks; our minds had to join it as well. Hence, the CGWC! The same commandant was quite adamant that our Marines required *no special training* for it. All Marines had to do, he believed, was to "saddle up and go." In his mind, that was enough to enter any war. The colonel on the Division staff had said it another way "We Marines fought the Japs in the jungles. We don't need this special training." It didn't matter to him that today's young Marines had not been there.

The type of training I would employ used traditional, progressive Marine training techniques that began with the individual, evolving to the small unit and then to the rifle company and battalion level. While I elected to use that proven evolution of training, the content was radically different. *It emphasized "sensing" and instinctively knowing what a guerrilla thinks and what he would do to destroy you in his environment.* There, the guerrilla was like anyone else in a hamlet or even a city. "The fish in the sea" was what Mao called the guerrilla. It was how General Giap employed *his* guerrillas. For sure it wasn't World War II, much less Korea! We would have a big job replacing Giap's "People's War, People's Army" slogan with our "People to People" slogan.

COUNTERGUERRILLA WARFARE CENTER
2d Marine Division FMF
Camp Lejeune, N.C.

RIFLE COMPANY TRAINING COURSE

MASTER TRAINING SYLLABUS

CRS	SUBJECT	HRS	HR OF DAY	1	2	3	4	5	6	7	8	9	10	TYPE
100	CGWC INTRODUCTION	1	1	x										L
101	COMMUNISM & INSURGENCY	1	2	x										L
102	GUERRILLA PITS, TRAPS, MINES & DEVICES	2	3,4	x										L,D
103	VC ORGANIZATION, TACTICS & TECHNIQUES	1	1				x							L
200	PATROLLING—VIET NAM	1	5	x										L
201	PATROL TIPS & TECHNIQUES—VIET NAM	2	6,7,8	x										L,D,A
202	PATROL ORDERS	1	19—2100	x										L,F
203	PATROL BASE OPERATIONS	3	1,2,3			x								L,D,A
204	PATROL FEX	6	4,5,6,7,8				x							A
300	IMMEDIATE ACTION—INTRO	1	1		x									L,D
301	IMMEDIATE ACTION—DRILLS	1	2		x									A
302	I.A.—REFLEX COURSE	3	3,4,5		x									A
303	I.A.—REACTION COURSE	3	6,7,8		x									A
304	MOTOR TRANSPORT OPERATIONS	1	2			x								L,D
305	M.T. "BAIL-OUT" DRILLS	2	3,4			x								A
400	AMBUSH—INTRODUCTION	1	5			x								L
401	AMBUSH—DEMONSTRATION	1	6			x								L,D
402	AMBUSH—APPLICATION	2	7,8			x								A
403	NIGHT AMBUSH—SQUAD	12	18—2400			x	x							A
500	COUNTERGUERRILLA OPERATIONS	1	1			x								L
——	CG OPERATIONS HANDOUT ISSUED WITH #500													
501	ATTACK ON GUERRILLA CAMP	1	4				x							L,D
502	ATTACK ON GUERRILLA CAMP (FEX)	4½	5,6,7,8				x							A
503	REACTION FORCE OPERATIONS	1	5						x					L
504	REACTION OPERATION (FEX)	4	6,7,8						x					A
601	FIRE SUPPORT IN GUERRILLA AREAS	1	1						x					L,D
602	VIETNAM, ITS PEOPLE & CUSTOMS	2	2,3						x					L,D
603	MEDICAL TIPS: VIETNAM	1	4						x					L
700	VILLAGE OPERATIONS	1	19—2000						x					L
701	VILLAGE CORDON & SEARCH ORDER	1	20—2100						x					L
702	VILLAGE CORDON & SEARCH (FEX)	16	0001—1600							x				A

Training syllabus (first page) based on Malaya Jungle School:
2 weeks of intensive 24/7 training; total: 150 hours

CRS	SUBJECT	HRS	HR OF DAY	1	2	3	4	5	6	7	8	9	10	TYPE
703	INSURGENCY TODAY: "THE THIRD CHALLENGE	1	19-2000	x										L,F
704	THE MARINE & CIVIC ACTION	1	20-2100	x										L,F
800	COUNTERGUERRILLA FEX	24	8,9,10day								x	x	x	A
900	COUNTERGUERRILLA TRAINING CRITIQUE	1	1500										x	L
	ADDITIONAL SUBJECTS													
	PHYSICAL TRAINING "MAD-HOUR" P.T.	4	0615-0700	x	x	x	x							P.T.
	COMPETITION	4	1700-1730	x	x		x[1]							P.T.
C-100	COMMUNICATIONS IN GUERRILLA AREAS	2	0900-1100			x								L,D
D-100	DEMOLITIONS, MINES & BOOBY TRAPS	2	ALTERNATE SUBJECT BLOCK											L,D[2]
S-100	SEARCH TECHNIQUES	1	2							x				L,D
T-100	CAVE & TUNNEL TACTICS	1	3							x				L,D
	FILM PROGRAM (EVENING)[3]													

1 – Conducted if Reaction Operation is completed by 1630.
2 – D-100 will be taught as an alternate subject when the primary schedule cannot be satisfied.
3 – Film program varies with new film footage available.

L – Lecture
D – Demonstration
A – Application

Training syllabus (second page)

I called the training "block training," and each session built upon a preceding block of instruction so that every Marine could see how he would function as an individual and how his unit also functioned. That part of the training concept was not challenged; everything else was. I knew I would have a hard time convincing the "old salts" that guerrilla fighting was unique. To many of them, my setting up the CGWC had departed from proven, historic Marine Corps training methods and techniques, which began in boot camp with individual hands-on training by exceptional drill instructors. Next, the basic Marine was sent to the Infantry Training Regiment, where he learned small unit tactics, fire and maneuver, weapons familiarization, and basic combat skills. The success of this training was confirmed by the uncommon valor of Marines in the island campaigns of World War II, the cold forbidding Korea mountains, and the many small wars we fought, even Desert Storm, with unique mobile warfare.

Vietnam was another combat dimension that my school would have to teach. We had almost forgotten that Chesty Puller, Smedley

Butler, Alexander Vandergrift, and earlier Marines had employed counter-guerrilla tactics many years earlier in the "banana wars." The Marine Corps had, in fact, written the first Small Wars Manual that was based on its successful engagements with Caribbean bandits. And the U.S. Army fought the Philippine Huk-Balahap and a wide assortment of unconventional conflicts.

Our first rifle company was scheduled to attend the CGWC in mid-January, in cold weather or not. Captain Joe Knotts, later a Marine General, would command the first rifle company through it. He had recently returned from Vietnam, where he had barely escaped death when his remote ARVN outpost of South Vietnamese soldiers was overrun by the Viet Cong. They destroyed it and almost got him as well. He really understood this war, and I received his full support. His combat experience and knowledge were greatly appreciated. I hoped I could rely on Joe to support and defend the type of training his Marines would receive.

Before the first training unit arrived, the Camp Lejeune CG, General Simpson, and his staff visited the CGWC. What he found there absolutely amazed him—I could tell by the look on his face. He had expected a few makeshift huts and some pop-up targets. What he found was a complete village with the actual look of the real Vietnam world. The booby-trap trail demonstrated over 50 different explosive devices that would blow up when triggered, simulating a real device. Corporal Harrington did an amazing job, so good that *True* magazine published an article titled, *The Devil Weapons of the Viet Cong* by Malcolm Browne, who was an experienced combat author that had just returned from Vietnam.

In addition to those two training sites, we had several guerrilla camps that platoons would attack, and pop-up targets that a Marine had to approach, size up, and counter instinctively. It was *not* what they had previously trained for, and certainly not the old two-up, one-back techniques. The Gurkha drill area (360-degree reaction to an ambush) was set up on a squad-sized ambush trail where Marines would have react quickly, in all directions, and fight their way out of a variety of well-laid ambushes they might encounter. This proved to be a very difficult task and hard to learn, as many untrained squads would find out. Finally, combat firing techniques emphasized actual fire discipline, which the frightened Marines at Camp Pickett never used. Fire discipline was critical in Vietnam where the Army's wasteful "recon by fire" became the norm. It remained that way throughout the war.

General Simpson said he was dumbfounded and had expected nothing like he saw. Besides the usual "well done" comment to me, the officer in charge, he announced that he was promoting my two staff NCOs one rank, immediately, for doing such an unbelievable job. I was truly elated—for the guys and the new gunnery sergeants who had done the job. They deserved their promotions. What a way to begin the CGWC—critical training for thousands of Marines that I knew would receive orders for the real thing. And it was not far off, for some of us that had also volunteered to go. We could train a full rifle company in two 5-day periods. There was a special training program established for the Seabees (members of U.S. Navy construction battalions), who learned how to counter and survive one-mile-long truck convoy ambushes. Special Forces Teams and Navy Seal teams also asked to attend, as did battalion and regimental staff men who were just beginning to get their orders to Vietnam.

By the summer of 1966, the CGWC was getting a reputation we enjoyed. It was a tough daily 24-hour course, with little sleep, like Marines experienced in actual combat, and a guerrilla force that scared heck out of some of the returning Vietnam veterans. "At night they look and act the same as the Viet Cong, and I have to admit I was scared as shitless as I was over there," said one returnee. That was exactly what I had intended, but I did not want them to relive their tough experiences. They had paid their dues and *were already trained*! It was unfair to pile more onto these actual vets. Instead, we asked them to work with our guerrilla teams, who appreciated hearing first-hand what Vietnam was like.

We were becoming the most popular training site on the whole base, as news of Marine deaths and even the first officer deaths began to trickle in. General Simpson's aide, Tom Kennedy, would leave for Vietnam that very spring. I still recall his last words to me the day the general made his visit: "I just hope I don't miss out on it." Tom was assigned to the same Vietnamese Marine Brigade that I would also join. The Viet Cong ambushed his battalion, overran its command post, and killed Tom and his whole Vietnamese Marine Corps group. In 1965 we also lost more Vietnamese Marine advisors, and others were badly wounded. Tom and his family had lived only a few doors down our street.

Now, the war was getting very real. Marine Corps mental blocks and the BLT mentality soon changed. I saw very different looks on the faces of those who had ridiculed my prophecies and warnings just a year earlier. One colonel even asked me if there was a book he could get so he could "read up" on Vietnam. He had *his* orders. I suggested *People's War, People's Army* by General Giap. As Viet Minh enemy commander, he defeated the French at Dien Bien Phu and he was well worth reading. Soon, others sought our advice even if it was late in the game. I got no pleasure out of being right, but did find it amusing to observe the many unbelievers that had now become believers—in a short time.

The great majority of the troops we sent to Vietnam had virtually no training for that kind of war and would learn how to fight a very different enemy the hard way. But great credit must go to the soldier, sailor, Marine, and Air Force crewmen who found a way to fight and survive, literally developing their own techniques as they went along. A high price was paid for our lack of readiness, and more so for our failure to understand the kind of war it was. An even greater price was paid in the thousands of lives we sacrificed due to this "historic" mindset.

This thinking has occurred before every war we have fought except Desert Storm. Then, another "radical" and visionary Marine, Colonel Mike Wyly, managed to introduce mobile, desert warfare into our Marine Corps training at some peril to his own career. Ironically, he also encountered resistance to this rank departure from our amphibious warfare doctrine. Who had ever heard of Marines playing Lawrence of Arabia, attacking over vast miles of desert? Where were the beachheads? How fortunate it was that a few visionaries actually foresaw the coming conflict in the Middle East and began to train for it at Twentynine Palms, California. As a result of this training, it is no surprise that Marines were the first troops into Kuwait. Yet this visionary colonel was passed over for promotion to general.

By the time our counter-guerrilla training was fully underway at the CGWC, Marines were already in Vietnam. The CGWC became an instant focal point for training all battalions and support units at Camp Lejeune. We were really into it. That was enough! But sycophants abound, even in my beloved Corps. Once the CGWC began operating, another order was promulgated by HQMC. General Wallace Greene, who was the new commandant, had toured all of our training sites at the CGWC. He was very impressed with everything my team had done to get our training started in such a short time. His major concern was the many booby-trap casualties we suffered on a daily basis in Vietnam.

General Krulak, the commander of FMFPAC and one of the finest professional, tactical minds in the Marine Corps, had begun disseminating "lessons learned" from Vietnam, where booby-trap and mine casualties ranked as the most critical problem. How the Marine Corps could effectively train for this was the question on his mind as well as General Green. Our booby-trap trail with its loud explosions did not disturb him, even though such training frightened the men that were heading to Vietnam. Instead, he said we must do *all* we could to instill such training into Marines—to save their lives. He studied each training area closely and could not seem to get all the information he wanted to know. There was so much that was new for all of us, as well as for HQMC. When he finished his tour General Greene praised our efforts and stated, "This is the finest training of this kind I have ever seen. You all have done a remarkable job in getting our Marines trained for this tough war in Vietnam." I knew that Major General Simpson had to be very pleased. Then, the most ironic thing began to happen. Many of my former adversaries, and those who had opposed and delayed my original proposal for the CGWC, began to "brown up" to the commandant. They acted as if they always supported the effort. My team and I thought it funny to see so many recent "conversions."

Yet not everyone would jump on the bandwagon and that disturbed my boss, especially when it included the very company commanders that had their Marines in training at the CGWC. A few of these Marine "leaders" would head home at 5:00 p.m., as if *their* training day was over. They left their men to us, and to my instructors, for the intensive training that took place every night—which is when the Viet Cong really operated. I still am puzzled by captains who command, but then walk away from that responsibility at a critical time in the training cycle of their own Marines. If I were that company commander, I would like to know *how* my squads and platoons performed in ambushes, guerrilla camp attacks, cordon and search operations, Gurkha drills, and so forth. As a company commander, I'd like to learn as much as I could because I also would have to fight in that new war, and probably very soon.

I decided to report this occurrence to my boss, who simply told me to tell it like I saw it and report that the company commanders left the CGWC nightly while training was ongoing. At least I had his backing for my critiques. I can see the heads (and butts) of the officer absentees rolling when my critiques reached a battalion CO, endorsed by none other than Major General Simpson and citing their absence during critical training *of their own unit*. The word soon got out. All future scheduled company commanders knew that they too were included in *all* of their company's training. Duh! I previously had made enemies of the senior officers; now it was with them.

The CGWC was getting into full-scale training, with one company scheduled each week. Staff and base support units arrived for the short indoctrination courses. Both ambush and village operations were very realistic, and feedback from all the training units confirmed that they had indeed learned valuable new techniques. The Gurkha drill, the booby-trap course, and unique search-destroy tactics used in a guerrilla environment also were high points in their CGWC training.

Years later, at a "happy hour" in Hawaii, my ears perked up when I heard the comments of a Marine officer who was sitting near the bar. He extolled a counter-ambush technique he had learned, called "the Gurkha drill." He had employed it in Vietnam and was raving about *that* school that had taught it. The CGWC began to get press notices, such as the *True Magazine* article on our booby-trap course. Other writers would visit our school to advertise the effectiveness of the training.

However, the best validation came from those who had employed our techniques in real combat, like the Seabee battalion from Quonset Point, Rhode Island, that wrote to request counter-ambush training and small-unit training against ambushes. We made certain that no Marine or Seabee unit would leave the CGWC unprepared to cope with that circumstance! So, we set up a one-mile long truck convoy ambush on a very winding road and put them through our own convoy ambush. We blew them away the first time they went through it, but then we taught them the most successful way to counter the ambush: get off the trucks immediately, run right through the trap, and then turn and attack right up the ambusher's own flanks. The shock and surprise would get them. After several drills, which took most of a day to complete, the Seabees had it down cold. It was no surprise that only one month after that same Seabee battalion arrived in Vietnam, it happened: the battalion was ambushed. The Seabee unit commander could hardly contain his exuberance in his letter to General Simpson. They not only escaped the ambush, they blew the heck out of that guerrilla ambush and turned what could have been a disaster into one of the most successful and morale-boosting assaults on a very large ambushing guerrilla force. We couldn't get any better feedback at the CGWC. They learned their lessons well and lived through their experiences to let us know the training really worked.

Yet we couldn't rest on our laurels. Within six months, the CGWC's reputation was rapidly rising, and validation was pouring in. Even unit commanders in Vietnam were requesting our syllabus and everything we could send that told how to fight this enemy.

The effective truck convoy counter-ambush technique must be credited to Lieutenant Doug McCaskill, who had personally survived a similar fate during his tour of duty in Vietnam. I had been looking for an early replacement for Lieutenant Willie, before Gunny Jordan did him in. Late that spring, a sharp, lean, young Marine officer appeared at my filthy tent at the CGWC. He told me that he had requested the new position at the CGWC. He'd heard I was looking for a combat-experienced officer, and Doug was a perfect instructor for the center. He had been in the long-range recon patrol units and had solid, proven combat skills against guerrilla units. He often escaped with his life when his small team patrolled miles away from the main base, barely making it aboard the rescuing choppers just as the Viet Cong were closing in for the kill. He wore a Silver Star medal for extreme heroism, which told me the kind of Marine Corps officer he was. Most importantly, my gunnery sergeants liked him immediately as did all of my guerrilla team.

My first introduction and conversation with Doug did not go well at all. I liked the look of this sharp officer, but when he placed a small jar (baby-food size) on my desk, I saw that it contained two human ears: Viet Cong ears. Body-count had become the most important measure of combat success, and Doug found that he could confirm their kills only by collecting the ears of their enemy and turning in the grisly things for "kill credit." These particular ears belonged to an unfortunate "woodcutter" that the Viet Cong posted at remote points around the countryside so they could report on Marine units like Doug's. It was far away from their base, and the area was ripe for Viet Cong ambushes and annihilation. As Doug explained to me, "We found we had no alternative but to kill those civilian sentries, or we never would have made it back alive They were there just to report our position."

I told him I understood what he had experienced. Then, I picked up the jar, walked out behind my office, and threw the jar (and the ears) as far as I could into the dense woods behind us. "Not in my school!" I told him. I could not teach that miserable part of combat. Though I was sure that all Marines would eventually find that kind of thing necessary, someone else could teach them *that*—but not us. There was enough sickness in a guerrilla war, with its terrorism, torture, and brutality. I told Doug that he had a choice: he could teach my way, or he could report back to division for assignment to a battalion. Fortunately, he decided to do it my way, and I welcomed to the CGWC one of the finest young Marine officers I would ever know. The value he added to our training staff was immeasurable. A brilliant instructor, he inspired his Marine trainees with factual, accurate, and experienced accounts of his own combat experience. The Seabee truck convoy's counter-ambush training was one of many techniques he introduced to our syllabus. Like the rest of my team, he was almost too good to be true, and proved it every day.

The CGWC's reputation had spread not only throughout the Marine Corps but to the Army, Navy and even some civilian and congressional sectors. Consequently, we began to hold "guided tours," which Doug and I barely managed to keep under control for the first few months. Then, the CMC published a directive. It stated: **"All Marine Corps commands will send representatives to the Camp Lejeune Counter-guerrilla Warfare Center to study the counter-guerrilla techniques and the training *oriented* toward Vietnam. The focus of training is the guerrilla war now being conducted in that *theater of operations.*"**

We received many requests for our syllabus and training plans, even from Marine commanders in Vietnam, where battalion commanders like Lt. Colonel Dave Clements had found that the Marines that integrated into the regional forces of the Vietnamese deterred guerrilla activity in many hamlets and villages. This logical strategy was supported by Marine commanders and was based on Lt. Colonel Bill Corson's CAP, where his small Marine teams were combined with local militias and regional forces to train them to deny the enemy access to food sources, roads, and even inside the villages and hamlets. As a strategy, it meant that Cong and PAVN forces would lack enough sustenance to conduct their own tactical schemes and have access to the villages, where they also had to recruit new guerrillas. The CAP strategy drew enemy units out of hiding spots to counter the CAP teams and regain village control.

Population and resource control (Corson's CAP) was successful in I Corps as early as 1965. But it too was countered by a Giap shift in strategy in 1966. During the 1964–1965 Dry Season offensive, it was General Nguyen Chi Thang who commanded the B-2 Front, which included most of South Vietnam from Tay Ninh south to the Delta. He also commanded the COSVN, the major headquarters for that region. Westmoreland would spend years trying to locate and destroy it. General Thang was also the chief PAVN strategist whose employment of his large, main-force attacks had almost decimated South Vietnam's best battalions. His objective was to bottle up all of Saigon's remaining forces in the larger cities and free up rural and agricultural areas where local Viet Cong forces would maintain control. Had America not sent its Marines in March 1965, Thang's strategy would have guaranteed the defeat of the South Vietnamese government. It came close.

That effective strategy was employed right through November 1965, until the PAVN 304th Division and a main-force Viet Cong unit stood and fought the technically superior Air Cavalry at the Ia Drang battle. Thang felt American units were inexperienced and that the best way to fight them was to have his main-force units stand and fight, creating a very large number of casualties. He believed that Americans could not accept or endure attrition warfare. Ho Chi Minh stated that he would accept the loss of ten of his soldiers for the life of one American. But Westmoreland eagerly sought main-force engagements, since his regiments and battalions had the advantage of mobility and could call on massive air and artillery support as well. By January 1966, three different strategies were on the table, but the chess master Giap soon would rearrange the chess board in his favor. The expanded Ho Chi Minh Trail was wide open on the west side of the Annamese Moutains in Laos. It poured huge numbers of troops and supplies to the south with no let-up. A pathetic political decision allowed no border crossing at all, and B-52 bombs could not stop it. But PAVN strength increased to match U.S. and Vietnamese strength when General Giap shifted to another strategic gear, revoking General Thang's "stand and fight" approach, which he felt would favor U.S. tactics and technologies, although it guaranteed attrition. His PAVN regiments and battalions adopted Phase I and Phase II guerrilla tactics that also would have heavy attrition, and (more importantly) the protracted war would wear down U.S. units. Then he would employ a stand-and-fight Phase III once again.

Giap reemphasized control of the rice lands, resources, villages and the "fish in the sea," even locating hard core, main-force units in many of the important areas of Vietnam. His terror teams made sure the locals remained a faithful "people's army" to deliver food, medicine, and other key supplies. They also dug their allocated tunnel footage. Our successful Marine Corps' CAP program in I Corps denied the enemy rice and other resources in 150 villages. It also kept them out of villages, denying them more recruits and their ability to conduct low-level Phase I tactics. Since CAP units mustered 2000 Marines from our various infantry battalions, it was a drain on maneuver units but still a very workable strategy (given the time to train local militias to handle their own security). The objective was to have roving CAP teams and expand village control. It became a trade-off between the time required to do this and Marine troop availability. Giap had an answer for this too. He soon placed large main-force units as decoys to lure U.S. forces to potential main-force battle sites along the demilitarized zone, where they would have to fortify and defend bases like Khe Sanh, Dong Ha, and Chu Lai. South Vietnamese units soon found themselves back in *defensive* enclaves, but like Marines in I Corps, they could still patrol out from their bases. Unfortunately, the CAP's successful population and resource control quickly diminished. Terrorized villages were left again in confusion and despair. Giap had won.

But General Giap had a strong ally in terminating the CAP programs: Westmoreland himself. He angrily attacked the Marines for their refusal to take the fight right to the enemy—based on all he knew, which was right from World War II. It was the worst decision he ever made. But then, he never understood his own war—nor would those who sent our first combat units into Iraq many years later. It was a display of the same ignorance! He still believed large PAVN and Viet Cong regiments were just waiting at some *fixed* battle site, ready to fight, as General Thang had led him to believe.

General Westmoreland had been an artilleryman in World War II, where *fixed*-position warfare meant facing your enemy along long, deep battle lines, and then taking the offensive and destroying almost everything that stood in the way of our big Army units. His approach was to employ the same strategy in Vietnam: the big main-force battle, *a lá* General Thang, and the search-and-destroy strategy he employed in Europe. He had cut his military teeth on attrition warfare in Europe, which likely was why body-counting was so appealing to him in this war. He knew it had worked against the Germans, as well as the civilian populations that were in the way. Through use of such logic, body-count became his bizarre measure of combat effectiveness, as did his aggressive search-and-destroy tactics in Vietnam. When Viet Cong and PAVN units were discovered in villages, his credo was, "I have to destroy your village to save you." It made no difference that these were ancient home sites, with ancestral graves and a long history. His aggressive strategy was like General Sherman's march through Georgia: Scorch the earth, kill as many as possible, but make sure the kill ratio favors us! His attrition and body-count war cost 58,000 lives.

What Westmoreland could not readily grasp was that American people, and even war veterans, had decided that such a large number of American dead and wounded was unacceptable. Having 50,100 (or even 200) young men killed each day was a very high price to pay for his lame strategy. He could not seem to grasp the simple fact that American dead cannot be traded for enemy dead, regardless of the ratios and how "successfully" Westmoreland felt his body-count war was progressing. Had he been a World War I general like the infamous British Field Marshal Haig, who ordered *one million* soldiers to be sacrificed to German machine guns, then it would have been considered "a good number." I can imagine them both saying, "March into the guns, men—this is how real wars must be fought." Yet the more soldiers we sent to Vietnam, the more resolved General Giap and Ho Chi Minh became, and the more they sacrificed greater numbers of soldiers. Ratios be damned, they knew Westmoreland's scorched-earth approach, his destruction of villages, and "acceptable" civilian deaths were exactly what would turn a majority of Vietnamese (even former friendlies) against a brutal eight-year war. Marines had a more humane (and successful) way to win their hearts and minds—by using CAPs, which became the strategic foundation for our future counterinsurgency programs almost 40 years later. Unfortunately, the CAPs they did not survive when General Giap decided to repeat Dien Bien Phu. He selected Khe Sanh for this endeavor, but it became a disaster for him.

By 1968 and the Khe Sanh battle, Marines had begun to understand the full scope of the war we were enmeshed in. Sadly, we had very few men like Lt. Colonel Bill Corson to direct and expand our counterinsurgency program. The many years Corson spent in Asia gave him insights and an understanding of "this kind of war" that few American military men had. He also spoke several languages, including Chinese and Vietnamese. He knew the cultures, religions, politics, and even their military tactics and techniques at the guerrilla level that Mao and Giap had introduced in the People's War. Yet Corson never was given the opportunity to expand upon his successful CAP program and heed the lessons the French gave us. It took this out-of-the-box thinker to give us an effective, comprehensive counterinsurgency doctrine and strategy, and even the required training program. What Corson did not know is that he had in fact laid the groundwork for effectively countering insurgents in Iraq and Afghanistan many years later, where COIN finally became an accepted strategy.

Fed up with Westmoreland's war, Bill Corson decided it was time to "open the kimono" and sacrifice his Marine Corps career. He wrote a blistering critique titled *The Betrayal*. Bill decided to do what Colonel David Hackworth (author of *About Face*) had done. He told the sick story of the grossly incompetent American Agency for International Development (AID) program and dissected the traitorous behavior of the early South Vietnamese military leaders, much as John Paul Vann had done a few years earlier.

At the CGWC at Camp Lejeune, I focused on the guerrilla and his tactics. I also taught the British version of countering guerrillas that was practiced successfully in Malaya, where *they won their war*. Marine generals like Krulak, Walt, Greene, and Simpson had studied that war and sought the counsel of Sir Robert Thompson, the architect of the British anti-terrorist program. His program had all the essential elements of an effective counterinsurgency strategy. Yet General Westmoreland's institutional military training and World War II experience overruled it. While he met with Sir Robert Thompson of Malaya and listened to his strategic hamlet (*kampong*) program, he was smart enough to know that President Diem's similar

Vietnamese program failed miserably because Vietnamese villages were ancient and sacred family sites. The "fish in the sea" bitterly opposed such relocation. The program ended abruptly with Diem's assassination in 1963.

U.S. military leaders continued to ignore the people of Vietnam and gave our best Vietnamese units (Marine, Airborne, and Ranger) demeaning lip service and a condescension they despised. These elite units also became pawns and victims of our faulty strategy as we pursued the "wrong war in the wrong place at the wrong time," as Lt. General Paul Van Riper would label the Iraq War almost 40 years later. Yet none of Vietnam's lessons were applied in Iraq. Again, another obtuse, arrogant Secretary of Defense (Donald Rumsfeld) ignored the lessons of that earlier war and, like McNamara and Westmoreland before him, put all his military eggs into the wrong basket: heavy, expensive weapons and a limited military force that enjoyed a very brief "shock and awe" phase. Then, as in Vietnam, their big bombs and endless operations became a burden as, once again, we fought the wrong war at the wrong time and in the wrong place. Bill Corson must have been spinning in his grave! Alas, the ominous predictions of General Shinseki and General Schwarzkopf came true. The necessary 300,000 support troops were not there: they had been left at home. This follow-on force was required to secure, control, and maintain infrastructures—*and the peace.*

Then, amazingly, like General Westmoreland had done in Vietnam when he insisted on totally separate, distinct chains of command for American and Vietnamese military and their paramilitary forces, Rumsfeld and his advisors shoved the Iraqis aside when a dozen divisions would have surrendered and joined us to save that war. Saddam's Shiite generals were ready to do it—to assist the U.S. forces, if their army was paid. One of the massive blunders of that war, says Tom Ricks in his book, *Fiasco*, was Coalition Provisional Authority boss Paul Bremner's thoughtless "decision" to disarm and dismiss the whole Iraqi army after Baghdad fell. But what else could we expect from a political appointee in such a demanding position? His witless, ignorant act created many thousands of new insurgents. Those former soldiers were left without careers, jobs, pay, or sustenance of any kind. For Bremner and Rumsfeld it had become an American war, just like Vietnam had become an American war under Westmoreland. He mistrusted the Vietnamese and never acknowledged that Corson, Hackworth, and Vann might have had it right. Vietnam was a "peoples' war," as future insurgencies would become. Three years after we entered the war in Iraq, the fact finally hit home (but not to Secretary of Defense Rumsfeld, Bremner, and their intimidated staffs): counterinsurgency must have popular support. At the time it was needed, it did not.

It should have been obvious, even in Vietnam, that the solution to winning an unconventional guerrilla war *must also include a comprehensive counterinsurgency program, and an important parallel strategy that includes the people—all the people.* The Marine Corps tried to initiate this early in the Vietnam War. But those "leaders" who had forgotten the lessons of the past had to relive them, even when the recent French Indochina experience was so relevant to the war.

In Vietnam we never integrated the Vietnamese military with our own; we kept them at arm's length with their own chain of command and obsolete institutional approach. As a Marine advisor, I witnessed this many times as our U.S. field commanders "spoke down" to professional Vietnamese officers, ordering them about as if they were subordinates. They ignored the fact that these officers had been fighting *their* war for 10 years before we entered "our war." Bremner's untimely dismissal of 400,000 Iraqi military in the earliest days of the Iraq War was a duplication of that ignorant Vietnam decision almost 40 years earlier. In Iraq we had a number of Shiite division commanders who despised the Sunnis and Saddam. They would have surrendered to our bare-bones military force, which instead remained overextended and devoid of any military resolution. It would soon become obvious how much we could have used those extra troops. We actually had the solution for full urban security and maintaining Iraq infrastructures. Instead, obtuse, obsolescent obstacles were managing a carbon-copy of our former war in Kuwait, in the same way, and with the same gleeful "shock and awe" strategy. But in Iraq there was no way to speed up, even charging about blindly attacking the enemy. Marines were willing to control the people and resources like we did in Vietnam, and draw the enemy to them. But Rumsfeld's ill-conceived "shock 'em and blast 'em" strategy guaranteed another long war—Vietnam all over.

In Vietnam, enterprising U.S. units developed their own successful tactics. The Army's Air Cavalry, its Special Forces, Marine Corps units, Navy riverine squadrons, Navy Seals, Air Force Forward Air Control, and other combatants were "getting it right" in "countering" guerrillas. Every combat battalion, swift-boat squadron, helicopter unit, and their "new guys" were soon blooded. Yet it was obvious that Giap's protracted war had set in. While our grunts lost few battles, we paid a heavy and bloody price for the victories. Sadder still, Westmoreland's credo remained the same: "I don't know where they are out there, but you go out there, find them, and keep racking up my body counts!"

Population and resource control (using Corson's CAP) was so successful that General Giap would try anything to stop regional control of the people, food, and especially his guerrilla control of the villages. Marine Corps pacification operations married and merged U.S. troops with Vietnamese troops at the local village level. Other large Marine combat units began to conduct "County Fairs" and then "Golden Fleece" operations where active Viet Cong villages were quickly surrounded and cordoned off (a move that was right out of Bob Atkinson's CGWC Village Operations lesson plan). Finally, they systematically searched for hiding Viet Cong, their weapons, and their caches. Corson set up combined Marine-Vietnamese defenders who lived and fought together in that village. It was an excellent way to gain local intelligence and loyalty, and also to understand exactly what was happening in a specific place, such as a village or hamlet.

This practice soon gained the attention of General Giap, who sent his hardcore conventional North Vietnamese units across the demilitarization zone to force U.S. Marines to counter them all along the 38th parallel. This move almost neutralized Lt. Colonel Clement's hamlet, village, and population control. Giap's objective was to lure Marines from the villages and into their careful traps. At first

Marines refused to take the tempting bait, but the enemy had an unwitting ally: General Westmoreland. He angrily attacked the Marines for their refusal to take the fight right to the enemy—based on all he knew, which was right from World War II. It was the worst decision he ever made. But then, he never understood his own war. Many of our units that he sent out had no intelligence but still were told to go out and attack—and to "develop" the situation. After our first early ventures into several enemy strongholds, we rarely found a large enemy force waiting to fight, but then we were also surprised when the Viet Cong or NVA quickly appeared. *They* had chosen the time and place to engage us. And, as bravely as our troops fought (and died) it seemed that *this* enemy had a special advantage. As a result, we suffered heavy casualties. This lasted eight years.

Corson's CAP, on the other hand, was very successful because we chose to secure a village, merge our troops with their local forces, train them to defend themselves, and thus ensure a peaceful and prosperous life for the villagers. It also denied the Viet Cong their former movement and control. Compare this to Westmoreland's self-defeating strategy: *We have to destroy their village to save them.* It demonstrated almost unbelievable ignorance. Yet many would argue that CAP was undoubtedly the most successful counter-guerrilla strategy employed in Vietnam. It was similar to what the British were able to establish in Malaya, where they actually defeated their insurgents—after 12 years of fighting them. But CAP was troop-heavy and took a much longer time to succeed. It had some merit because it was almost the same strategy that Generals Petraeus and Mattis would employ in Iraq and Afghanistan.

We also incorporated Lt. Colonel Dave Clement's successful village "County Fair" techniques into our training, but the success was short-lived when we took Giap's bait and succumbed to Westmoreland's demands—more blundering! Marines were ordered to continue the attritional body-count war and chase NVA units all over I Corps. However, 2000 CAP Marines remained in the villages. Population and resource control and village security was still successful. Giap was desperate to counter this stalemate, and in 1968 he began sending large conventional units to attack across the demilitarized zone with the objective of destroying a large U.S. unit, as he had done to the French at Dien Bien Phu. The Marine base at Khe Sanh was the ideal target, and he sent his best divisions to destroy that isolated bastion. But he also preempted our successful counterinsurgency program. So, we abandoned the CAP team strategy and Corson's combined-unit approach, even when it was the most effective way to fight insurgents. It would take many years of post-war analysis to finally recognize that it may have been *the only way*! As proven in Iraq many years later, joint deployment of our CAP equivalent forces, with local Iraq army troops, finally began to wear down that insurgency—the same way it would have done in Vietnam. But again, it would take years.

Corson's approach was more successful but did not have the "shoot 'em up" appeal of the Army search-and-destroy tactics. Westmoreland pursued that futile strategy until he was relieved after the Tet Offensive in 1968, after four futile years wasting young lives in his inane body-count strategy. In Malaya, the British, with their infinite patience and usual analytical approach, plus a studious understanding of the guerrilla war, successfully employed exactly what Clements and Bill Corson later employed. Even worse, Westmoreland continued to severely criticize the Marines for our "cautious reluctance" to engage the enemy by chasing him down in his sanctuaries, running up body counts, and often getting our own units badly mauled—to the tune of 100 to 200 young men killed daily. Unbelievably, Westmoreland had reduced his *own* combat results to the ridiculous and futile "body count" measure of effectiveness. In this view, 1000 U.S. casualties was a good trade for 3000 of the enemy. Giap accepted a loss of 5000 to our 1000. It *was* a war of attrition, including *our* bodies! Too many were sacrificed.

What Westmoreland could not readily grasp was that the American people, and even war veterans, had decided that such a large number of American dead and wounded was unacceptable. Having 50, 100, and even 200 kids killed each day was a very high price to pay for his lame strategy. He could not seem to grasp the simple fact that American dead cannot be traded for enemy dead, regardless of the ratios and how "successful" Westmoreland felt his body-count war was progressing. Had he been a World War I general like the infamous Field Marshal Haig, no doubt one million soldiers sacrificed to machine guns would have been considered "*a good number.*" I can imagine them saying, "March into the guns, men—that is how real wars must be fought." Yet the more soldiers we sent to Vietnam, the more resolved General Giap and Ho Chi Minh were to sacrifice greater numbers of their soldiers to win the war. They knew Westmoreland's scorched-earth approach, massive destruction of Vietnamese villages, and "acceptable" civilian deaths was exactly what would turn a majority of Vietnamese (even former friendlies) against a brutal war. Marines had a humane (and successful) way to win their hearts and minds—by using our CAPs.

Television and other news media highlighted the many medical evacuations, dead soldiers, and hometown funerals that we regularly saw on America's news. For Westmoreland, the answer was to send more men. General Giap knew how to execute a drawn-out attritional war (as he had against the French), where he chose the moment to attack or ambush a vulnerable American unit. He deduced that the American public wouldn't stand for a long, protracted war that slowly consumed our finest youth. Ho Chi Minh also stated "you will kill ten of us; we will kill one of you, but in the end you will tire of it first." It soon became like being "between a rock and a hard place."

The fundamental difference between the two conflicting concepts lay in the understanding of our enemy, which already had the solution that escaped us. Their kind of insurgent-guerrilla-terrorist war *was a protracted war*. It was purposely drawn out and frustrating, so that the superior military force (ours) would soon tire of the slow attrition and depletion of our military units, sapping our will to continue fighting. But it took the people back home to make the decision to end it. Ho Chi Minh and Giap counted on that. They also knew that their enemy commander, Westmoreland, would fall into their trap and make the same mistakes the French had made just a few years before, on the same ground and against the very same enemy, but better equipped by China and Russia. Worse yet, *they* had written down exactly how they would accomplish it—and it was there for our reading, and more importantly, for our understanding.

By 1966, Marines in Vietnam had begun to understand the full scope of the war we were enmeshed in. Sadly, we had very few men like Lt. Colonel Bill Corson to take us all the way and develop a workable *counterinsurgency program*. The many years Corson spent in Asia gave him insights and an understanding of "this kind of war" that few American military men had. He spoke their languages, Chinese and Vietnamese. He knew the cultures, religions, politics, and even their military tactics and techniques at the guerrilla level that had been established by Mao and Giap in the People's War. Yet Corson was never given the opportunity to expand upon his successful CAP and heed the important lessons the French had provided us. It would have taken a Bill Corson to develop an *effective, comprehensive counterinsurgency doctrine and strategy, and even the type of training program* that would include *all* U.S. civilian and military personnel involved in the war. Apparently it asked too much from institutionalized leaders whose "last war" mentality and inability to see past briefing charts gave Corson no alternative. It remained an Army-Marine issue.

Had he not written *The Betrayal*, Bill Corson probably would, like Colonel David Hackworth (author of *About Face*), have written a blistering critique of the whole mess we had gotten bogged down in. Instead, Corson decided to open the kimono, tell the sick story of the incompetent American Agency for International Development program, and dissect the traitorous behavior of the South Vietnamese military leaders, much as John Paul Vann had done before that. At Camp Lejeune. I had focused on the guerrilla and his tactics—the British version practiced successfully in Malaya where *they won their war*. Marine generals like Krulak, Walt, Greene, and Simpson had studied that war and sought out Sir Robert Thompson, the architect of the British anti-terrorist program. It had all the essential elements of an effective counterinsurgency strategy. General Westmoreland's institutional military training and World War II experience would predominate. While he met with Sir Robert Thompson of Malaya fame, and tried to employ limited village

174

security, nevertheless, his search and destroy and body-count measures remained his credo for his four years. He remained a "big war" advocate to the very end.

U.S. military leaders also continued to ignore the people of Vietnam, who became pawns and victims of our faulty strategy as we pursued the "wrong war in the wrong place at the wrong time"—as Lt. General Paul Van Riper would label it almost 40 years later. Those very same lessons were not applied to the war in Iraq. Once again, an obtuse, arrogant Secretary of Defense ignored the lessons of that earlier war and, like McNamara and Westmoreland, put all of his military eggs into heavy, expensive weapons and a limited military force that enjoyed a brief "shock and awe" phase. Then, like in Vietnam, the big bombs and endless operations became a burden as once again we fought "the wrong war, in the wrong place at the wrong time." Corson was spinning in his grave! The ominous predictions of General Shineseki and General Schwarzkopf came true. The missing 300,000 were left at home. They were the follow-on security and administrative elements required to secure, control, and maintain infrastructures—*and the peace.*

Then, amazingly, like Westmoreland also did in Vietnam when he insisted on separate, distinct chains of command for American and Vietnamese military and paramilitary forces, Rumsfeld and his advisors shoved the Iraqis aside when a dozen divisions would have surrendered and *joined us* to save that war. Saddam's Shiite Generals were ready to do it. One of the massive blunders of that war, says Tom Ricks in his book, *Fiasco,* was Coalition Provisional Authority boss Paul Bremner's "decision" to disarm and dismiss the *whole* Iraqi Army after Baghdad fell. His witless act created many thousands of insurgents, those former soldiers who would be left without pay and sustenance of any kind. Instead, it had become an American war just like Vietnam, never acknowledging that Corson had it right all along. Three years after we entered the war in Iraq, it finally hit home (to all but Secretary of Defense Rumsfeld and his staff) that the real solution to winning that *unconventional war had to include a complete, comprehensive counterinsurgency program* that—unbelievably—the U.S. Army and Marine Corps tried to

175

initiate early in that war. Those "leaders" who *forgot the past* were reliving it. They would have to re-learn lessons that history provided.

While we never integrated the Vietnamese military with our own (and we kept them at arm's length with their own chain of command and institutional approach), Bremner's untimely dismissal of 400,000 Iraqi military in the early days of that war was a duplication of that ignorant Vietnam decision almost 40 years earlier. In Iraq we had a number of Shiite division commanders who were willing to join our bare-bones military force, which would remain overextended and devoid of any military resolution in that insurgent situation. Yet we had the solution to maintaining the full-blown security and sustaining the local Iraq infrastructures that a successful counterinsurgency program demands. Instead, these obtuse, obsolescent obstacles were managing a carbon-copy of our former war in Kuwait, in the same way, and with the same "shock and awe" approach. There was no way to speed up the Iraq war, even by charging about and blindly attacking the enemy. Marines were willing to control the people and resources, and to draw the enemy to them. We already knew that it would be a long attritional war.

In Vietnam, the Marine way (formulated by General Krulak and CMC Greene) could have taken many years, but it would have saved many young lives. And buying that time would allow advisors and Special Forces teams to train, equip, and motivate Vietnam's own military units to fight *their own* war. Ironically, it was also the U.S. Marines that first used tactical envelopments and heli-borne blocking positions by employing ready reaction forces when large-scale contact was made. Our earlier 1950s and 1960s Marine Corps test and development of heli-borne assault and vertical envelopment tactics laid the groundwork for its use in Vietnam. We also had experience in the years before the war, when our Shu-Fly heli-lifts of Vietnamese units gave us a better understanding of it.

Unfortunately, General Westmoreland didn't see it that way. He saw every major military unit as a World War II combat force, with front lines, two units up, one back, and hot chow in the rear. Alternatively, he and LBJ sent out battalions to "develop the situation" with virtually no intelligence as to how big an enemy force was. But he was positive that large NVA and Viet Cong units were simply waiting for his U.S. units to engage them. His antiquated World War II Army tactics kept soldiers frustrated and exhausted, mentally and physically, as they executed one major action after another—*for four years*. Even the Army of Vietnam (ARVN) small unit training at the National Training Center at Van Kiep (where my own Vietnamese Marines wasted more than a full month) had virtually no counter-guerrilla tactics taught or considered. Instead, conventional squad, company, and battalion tactics, right out of World War II and Korean War training manuals, were still taught as the gospel and doctrine for that war.

My Vietnamese Marine Corps officers who witnessed this obsolete training were doubtful and critical. At least the Army's Air Cavalry, its Special Forces, and Colonel Dave Hackworth had gotten it right in "countering" guerrillas. And there is no doubt that most American combat units learned their lessons the hard way. Each battalion, swift-boat squadron, helicopter unit, and the "new guy" was soon blooded. Yet it is a fact of that war: our grunts rarely lost a battle, but we did pay a heavy, bloody price for those victories. Sadder yet, Westmoreland's credo still remained the same: "I don't know where they are out there, but go out there and get 'em. Keep racking up my body counts!" Our price (count) was 58,000 American lives. Like General Harkins before him, he would not hear any criticism and certainly had not read the "French Lessons Learned in Southeast Asia." He adamantly refused to admit that his blitzkrieg combat assaults had destroyed too many villages—as well as the potential loyalty of the many villagers he blasted. Those villages and graveyards were ancient and sacred ground. It seems that he truly believed all villagers were "Viet Cong sympathizers." During his time, he never merged U.S. and Vietnamese units, preferring separate chains of command that puzzled most Vietnamese officers.

Other unique, individual Marine initiatives like Captain Steve Illes's "smoke 'em out" technique suffered a similar fate. Steve discovered that a neat mixture of itching powder and tear gas (CS) could be employed very effectively. He began using it in the caves that Marines discovered on Marble Mountain, right next to the

Marine perimeter at Danang. Smoked out, the Viet Cong were forced to flee their many hiding places underground, itching like hell as they ran. Only after the war would it be disclosed that the Viet Cong had "thousands of miles" of trenches and tunnels to hide in. Then, we found out that the guerrilla armies literally lived in those burrows, right under our military bases.

I was really surprised to learn that one of the biggest tunnel complexes was right next to my Vietnamese Marine base camp at Thu Duc, where I would win my Tet party yo-yo drinking prize. Big Red One, a camp just up the road, was literally on top of a huge 50-square-mile tunnel complex that would not be "discovered" until a few years after the war. Saigon was controlled from that cave and bunker complex. After the war, visitors to Vietnam crawled through the tunnels, like a Disneyland guided tour. We never found them when we routinely chased fleeing guerrillas from one village to another. The guerrillas just disappeared, or so it seemed. Why not? It was a tactic that worked for them: *dispersion*. We eventually learned to locate the tunnels and a dozen other underground structures used.

Alas, Steve's life-saving inventiveness would also be for naught. The North Vietnamese (not the Viet Cong, the ones we were smoking out) immediately presented this "violation of the rules" of war to the Geneva Convention, where disputes over weaponry were highlighted—as if *any* of our enemies played by such rules. The effective smoke-and-gas mechanism was ruled inhumane, and Steve was put out of business. We soon learned that we were almost helpless in ferreting out the Viet Cong, except by sacrificing our "tunnel rats," the brave young Marines who crawled in after them. Other military options also were negated, such as bombing the Red River dikes to flood Hanoi. Worse yet, all efforts failed to cut off the Ho Chi Minh trail and end the war.

The tunnels concealed many thousands of Viet Cong, and even the hardcore North Vietnamese troops throughout Vietnam. They had been digging those tunnels for 30 or 40 years. Many had been dug during battles with the French, and then were continued during the U.S. involvement. We would learn that many villagers had a tunnel-digging schedule of a set number of meters each week. Later,

I watched a column of unarmed civilians trek up into the hills of Bong Son each evening to dig their three meters per night. It was Giap's *People's War, People's Army* in practice. The North Vietnamese had terrorists who would practice some of the most inhumane and illegal forms of warfare on their own people and on our downed pilots, and *that* never seemed to faze the Geneva folks. We rolled over, kissed their butts, and watched our leaders take garbage as we blundered into our worst war in history."

Steve Illes's machine would have forced this elusive enemy out of the ground, where we could easily have defeated them by massing forces by helicopter and other mobile means as we caught them in the open. They would have retreated into the villages, and we had a plan for that as well. Highly effective village cordon-and-search techniques developed by the British and introduced at the CGWC would have been successful in ferreting them out of their village holes and destroying them. *This was possible very early in that miserable war!* Instead, we relied on a worse solution—Agent Orange, which harmed thousands of Americans and "innocent" Vietnamese civilians. We still lack the real count.

As I read the weekly reports coming from Vietnam, it was obvious that we knew almost nothing about fighting "this kind of war." Marines were learning firsthand the horrors of the booby trap: thousands of missing limbs and immobilized paraplegics in veteran's hospitals. We continued to pay a very high price while ignorant politicians and top generals waged "yesterday's war" in their futile and obsolete way. Bill Corson, Dave Clements, and Steve Illes were imaginative thinkers whose ideas were rejected.

As I mentioned previously, another military man whose sound facts and recommendations were totally rejected was John Paul Vann, an Army advisor who tried to tell everyone in Washington about his factual experience with the real enemy: the Army of Vietnam. He was in Vietnam well before the first Marines landed at Danang, and what he found was an enemy we didn't know existed. He watched an inept Vietnamese Army general employ a useless military approach, destroyed a village, and underestimated the Viet Cong. Then, this same general and his ilk boasted to Washington that "we were winning the war." Not only did in-country U.S. generals kowtow to these frauds, but Washington politicians flooded these crooks with massive amounts of U.S. aid and money, which they pilfered with no accountability at all.

This early ignorance would continue during General Westmoreland's tenure, and it led us to the very disaster that Vann had predicted before we had even entered the war in 1965. What he tried to warn us about came true only a few years after his first warning. Our politicians and generals dismissed everything he said because *they knew better*. History would soon document our total failure to understand and correctly prosecute that "different, difficult" war. It was virtually unknown to most military men, even those with orders to Vietnam. They learned it the hard way.

One lesson was obvious: the old ways are not effective! The attitude of "all ears must stay closed while we continue to make the next rank" and "we must be sure to fight the *last* war" led to disastrous consequences. It would be more accurate to repeat "War is too important to be left to the generals." The tragic failure of our generals to even read the *French Lessons of the War in Indo China*, as translated by Colonel Victor Croizat, underscores the colossal ignorance of General Westmoreland and many others.

Colonel Dave Hackworth, one of the most decorated and best combat leaders in Vietnam, would surrender his own career after four years of trying to educate the Army brass in how to effectively fight that war. His book, *About Face*, tells the sad story. It is a tragic account of our blind political leadership, combat arrogance, and our failure to know the enemy we were fighting. No grunt was as successful as Dave Hackworth in fighting and defeating the guerrillas and NVA, with very light casualties to his own troops. Yet he was totally ignored when he tried to tell it like it was. He gave up a brilliant Army career to let America know on ABC television how badly the war was being fought, with few real leaders. With three wars under his belt, he had to quit a career he loved. Later, he was back telling his story again, and some of us listened. Lessons are learned the hard way.

The generals arrive to check out CGWC training.
(Official MCB Camp Lejeune, NC, photos, 1966)

In 1964 when I proposed the CGWC, I knew nothing about the earlier Vann conflicts. Even though some of us at the CGWC were enjoying its new role, and our commandant and my division commander believed in it, there was still great opposition to "that kind of training." It was still anchored in the minds of the old Corps. It was the summer of 1966 when I received a message from the division that a group of retired Marine generals would visit the CGWC to see and evaluate what was going on there. They also wanted to gain some insight into this Vietnam "situation" that active duty generals like CMC Greene, Krulak, Simpson, and Robertson were emphasizing, and then supporting at Camp Lejeune. They arrived in two helicopters in civilian clothes. I recognized most of them as very distinguished Marines with proven combat records in World War II and Korea. They were officers we respected and admired. They fought the real wars and were true heroes to us younger officers. They were, in our eyes, the best of the Marine Corps! I had committed my life to their Marine Corps. So, I looked forward to meeting and briefing them.

First, I gave them an overview of the guerrilla war we were fighting and why the CGWC mission was so important for the unique training of young Marines. My introduction would be followed by a short tour of the village, the booby-trap trail, and the other training sites. I had hardly started my presentation before their penetrating questions flew at me—followed by their critical remarks. "Why do we need this specialized training? Marines have fought in these kinds of wars before, with traditional training. Why are you focusing this type of training on a single theater of operations, when Marines can 'fight in every clime and place, from dawn to setting sun'—right out of our Marine Corps hymn?" They were obviously bothered by the commandant's directive that supported our specialized training at the CGWC (focused only on Vietnam), and also that he had ordered all the other Marine Corps commands to come review it for incorporation into their training syllabus. There was no way this upstart Marine officer would ever convince these distinguished officers of the uniqueness of this different war, and I darn well didn't! They would have to learn it the hard way, and I am sure they did a few years later.

Ten years later, every single general would look back, puzzled and confused, to try to fathom that very different war we "lost"—and one they truly failed to accept, much less to even try to understand. Each of them had trained in the same basic courses I had taken at Quantico, which taught strategies that had been effective in fighting wars prior to Vietnam. But there were major differences! In their former wars, they could actually see their enemy. He was waiting for them on a hill, a mountain, or a beach. He was there, and you found him any time you wanted to. You fought him and shot him when you chose to. You recognized him when you saw him, face to face. This approach was good enough.

I knew it would be futile to try to press any points and explain the differences, especially when so many *stars* were falling on me that day. So I chose to exit gracefully and let the sergeants take the generals on short tours of the training areas and village. When they were done, they left as angry and hostile as when they had arrived.

Within a week of their visit, two VNMC *covans* that had just returned from their first advisory tours paid me a visit. My friend Captain Jim McWilliams and Lt. Col Bill Leftwich were assigned to the Tactics Section at the Marine Corps Basic School, Quantico, Virginia. They were checking out our CGWC program, especially the village, where we stepped each company through the cordon-and-search operation after being heli-lifted (simulated) into positions around the target, our Vietnamese village. Marines would then learn how to screen off and secure villagers, gain intelligence, and search out Viet Cong hiding in the many clever places that we gleaned from Marine combat action reports.

I had already heard of the exploits and near-death experience of Bill, who now wore a Navy Cross and a long pale scar across his face. He also had been awarded the Vietnamese Cross of Gallantry (with palm), which is equivalent to the U.S. Medal of Honor. Bill's VNMC Task Force Alpha had engaged and defeated large enemy units in his intense combat tour as the senior advisor to the famous VNMC Lt. Colonel Yen. Bill's heroism, combat skill, and capacity to outwit and out-fight the best of General Giap's combat forces had earned him the distinction of being named "the best advisor in Vietnam" and the one U.S. military leader that dozens of our correspondents sought to join on operations. Westmoreland also heralded him as the best combat officer we had in Vietnam. During this visit, Bill told us how well our U.S. Marine Corps advisors were organizing and training the Vietnamese Marine Corps, ensuring that it was an exact copy of our own U.S. Marine Corps. Its organization, tactics, and techniques were virtually the same as ours, but its growth would be much slower—that would take many years and many *covans*. When Bill returned in early 1966, the Vietnamese Marines had just four battalions.

At the time of his visit, I was unaware that Bill had already made dozens of speeches about his *covan* tour and had authored a number of articles that I later read. How I wished that Bill could have been there when the generals visited, to give them a firsthand view of how different this war was and why we really needed the training at the CGWC! As it turned out, Jim and Bill also established a Vietnam

Village at the Basic School, and every Marine lieutenant who went to Vietnam knew how to conduct the very intricate but effective cordon-and-search procedure. Bill was a firm advocate of Bill Corson's and General Walt's CAP program and the cordon-and-search tactics. In August 1970, on his second tour, and as the CO of 2nd Battalion, 1st Marines, he and Major John Grinalds (his S-3 officer and another former *covan*) executed an almost perfect heli-borne cordon-and-search raid at Cam Sa. The operation resulted in the killing and capture of 24 Viet Cong commanders and a key guerrilla cadre with a large number of documents that detailed the operations and activities of Viet Cong District III. It was heralded as a counter-guerrilla classic, and Bill was once again cited as the most imaginative Marine CO in Vietnam.

It also was Bill Leftwich who demonstrated that he could "shift the gears" in a guerrilla war and match anything Giap threw at him. Whether it was main-force Viet Cong, NVA PAVN regiments, or the local village guerrillas, Bill understood that enemy and employed the most effective "countering" tactics and techniques required at the time. He took the fight to the enemy, which is exactly what we taught Marines at the CGWC. Village cordon and search tactics, the Gurkha drill, ambush techniques, and attack on a guerrilla camp were *offensive* (not defensive) operations. No war can be won relying solely on the defense, nor can a football team win with just defensive players. Yet by the time I would get to Vietnam, General Giap's strategy had most U.S. and Vietnamese units relegated to *defensive* positions.

Later, in his second tour, Bill became the 1st Reconnaissance Battalion CO. True to his heroic and professional character, he flew out to a difficult mountain site to attempt the extraction of one of his reconnaissance teams. Tragically, the helicopter crashed, killing Bill and 11 Marines. I knew and admired Bill Leftwich at Annapolis, where he was brigade commander. That he would excel in the Marine Corps as the perfect Marine officer was never in doubt, nor would any of us ever doubt he would one day become the commandant. To me, Lt. Colonel Bill Leftwich was the essence of the guerrilla grunt that knew and understood his enemy at every level of combat in that difficult and different war. Thankfully, he also thought outside the conventional box and quickly executed sound, effective counter-guerrilla tactics and techniques that outmaneuvered and defeated main force enemy units. A true professional, he set the example for CGWC trainees, who learned to use those successful tactics and techniques as our motto stated: *to defeat the guerrilla in his own environment.*

In the summer of 1966 the CGWC was in full operation, and each training battalion would assist us in putting the village back together once one of its rifle companies had completed that phase of the training. They also acted as guerrillas on our final field exercise, when a rifle company had to demonstrate exactly what we had taught them. Gunny Jordan showed no mercy in his night ambush training. Unfortunately for the squads and platoons, executing an ambush was a skill held by my own young men, who had grown up on the land and moved like panthers at night. The ambush was a difficult tactic to learn. Dog tags were removed and canteens were taped, but a low cough or slight movement would alert the guerrillas, who were to move down a road through the ambush. When an ambush failed, Jordan mustered the noisy unit, chewed some butt, and had them set it up again. This procedure had to be repeated several times before they got the point. *There is only one good way to conduct an ambush—that is as silent as the night!* Even "noisy" Seals and Special Forces did it many times.

Years later, the toughest Seal of them all, Dick Marcinko, belittled the CGWC ambush course by writing in *Rogue Warrior* that it was no challenge. I don't know what he thought an ambush involved; my pros knew better! The "rogue warrior" hadn't been to Vietnam as yet, but Jordan, Bob, and Doug had. They were the experienced ambush experts and conducted successful ambushes and combat patrols with more kills than most ever made. They told a different story about the training—one Marcinko didn't like.

Village operations were the same with Bob Atkinson. Having already experienced this sort of activity in Vietnam, he allowed no half-hearted efforts. Bill Leftwich and Jim McWilliams also gave him very high marks for the exceptional work he had put into the authentic village. Excellence was not only expected in training, it was *demanded* of everyone, including our own guerrillas. By the time a rifle company had finished our 75-hour, day and night training, their butts were dragging. Everyone praised our CGWC training as the best they'd ever had. In addition, it assured us that these trainees would understand what they might face in Vietnam.

I would soon have evidence of the usefulness of this training. It came when I was on Deckhouse V, the first amphibious landing in the Delta, which was my first actual combat action just a few days after I arrived in Vietnam. Back on board the LPH-2 (the Iwo Jima, a new amphibious assault ship of the Navy) after the landing and the 10-day operation in Kien Hoa, I was getting hosed down to remove the mud that covered me from my waist to my boots. Many Marines of the 1st Battalion, 9th Marines were also returning to the ship. Several of them spotted me and came running over. "Major, it was exactly like you taught us at the CGWC—the booby traps, hiding places, tunnels, and even the village itself was like yours. We were ready for them, thanks to you and the guys at Lejeune." How I wished those visiting generals could have been there to hear them! It's not often that someone like me or a training officer gets real feedback (and an actual combat critique) of the training we gave them. But there on the Iwo Jima, right after a major landing, those Marines I had previously trained made my day, my month, my year, and even my young Marine Corps career. I hoped this news would make it back to Camp Lejeune.

After the CGWC's reputation surfaced, we were deluged with requests from other Army and Navy units to attend the course. Many foreign and U.S. civilian visitors also wanted to see it for themselves, as did a dozen or more newspaper, magazine, and media teams who wrote and filmed our story. But our finest comment came from a former French officer who had served in Vietnam, fighting against the Viet Minh. He also was born there, so he knew that unique Asian world. His comment upon leaving was, "This is the best training center I have ever seen. The training is the best that any soldier could ever get if he is going to fight in Vietnam and defeat the enemy there." Finally, our efforts and difficult work paid off!

Not everyone, however, was so complimentary or supportive of our training, or of the center itself. We had forgotten about some of the local guys. Unfortunately, the CGWC was many miles from the base, way out in the boonies where the boozed-up locals could easily get their drunken kicks. But this time, they would regret it! One weekend night, someone decided that our sign had to go, so they pushed it over and drove a truck over it. We had it repaired and assured the carpenter shop that this would *never* happen again. I told Corporal Harrington to rig the sign with his best booby-trap trigger. I wanted metal plates on the posts in the ground and metal plates one inch away from them, so that if anyone pushed over the sign, the plates would touch and an explosion would occur. In the trees above, Harrington rigged a C-4 "necklace." It hung 20 feet above the sign in a semi-circle. I had to admit that Harrington knew his stuff.

Several days later, a nearby farmer told us he had heard one heck of an explosion at about 2:00 in the morning. It rattled his windows even a few miles away, scaring his poor wife so badly that she thought the U.S. was being invaded that night. But somewhere near Sneads Ferry, a few disoriented drunks were trying to get the loud ringing sound out of their ears. Even today, they may still be babbling incoherently to strangers, wondering what really happened that scary night. The sign was never touched again, or probably even breathed on by anyone. I am sure *that* bar story was never told! I can almost hear the babbling, brain-dead vandals still yelling "Man, was that a f------ blast! Let's try some outhouses next."

In the fall of 1966 I visited HQMC to inquire about my own status and assignment to Vietnam. Since I had just returned to the States from my flagship tour in 1963, I was told that I was not due for orders for a year or more. Then I asked the infantry monitor if there was any other way I could get orders to Vietnam. He told me that I could request advisory duty. I asked for the Vietnamese Marines, and just six months later would join Bill Leftwich's Task Force Alpha as a VNMC *covan* in the biggest operation of the war, which was called Junction City. But unlike Bill's heavy combat experience against Giap's superior PAVN regiments in 1965, this massive, 30,000-man operation was too big to succeed. It didn't!

Westmoreland was positive that we would fight Giap's regiments all along the Cambodian border.

At that time few Marines had any idea that General Giap was implementing a major logistic strategy and had the Ho Chi Minh trail extended well inside Laos, on the western side of the Annamese mountains. By supporting the Pathet Lao and seizing parts of Laos, Giap's massive resupply and troop reinforcement of PAVN forces in the south was no longer constrained by the narrow and vulnerable trails along the 700-mile borders (Laos and Cambodia). *This other brilliant strategy of Giap proved to be the most important of the war.* An ill-conceived U.S. political and military mandate denied our U.S, forces entry and access to Laos, Cambodia and North Vietnam. It also included the entire Ho Chi Minh Trail. That ignorant strategic and tactical decision and our failure to bomb the Red River dikes and flood Hanoi ensured that Giap's protracted, drawn-out war could be sustained—and "won." He knew that Americans at home would tire of a long, endless war and rebel against our large daily casualties. This is the Vietnam War I entered, to do my job as a *covan*.

On the heels of my request for orders to Vietnam came another set of orders to Notre Dame University as the Assistant Military Officer Instructor (MOI). What a bizarre thing to happen! At any other time, I would have loved to be part of legendary Rockne history and see one of the best teams in the country play football. To the amazement of my buddies, I turned down the orders. An old Fort Benning Marine friend received them instead.

That fall I began to look for my replacement as the officer in charge of the CGWC. That officer was Charlie Sampson, and I was elated. He really liked what we were doing, and I knew he would carry on the work I had started. Much later I would run into Charlie again, after Vietnam, where he had been a junior aide for General Westmoreland, the overall commander of all U.S. forces in Vietnam. He confirmed many things that we all suspected—such as LBJ looking over Westmoreland's shoulder and telling him when and where to commit his units that he (LBJ) never knew, never commanded, and had no clue how they (or any U.S. military unit) should be deployed! Hell, it was tough enough doing just that when you were on the ground. War was too important for the lieutenants! Likewise, Westmoreland had a "big war" syndrome. He was convinced he could bait or trap very large NVA and Viet Cong units into set-piece battles. So, we chased about madly for *four years* in that totally useless tactical approach. Charlie's inside tales of that tour would fill another large book.

The time drew nearer for me to leave for Vietnam. I would receive my orders to report to the Vietnamese Marine Corps before Christmas of 1966. It was a very hard time for Gwenny and my family. The news from Vietnam was not good. She was just barely adjusting to the news of Captain Tom Kennedy's death. He had lived just down the street from us and was killed in the same Marine organization that I was reporting to. Worse, I wouldn't be home to enjoy Christmas with my four girls—a real bummer. Many Camp Lejeune Marines had orders. It was the price we paid.

Gwenny's sister, Joy, had come to visit again. The 20-year-old Australian beauty had numerous young officers at Camp Lejeune standing in line to date her, with Gwenny acting as chaperone and "mother hen" to ensure that her kid sister escaped with her life—and she did. There were few single girls at Camp Lejeune. My mother also had come to visit and see her son off to the war. So, I had a trio of women to worry about me, plus my four little girls who were too young to even remotely understand why daddy was leaving again. For them, it would be exciting to go to Australia.

I had been away a lot at Lejeune, just as my daughters got used to my being home with them. Now I was leaving for some new place—and their mommy and grandmother were crying about it, a lot! I tried to minimize my own concerns, and Gwenny's, by taking her on a trip to Annapolis to re-experience where we were married and what we had done on our honeymoon route. While we enjoyed the time alone, the knowledge that I was leaving hung heavily on everything we did. Sadly, we had to go back to Lejeune.

There was no easy way to go to war; I was one of the many thousands who would have to experience that fate. The families suffer the most when the "soldier" leaves because it is a duty that only he can understand. I had some very mixed emotions. I was a professional Marine officer and my duty called for me to go to war like my friends were doing. My profession was war, and I had trained myself and thousands of others to fight in the worst war we would ever enter. But my girls were also my life, and I can only say that the professional soldier also finds it very hard to leave his children and rush off to war. Now, it was my turn.

The CGWC training days and the pretend days were no longer my single focus. I had done everything in my power and imagination to get the CGWC started, and I knew I had succeeded. My job there was over, and the CGWC was going great guns. I also knew it was in the hands of exceptional, dedicated Marines like Captain Charlie Sampson, who had relieved me. Charlie would later be assigned to General Westmoreland's staff in Saigon and witness even more unbelievable Westmoreland-LBJ lunacy and ineptness. Since it was now my turn to head for Vietnam, I remember looking into the faces of the young kids I had been training for more than a year, I recall feeling a deep sadness in knowing that some of them would not return alive. I only hoped I would! But I put the thought aside as I packed my bags to leave and started focusing on the tasks that lay ahead of me. It had been two years since Grassroots '64, and now it was the real thing. I knew I had done my best to teach some Marines how to survive.

The top hit song that fall was *Softly as I Leave You* by John Gary. It was a plaintive, beautiful verse about a man leaving behind those he loves. In my case, it reduced three women to a waterfall of tears, while I could only try to minimize their sadness. My little girls were so young and so innocent; they didn't grasp the gravity of my situation. Gwenny would take them home to Australia (with Joy's help) on the Oransay, an Australian ocean liner. Gwenny's mother insisted on having my family visit while I was in Vietnam so she could enjoy her grandchildren.

By Thanksgiving, all the plans were in place, and we would drive cross-country in early December, taking the southern route to escape the ice and snow. At Camp Lejeune, just two years after I had warned the unbelievers at Tom Glidden's home that all of us would be fighting in Vietnam, it was my turn to go. Many officers at Camp

Lejeune were also getting their orders. There were many believers this time. The fortunate ones were those who had an opportunity to train at the CGWC. In the time that I was officer in charge of the school, we trained thousands of Marines, Seabee battalions, and a few volunteer Navy Seals and Army Special Forces. Other Army, Navy and Air Force visitors had heard of our reputation for realistic counter-guerrilla training and requested to attend. But we could handle only our own rifle companies and supporting units, as well as Marine visitors from other commands. Two years later, after I left, that total would exceed 20,000. Doug and Charlie were deluged with requests to train any and all that they could squeeze into their busy schedules. I would later meet and serve with many CGWC "graduates" in Vietnam. Yet I had to put this part of my life behind me and begin applying these lessons and techniques to a real guerrilla war I would soon begin.

In 2003, the U.S. invaded Iraq to depose Saddam Hussein and continue our search for his weapons of mass destruction. At that time, the majority of our congressmen and Americans in general supported this act of war that came after our 100-hour war liberated Kuwait in 1991 (Desert Storm) where a powerful, superior allied force of arms overwhelmed Saddam's military. They sent the lucky survivors in pell-mell retreat back to Baghdad. Order was restored in Kuwait and the Arab nations in the Middle East breathed a sigh of relief. It seemed simple: employ the latest weaponry in our arsenal, and fast "shock and awe" seemed to be the answer to any conflict.

What we failed to remember was the muster of 650,000 U.S. and coalition troops and weaponry that took almost a full year. Then, General Norman Schwarzkopf took his time and put his conventional forces in place, executing an almost flawless assault upon the outgunned, outfought Iraqi army units. The end came quickly, and our Desert Storm heroes returned to a grateful and celebrating America. There was no "Vietnam return" this time! However, the top combat commanders, including Schwarzkopf and Powell, were all Vietnam veterans. They made damn sure the earlier Vietnam mistakes were not made, and knowing exactly how this enemy would fight, on a classic desert battlefield, our prior training for this kind of warfare paid off in spades. This time we did not "fight the last war" (in this case, Vietnam). We adapted to this new conflict, and trained and prepared for it when we had solid intelligence and specific knowledge of our enemy's strategy.

When America's military was so successful in its execution of Desert Storm, our own military establishment—specifically the Pentagon—spent the next decade testing, buying, and building the most expensive, technical, and destructive military machine in our history. No future enemy would dare stand up to it. Didn't the "shock and awe" that it produced guarantee a quick, decisive victory in Kuwait? Saddam's million-man Iraqi army would be no match for the same tactics and technology once they experienced the same overwhelming force of arms. As it turned out, the Pentagon powerbrokers forgot another past and put all their destructive eggs in one bountiful basket of billion-dollar bombers, smart bombs, and mechanized mobile forces, *with minimal combat troops on the ground*. They truly believed that "shock and awe" guaranteed a decisive "victory." It did—for just a moment. It ended in Baghdad when Saddam's statue was toppled, the Iraqi military folded, and its surrendering soldiers quickly became insurgents. It was the same old lesson we failed to learn—unable *to shift the gears of war*—just as we did in Vietnam 40 years earlier.

Those who forgot the past were pompous Pentagon puppet masters. Unfortunately, the military men who brought up the past and warned that we had a very different war to fight (as we did in Vietnam) were dismissed, ignored, humiliated, or forced into early retirement. It was a few experienced Vietnam veterans like Generals Schwarzkopf, Powell, and Shinseki who saw the need for enhancing the depth of our thin military machine. It lacked the additional several hundred thousand troops that were required to secure, patrol, police, and maintain the complex urban infrastructures and sources of intelligence. Every town and city in Iraq required this attention if it was to survive and remain a stable society. Those few veterans knew that a bare-bones "shock and awe" force could not accomplish that larger job. And it damn well didn't.

That same conventional shock action was also tried in the early years in Vietnam. Westmoreland ordered us to execute his massive (30,000 troops—Operation Junction City) and other large, useless, and wasteful operations that leveled the villages, destroyed social and economic infrastructures, alienated the populace, and failed miserably. We ignored the growing, hidden enemy that eventually outlasted us. Giap's strategic shift from Phase I (the People's War and its guerrillas) to Phase III (conventional army warfare) was unmatched even as it evolved. It was his modern PAVN army, with tanks and artillery, that fought us at Khe Sanh and later swarmed into Saigon in 1975. For most of the war, they had a smaller military machine than ours.

Years later in Iraq, we initially encountered a Phase III military force in "the Queen of Battles" (Saddam Hussein's pompous boast). But that main-force army dissolved into an insurgent army, the exact reverse of what Giap had done in Vietnam almost 40 years earlier. Yet, having learned no lessons from the Vietnam War, our military units were *unable to shift the gears of war*. It was the same scenario we experienced when we entered Vietnam: there were simply not enough troops to do the larger job. Westmoreland continually appealed to LBJ for more troops until 500,000 were in the country. It still was not enough—and the situation was the same in Iraq. We learned the hard way that sparse, front-line combat units had their hands full and became bogged down in protecting our own supply lines, equipment, bases, hotels, and hooches. Giap's Phase I and II guerrilla focus worked in Vietnam. Surprisingly, Saddam made a similar shift in Iraq.

General Shinseki, the Army Chief of Staff, had tried to warn Rumsfeld that *his* meager forces lacked the depth (300,000 to 400,000 more security and infrastructure control troops) that General Schwarzkopf made certain he had before going into Kuwait. One Army commander, who was attacking along the main road leading to Baghdad, with his brigade strung out for miles, saw insurgents drive into nearby ammo dumps and haul away tons of shells. When asked why he did not attack them, he lamented that he barely had enough troops to secure his own convoys. But later he suffered improvised explosive device (IED) casualties from the same shells the insurgents placed on other roads. Security was hardly a consideration when using "shock and awe."

It is obvious today that several hundred thousand Iraqi troops, combined with our own U.S. forces, could have secured and controlled those vulnerable roads and the many ammo dumps (with Shinseki's thousands). It would have denied the insurgent those deadly IEDs, sparing us many casualties. They also would have controlled the population, the urban centers, and all resources. Most importantly, we would have had superior intelligence when they maintained and controlled the population and infrastructures. Combined U.S.–Iraqi military teams would have culled out the insurgents with the help of the secure, non-terrorized people. Much like his predecessor, General Westmoreland, the obtuse, arrogant Secretary of Defense Donald Rumsfeld dismissed this effective strategy, which was the only solution that would have worked. His limited "shock and awe" strategy blew up in his face. It turned out to be a momentary military orgasm.

Finally, what occurred when I attended the prestigious Naval War College in 1975 added credence to the fact that our propensity was to simply ignore and "forget the past." Since I had MBA teaching experience in evening programs for the University of Southern California, the University of Maryland, Golden Gate University, Chapman University, and other colleges and universities. I was asked to teach at the war college. I had assumed that my background in counterinsurgency, as well as my experience as a Vietnamese Marine Corps advisor, would qualify me to teach in the Strategy Department. Imagine my surprise when the head of that department announced, "We will not be discussing the Vietnam War this year. It is just too controversial." And we didn't—not for an hour, not in a single lecture! Visionary admirals who planned the Navy's successful strategy in World War II must have been spinning in their graves at that amazing pronouncement! If this was a war college, then why could we not even mention *my war*?

The college had on its staff a distinguished, experienced Vietnam combat veteran with both Marine Force recon and CAP village experience. Bing West, a former Assistant Secretary of Defense, was a professor and dean of Research from 1970 to 1980. He would have taught us many lessons. I met him and was very impressed. His writings, *Small Unit Action in Vietnam* and *The Village,* are still bestsellers today. Later, he covered Iraq by visiting the most difficult combat areas and wrote, *The March Up, Taking Baghdad with the U.S. Marines,* and *A Frontline Account of the Battle of Fallujah.* He also was named by the Los Angeles Times as "one of the top ten journalists covering Iraq." What an education Bing West could have provided, so we would not "forget the past." Instead, we rigorously studied an ancient war: Peliponnesian, followed by World War II. Instead we studied ancient wars, then World War II. The abstruse operations research and math left 80 percent of the class baffled.

Instead, at the request of the attending foreign students that they receive counterinsurgency instruction, I was tapped by the admiral to prepare a lecture series after he had reviewed my military record. I was elated, but soon found myself in deep trouble when they challenged me with the question, "What do you know about this subject? You lost the war!" Other queries were almost as bad, and I felt like I had stepped into an academic fiasco. Yet once they gave me a chance to tell it like it was and use my CGWC lecture subjects and my combat experience in Vietnam, they loosened up and it was great. For my efforts (and the excellent instructor critiques), I received a Letter of Commendation from the War College admiral.

That year, 1975, Saigon and Vietnam fell to Giap's conventional army assault into the south. But in 1972, the South Vietnamese military forces had defeated his army during the 10-month Easter Offensive in Quang Tri. Giap retreated and took three years to recover. He played Westmoreland's body-count game so well that it cost him his best soldiers—the heavy price he chose to pay. With few of his previous soldiers left to muster another big offensive, he began recruiting 14- and 40-year olds. Then, Russia provided massive equipment support to outfit his depleted weaponry and helped train new troops.

In 1973, Henry Kissinger (much to the amazement of President Thieu) sold out our Vietnamese ally and negotiated a *separate* political surrender that sold out the rest of us as well. Although the South Vietnamese "victors," led by my own Vietnamese Marines with the best ARVN units, proved they could defeat the last of Giap's remaining forces, another level of betrayal was at work: Senators Kennedy and Frank Church led the charge to immediately cut off all financial aid, resupply, repair, and re-arming. That left them totally destitute and easy prey for Giap's last 1975 offensive. But in 1972, just a limited show of force by our U.S. troops that still had the capacity to enter the combat scene would have led to a quick negotiated settlement. Many years later, this outstanding fact was readily admitted by General Giap's own generals when interviewed by Michael Lind, author of *Vietnam, the Necessary War*. Not a single soldier, sailor, airman, or Marine was defeated! We had no part in that political surrender.

Yet all of this was quickly forgotten and buried by a hostile American public and our posturing politicians. Worse, our biased news media had long lost faith in winning our longest war, although the Vietnamese had an arguable "victory." Instead, retreating political "leaders" abandoned an ally who fought and died for eight long years, leaving them to the recriminations that followed. It is part of a sick, sad past that some of us would never forget—ever.

A few of us stuck out our necks in a bold attempt to educate people and change the status quo. Was it worth it? You bet it was! Today's Marines are trained in both counterinsurgency and our amphibious operations. And you can bet our war colleges, military universities and schools are now teaching both conventional and COIN strategies today so future officers and NCOs will be able to "shift the gears of war" and employ proven tactics, techniques, and technologies that lets them fight and survive in any clime and place. Our lessons are finally learned. We won't forget the past!

DEPARTMENT OF THE NAVY
HEADQUARTERS UNITED STATES MARINE CORPS
WASHINGTON, D.C. 20380

MCBul 1510
AO3C21-mek
10 Jun ,1966

MARINE CORPS BULLETIN 1510

From: Commandant of the Marine Corps
To: Distribution List
Subj: Counterguerrilla Warfare Training, Conduct by the Commanding
       General, 2nd Marine Division, Fleet Marine Force, Atlantic

Ref: (a) MCO 1510.10

1. <u>Purpose</u>: To promulgate information concerning the subject training
and invite CONUS commanders to tour the training area established at
Camp Lejeune, North Carolina.

2. <u>Background</u>. As a part of program to implement reference (a), the
Commanding General, 2nd Marine Division established an Infantry Unit
Course and a Counterguerrilla Warfare Training Team. The Infantry Unit
Course is a ten day block of instruction designed to train rifle and reconnaissance companies in counterguerrilla warfare. The Training Team
provides instruction and assists the assigned unit in the conduct of the
course. An authentic Vietnamese environment, including a village, was
constructed to add realism to the training and increase troop motivation.

3. <u>Information</u>. The training facilities developed in conjunction with this
program are considered excellent vehicles to orient training towards RVN
operations. CONUS commanders are invited to send representatives to
observe the training and training facilities developed by the 2nd Marine
Division to assist in developing their own RVN oriented training programs.
Temporary additional duty costs must be borne by local commands.

4. <u>Action</u>. CONUS commanders desiring to send representatives to observe
this training submit requests directly to Commanding General, 2nd Marine
Division. Requests should be submitted two weeks prior to the date desired.

5. <u>Reserve Applicability</u>. This bulletin applies to the Marine Corps Reserve

CMC "suggests" that CONUS Marine commands send their representatives to visit our *authentic* training center. A large number of foreign visitors, including veterans of British, French, Philippine, Danish, and Dutch insurgencies, also visited, as did the Swedish ambassador and his staff.

CLARK W. THOMPSON
9TH DISTRICT, TEXAS

MEMBER COMMITTEE ON
WAYS AND MEANS

Congress of the United States
House of Representatives
Washington, D. C.   20515

September 19, 1966

Captain Robert L. Fischer
Officer-in-Charge
Counterguerrilla Warfare Center
2d Marine Division, FMF
Camp Lejeune, North Carolina

My dear Captain Fischer:

The time spent with you last week, even though
it was all too short, left me with a new and grati-
fying outlook on the war in Viet Nam. I realized as
never before how completely prepared our Marines will
be when their time comes to go into action over there.

Thanks for showing me around and thanks for what
you are doing for Americans young and old.

With kindest regards and best wishes.

Sincerely yours,

Clark W. Thompson

CWT/at

A visiting congressman gives the CGWC his approval.

THE SECRETARY OF THE NAVY

WASHINGTON

COMMENDATION FOR ACHIEVEMENT

The Secretary of the Navy takes pleasure in commending

MAJOR ROBERT L. FISCHER
UNITED STATES MARINE CORPS

for outstanding achievement in the superior performance of his duties in the field of training as set forth in the following

CITATION

Demonstrating exceptional initiative, foresight and resourcefulness, Major Fischer, as Officer in Charge, Second Marine Division Counterguerrilla Warfare Center, Camp Lejeune, North Carolina, recognized the desirability of centralized instruction on the subject of counterguerrilla warfare. With the assistance of a small staff of veterans of the Vietnam War, he developed a program for the Second Marine Division which trained 15,500 Marine and Navy personnel during the period of 21 January to 31 July 1966. Associated with this program was the building of a Vietnam village; trails demonstrating the mines, traps, pits and devices used by the Viet Cong; courses for improving individual reflexes and reactions, and the development of training programs tailored for both individual and unit training. Major Fischer's energy and imagination were of incalculable value to the individual Marine ordered to duty in the ground forces of the Western Pacific and to the increased readiness of the Second Marine Division. By his leadership, professional ability and dedication to duty, Major Fischer reflected great credit upon himself and the Marine Corps and upheld the highest traditions of the United States Naval Service.

Paul H. Nitze

Secretary of the Navy

An award I never expected, written up by my gunnery sergeants. I am more proud of this award than of any other medal or citation I have received.

DEPARTMENT OF THE NAVY
HEADQUARTERS UNITED STATES MARINE CORPS
WASHINGTON, D. C. 20380

IN REPLY REFER TO
DLA-cbd
2 2 MAR 1967

From: Commandant of the Marine Corps
To: Major Robert L. FISCHER 067809 USMC

Subj: Award

1. I wish to congratulate you on being awarded the
Commendation for Achievement by the Secretary of the
Navy in recognition of your outstanding achievement
as Officer in Charge, Second Marine Division Counter-
guerrilla Warfare Center, Camp Lejeune, North Carolina.

2. Be assured of my deep appreciation of your leadership
and professional skill which were in keeping with the
highest traditions of the United States Marine Corps.

WALLACE M. GREENE. JR.

**Navy Achievement Award (the medal was later awarded) for
the Officer in Charge of the CGWC, Camp Lejeune, NC**

200

NAVAL WAR COLLEGE
NEWPORT, RHODE ISLAND
02840

1 March 1976

From: Director, Naval Staff Course
To: Lieutenant Colonel Robert L. Fischer, USMC, CNW
Via: Dean of Students, NWC.

Subj: Letter of Appreciation

1. The Naval Staff Course includes Revolutionary Warfare as
part of the Strategy Study by the middle grade international
officers who are at the War College for a five month period.
Your lecture on "The Strategy and Tactics of the Insurgent"
and participation in a panel discussion on counterinsurgency
added significantly to student understanding of the subject.

2. The candor with which you responded to questions was
most appreciated by our international students. They felt
that you were sharing more than just a rhetoric of textbook
coverage of the area. Your professional knowledge of this
difficult area of warfare not only impressed them, but also
gave them a new perspective in considering counterinsurgency
problems.

3. Since you are also a student at the War College, this
served as a point of identification for our international
officers. The fact that you volunteered this time from your
busy schedule is greatly appreciated and deserving of recognition. Accordingly, a copy of this letter is forwarded for
inclusion in your next report of fitness.

J.Q. QUINN
Captain, U.S. Navy

**The foreign students really liked my COIN
(counterinsurgency) lectures.**

201

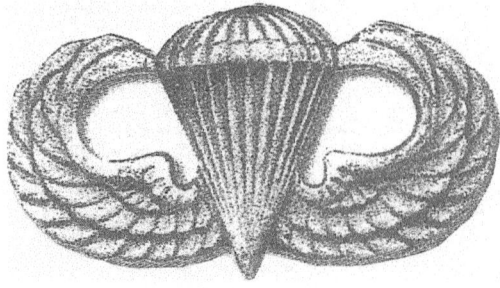

Grunt Glossary

3/8 – 3rd Battalion, 8th Marines

AID – American Agency for International Development

ARVN –Army of Vietnam

Bivouac *(biv-wak)* – a temporary encampment

BLT– Battalion Landing Team

CAP – Combined Action Program

CEP – an atom-bomb radius, identified by the acronym for the French *Centre d' Expérimentations Nucléaires du Pacifique*

CG – Commanding General

CGWC – Counter-Guerrilla Warfare Center

CIA – Central Intelligence Agency

CMC – Commandant of the Marine Corps

CO – Commanding Officer

COIN – counterinsurgency

CONUS – Continental United States

CORDS – Civil Operations and Revolutionary Development Support

CT – Communist Terrorist (Malaya insurgent)

Cumshaw – to obtain something through unofficial means

FBI – Federal Bureau of Investigation

FMFLANT – Fleet Marine Force, Atlantic

FMFPAC – Fleet Marine Force, Pacific

G-3 – Operations of a division

Gitmo – Guantanamo Bay, Cuba

Hooch – a dwelling, typically a thatched hut

HQMC – Headquarters Marine Corps

IED – Improvised Explosive Device

ITR – Infantry Training Regiment

LBJ – Lyndon Baines Johnson, U.S. President

LCVP – Landing Craft, Vehicle, Personnel

LHA – Landing Helicopter, Assault

LPH – Landing Platform, Helicopter

LST – Landing Ship, Tank

LVT – Landing Vehicle, Tracked – amphibious tractor

LZ – Landing Zone

MAAG – Military Assistance Advisory Group

MAU – Marine Amphibious Unit

MBA – Master of Business Administration

MCB – Marine Corps Base

MEB – Marine Expeditionary Brigade

MEF – Marine Expeditionary Forces

MOI – Military Officer Instructor

MP – Military Police

NCO – Noncommissioned Officer

NVA – North Vietnamese Army

OIC – Officer In Charge

PAVN -- People's Army of Vietnam

Pinko – a person with leftist political views, particularly those that favor communism or are derogatory to the U.S.; an extreme liberal

Pogue – a derogatory military slang term used to describe non-infantry, staff, and other rear-echelon or support roles

PT – Physical Training

PTSD – Post-Traumatic Stress Disorder

S-3 – Operations and Training office (and officer)

S-4 – Logistics and Supply office (and officer)

Sapper – a combat engineer who specializing in explosives

SEATO – South East Asia Treaty Organization

SLF – Special Landing Force

TAOR – Tactical Area of Operation

TBI – Traumatic Brain Injury

U.S. – United States

UCMJ – Uniform Code of Military Justice

USMC – United States Marine Corps

XO – Executive Officer

Bibliography

Advisor Handbook for Counterinsurgency – FM-31-73. Washington, DC: HQ. Dept. of the Army, Used in Advisor Course, Fort Bragg, NC, 1965.

Anti-Guerrilla Operations in Southeast Asia. Commander in Chief, British Far East Land Forces. Printed for H.M. Stationery Office by D.R. Hillman & Sons Ltd, Fromme, Australia, 1952.

Asprey, Robert. *War in the Shadows: Napoleon's Peninsular War*. New York, Doubleday, 1975.

Boot, Max. *Invisible Armies: An Epic of Guerrilla Warfare From Ancient Times To The Present*. New York. W.W. Norton & Company Inc., 2013.

Chapman, Spencer. *The Jungle is Neutral: The War of Running Dogs, Malaya, 1948-1960*. Cassell Military Publications, 1960.

Caputo, Philip. *A Rumor of War*: New York, McMillan and Company, 1977.

Chinh, Truong. *Primer for Revolt – The Communist Takeover in Vietnam*. As translated by Bernard Fall. New York, Praeger, 1963.

Corson, William R. Lt. Col. USMC (Ret.). *The Betrayal*. New York, W.W. Norton & Co., 1968

Counterinsurgency Planning Guide, ST 31-176. United States Army Special Warfare School, Fort, Bragg, NC, October 1963.

Croizat, Victor, Col. USMC (Ret.). *A Translation from the French Lessons of the War in Indochina*. Santa Monica, CA, the Rand Corp., 1967. Original review, 1964, Vietnam.

_____. *Journey Among Warriors – Memories of a Marine*. Shippensburg, PA, White Mane Publishing Co., 1997. First advisor (covan) to the Vietnamese Maine Corps, 1954.

Eller, Franklin P., Colonel USMC (Ret). "Binh Gia: Before the March 1965 Landing," Marine Corps Gazette, November 2009, and personal interview, April 2013.

Fall, Bernard. *Street Without Joy*. Harrison, PA: Stackpole Company, 1961.

Fitzgerald, Frances. *Fire in the Lake: The Vietnamese and Americans in Vietnam*. New York: Little, Brown and Company, 1972.

_____. *Hell in a Small Place*. Washington, DC: Potomac Books, 1961.

Giap, Vo Nguyen. *People's War, People's Army: The Viet Cong Insurrection Manual for Underdeveloped Countries*. University Press of the Pacific, 2001.

_____. *Victory at Any Cost*: Washington, DC: Potomac Books, 2005.

_____. *How We Won the War*: Philadelphia, PA: Recon Publications, 1976.

Galula, David. *Counterinsurgency Warfare: Theory and Practice*. London: Praeger, 1964.

Gettleman, Marvin E. *Vietnam, History, Documents and Opinions*. New York: Fawcett, 1965.

Guevara, Che. *On Guerrilla Warfare*. New York: Praeger, 1961.

Komer, Robert. *Bureaucracy Does Its Thing: Institutional Constraints on US:GVN Performance in Vietnam*. Washington, DC: Rand, 1972.

Hackworth, David, Col. U.S. Army (Ret.). *About Face. The Odyssey of an American Warrior*. New York: Rugged Land Inc., 1990. (Also authored *Steel My Soldiers Heart*, Touchstone, 2002.)

Kellum, Michael Dan. *American Heroes-Grunts, Pilots and "Docs"* (2 vol.). Longview, TX: Navarro-Hill Publishing Group, 2011.

Kilcullen, David. *The Accidental Guerrilla: Fighting Small Wars in the Midst of a Big One*. New York: Oxford University Press, 2011.

Krepinevich, Andrew. *The Army and Vietnam*. Baltimore, MD: Johns Hopkins University Press, 1986. (Note: The U.S. Army never adapted to the insurgency in Vietnam, preferring a conventional war.)

Larteguy, Jean, *The Centurions*. New York: Dutton, 1962. The French experience with counterinsurgency in Vietnam and Algeria. Followed by *The Praetorians*, 1964.

Linn, Brian McAllister. *The Philippine War, 1899-1902 (Modern War Studies)*. University Press of Kansas, 2002.

Mao Tse-tung. *On Guerrilla Warfare*. New York: Praeger, 1961.

Marlantes, Karl. *Matterhorn*. New York: Atlantic Monthly Press, 2010.

Nagl, John A. *Learning to Eat Soup With a Knife: Counterinsurgency Lessons from Malaya and Vietnam: How to Defeat an Insurgency*. University of Chicago Press, 2005.

Pike, Douglas. *PAVN: People's Army of Vietnam*. Novato, CA: Presidio Press, 1986. Considered the most important account of the Viet Cong of any published work on the subject.

_____. *The Viet Cong: Strategy of Terror*. State Department historian; his staff paper published by the U.S. Mission in Vietnam, 1970.

Reporting Vietnam (two volumes, 1959-1969 and 1969-1975). A comprehensive anthology by America's leading Vietnam War correspondents. New York: Literary Classics, Penguin-Putnam, 1998.

Stubbs, Richard. *Hearts and Minds in Guerrilla Warfare: The Malayan Emergency, 1948-1960*. Oxford, UK: Oxford University Press, 1989.

Sun Tsu. *The Art of War: Small Wars Manual*. Manhattan, KS: Sunflower University Press, 1996.

Taber, Robert. *War of the Flea. The Classic Study of Guerrilla Warfare*. Washington, DC: Potomac Books, 2002.

U.S. Army – Marine Corps Counterinsurgency Field Manual: University of Chicago Press, 2007.

Tanham, George K. *Communist Revolutionary Warfare: From the Vietminh to the Viet Cong*. New York: Praeger, 1961.

The Conduct of Anti-Terrorist Operations in Malaya: Director of Operations Malaya, 1960.

Thompson, Robert. *Defeating Communist Insurgency, The Lessons of Malaya and Vietnam*. New York. Praeger, 1966.

Trinquier, Roger. *Modern Warfare, A French View of Counterinsurgency: Indochina, 1940s and 1950s*. New York: Praeger, 1984.

U.S. Marine Corps. *Small Wars Manual*. Washington, DC: Government Printing Office, 1940.

Valeriano, Napoliano, Col., U.S. Army (Ret.) and Bohannon, Charles, T. R. Lt. Col, U.S. Army (Ret.). *Counterguerrilla Operations, The Philippine Experience*. New York; Praeger, 1962.

Webb, James. *Fields of Fire*. New York: Bantam Books, 1979.

West, Bing. *The Village*. New York: Simon and Schuster, 1972. Small Unit Advisors with the Combined Action Program–Vietnam.

_____. *Small Unit Action in Vietnam*. New York: Arno Press Inc., 1967.

Author Biography

Robert L. Fischer, Colonel, USMC (Ret)

Colonel Robert L. Fischer, a 1955 graduate of the U.S. Naval Academy, was a career Marine Corps officer. He has commanded Marine units from platoons to a battalion, and was Captain of Marines aboard the USS St. Paul, 7th Fleet flagship. He attended seven Army schools including Career Infantry, Nuclear Weapons Employment, Airborne, Panama Jungle, Advisor Course, and Special Warfare. From 1961 to 1963, he closely studied four Asian insurgencies and obtained the Malaya Jungle School syllabus. It was used at the Counter-guerrilla Warfare Center (CGWC) at Camp Lejeune, North Carolina, that he proposed and established in 1965. By 1968, the center had trained 20,000 Marines, 4 Seabee battalions, Navy Seals, and Army Special Forces teams.

From 1966 to 1968, Fischer was a Vietnamese Marine Corps advisor (*covan*). He and his assistant, Lieutenant Bob Whited, developed successful hunter-killer tactics employing helicopters and small-boat saturation patrols in dense, riverine terrain of the Rung Sat Special Zone. Their discovery of the afloat T-10 Psychological Operations and Political Warfare Headquarters was a major setback for Viet Cong operations in the entire district, as was the destruction of 20 Viet Cong camps and jungle factory sites. As the assistant senior advisor, Task Force Bravo, he made the first Marine Corps amphibious landing in the Delta and later successfully merged his own Vietnamese Marines with the U.S. Army's Air Cavalry for joint operations in Bong Son. He earned two Bronze Stars (with V for "valor"), the Vietnamese Marine Cross of Gallantry, and Honor Medal, First Class. His book, *Covan*, describes this advisory experience. In 1975 he attended the Naval War College, Newport, Rhode Island, where he was a student and also served as a lecturer on "The Strategy and Tactics of the Insurgent" for the foreign students' course.

In 1969, he received a Master's degree in Management Science from Rensselaer Polytechnic Institute, Troy, New York, where he specialized in plant, depot, and project management. Colonel Fischer later commanded a battalion on Okinawa and the **Defense Electronics Depot, Kettering, Ohio,** where his **workforce** set the all-time performance record in the history of the Defense Logistics Agency. For this he was awarded the Defense Superior Service Medal. During his off-duty hours in Dayton, Ohio, and at four other military bases where he served, he was an adjunct professor in the evening Master's degree (MBA) programs. There, he taught production and operations management, organization theory, project-program management, and analytical methods.

Fischer retired in 1982, when he and "a few Marines" developed and marketed reverse-vending (cash for cans and bottles) machines for Environmental Products Corporation, where he was vice president of Engineering and Production. In 1985 he became a program director for Grumman Corporation and helped **win the 250-million-dollar DMMIS (depot maintenance) contract** with the U.S. Air Force. As vice president of Defense Systems, Office of Government Services at Price Waterhouse, he authored their *Project Focus* and *Functional Engineering* methodologies. In 1988, Fischer teamed with an Air Force friend to found Computer **Engineering Associates,** a management consulting firm in the Washington DC area that specialized in logistics systems.

Today, Fischer and his wife Karen reside in Arvada, Colorado, where he devotes his time and effort as a military advocate helping veterans with traumatic brain injuries (TBI) and post-traumatic stress disorder (PTSD) by assisting them through treatment and healing at the Rocky Mountain Hyperbaric Institute in Louisville, Colorado. For this effort, he was cited by the American Legion of Colorado as the Military Advocate of the Year in 2012. In 1996 he helped found Cooper's Troopers, a group of Marine and Navy veterans of Marine Corps battles in World War II, Korea, and Vietnam. His book about these veterans, *Voices of the Corps,* documents their military experience.

www.ingramcontent.com/pod-product-compliance
Lightning Source LLC
Chambersburg PA
CBHW062059090426
42741CB00015B/3280